FREE PEOPLE

FREE PEOPLE

A Christian Response to
Global Economics

Tricia Gates Brown

To order additional copies of this book, contact:
Xlibris Corporation
1-888-795-4274
www.Xlibris.com
Orders@Xlibris.com
24342

CONTENTS

What is the "global economy"?
Key Tenets of Neoliberal Economics
Export Processing Zones: Backbone of the Global Economy
Invisible Injustice
Structural Adjustments as a Feature of Neoliberal Economics
The Debt Crisis
Moral Incapacitation?

The Global Trade System; A Thorn in the Side of Democracy
Seattle, Washington, USA, December 1999
Washington, DC, USA, April 2000
Prague, Czechoslovakia, September 2000
Davos, Switzerland, February 2001
Quebec City, Canada, April 2001
Genoa, Italy, July 2001
Cancelled Meetings/Protests in Washington, DC, September 2001
Qatar, November 2001
What is Freedom?

This book is dedicated to my
"Sunday night friends"—for sharing the journey

Preface

I cannot pinpoint in my memory the decision to write this book, or recall what factors precipitated that decision. What I can remember is the burning curiosity I had about global economics, and about how my lifestyle impacted people around the world. Several experiences fostered that curiosity.

One such experience was living in Scotland for two years as I worked on a PhD. While in that western country so distinct from and yet so like the United States, I discovered such things as the fair trade movement. Nearly every Scottish town seemed to have its own fair trade shop, and fair trade coffee and tea were readily available at most supermarkets. It was in Scotland that I began researching sweatshops and wondering why I had not seen many fair trade shops in the US. While in Scotland I also learned about the debt relief campaign, Jubilee 2000, which was getting underway at the time, and about the global debt crisis. I lived in international postgraduate housing with my husband and daughter, and developed close friendships with families from Kenya, Japan, China, Turkey, and Egypt. These friends—whose lives seemed a paradoxical intertwining of the beautiful, unique cultures of their home countries, and of western pop culture—raised questions in me. In most cases, western pop culture seemed to be the dominant thread. The questions cropping up in my mind had to do with culture and values, and with what market forces and western dominance were doing to both.

I watched current events closely at that time, and followed critically the wars of the day. I showed up at my first protest in Scotland, and became active in the student movement opposing the economic sanctions against Iraq. I began to analyze the worldwide impact of my country, the United States, more in-depth. Eighteen months after returning home, I started this book.

Around that same time, I began meeting regularly with a couple of friends to discuss simplicity, as well as ideas on economic justice and living sustainably. We shared rich discussions (and good food) and inspired each other. This trio soon grew into a much larger group that has been meeting ever since fall of 2001, every Sunday evening—sharing meals and hospitality, enjoying each others' kids, figuring out together how to "live lightly on the land." These are the "Sunday night friends" to whom this book is dedicated. These individuals strive to live examined, just, and peaceable lives which are also characterized by freedom and creativity. They share my passionate concerns. I value their unwillingness to accept simplistic answers, and their belief in alternatives to the dominant economic model described in this book. My exchanges with this group have fed my curiosity, and helped to keep me moving forward on this project.

This book is the outcome of a curiosity fostered, in part, by these experiences and relationships, or an outcome of the journey that curiosity led me into. But the completion of this book is by no means an indication of satisfaction. I still hold a wealth of questions in the satchel of my heart. Working on this book has, in some far-reaching ways, changed my life, and the whole journey, it seems, is just beginning.

Acknowledgements

First of all, I thank the "Sunday night friends" to whom this book is dedicated, and who are described in the Preface. They are Jared, Jody, and Ethan Jones, Karah Fisher, Kim, Bryan, and Emma Boyd, Janine Saxton, Brendon Connelly, Amy Lutz, and Truman Connelly, Colby Spell, Brenda, Bill, Jake, Rebecca, and Anna Jolliff, Darryl Brown, and Madison Sturdevant.

Many people gave generously of their time to read and comment on portions of this manuscript, including Roger Newell, Karah Fisher, Walter Wink, Colby Spell, Darryl Brown, Peter Illyn, and Tom Head. I thank them for their critiques, encouragement, and good ideas. Preeminent among these readers was Karah Fisher, who also served as editor. Her careful eye and writerly insights contributed much to the refinement of this book.

While working on *Free People*, I participated in a delegation to Chiapas, Mexico with Christian Peacemaker Teams. I thank the Mayan people of Chiapas, and especially the Abejas, for allowing me to enter into their lives and see the effects of global economics firsthand. Their generosity, humility and resistance were moving, and were a strong inspiration to tackle the topic of this book.

To the many colleagues within Christian Peacemaker Teams (CPT) who have encouraged me in this project and convinced me that a Christian response to global economics is needed, I am thankful.

Several people agreed to be case studies for the last chapter of this book, allowing me to interview and "make examples" of them. These are unpretentious people who are, I am guessing, not entirely comfortable with publicity. I appreciate their openness and willingness to contribute to this project. They are Bill and Brenda Jolliff, Jody and Jared Jones, Jessica Phillips, the folks at Right Sharing of World Resources, and Jerry and Molly Mechtenberg-Berrigan (who also extended exceptional hospitality to me).

To my family, all of you, and to my CPT family, thank you. I especially thank Darryl for believing in this book so wholeheartedly, and for caring about living justly. He has shared this journey with me from the beginning, and been a wonderful friend along the way.

Finally, I wish to thank Brother Martin Gonzales, Sue Newell, and Karah Fisher for exemplifying Christian community to me over the past year. Your trust in me, the way you always see my best, your unwavering love and grace—these have been among my greatest blessings.

Chapter One

Bought and Sold:

The Global Economy Introduced

... I look up to the people who are less bought than I,
You can show them what you're selling,
and they'll only ask you why.
And their paychecks don't have lots of zeros.
They're my friends and they're my heroes.
And the TV sets are angry cause they just can't make 'em pay,
but I like the way these people read the signs and walk away.

Dar Williams, "Bought and Sold"[1]

I am not an economist. I am a middle-class individual living in a middle-class neighborhood in a small but expanding town in America. I shop at supermarkets. I buy my gas at national gas station chains. I am an abstraction: a consumer.

Every day I wake up as enmeshed in the global economy as I am wrapped in my bright blue sheets tailored in Indonesia. On a typical day I will have used a myriad of products produced in such unfamiliar lands as Macau, Nepal, and Bangladesh, before my made-in-China clock says 10:00 a.m. I would guess this is true for most of my readers.

Of course, I am more than just a consumer. I am a great many other things, including a Christian. Nothing drives my interest in the global economy more than my Christian worldview. As a Christian I have something to say about it, despite the fact that I am not an economist. I hope many more will find they have a voice in the matter, whether as parents, Buddhists, engineers, humanitarian aid workers, plumbers, Native Americans, children, business owners, or farmers. We all have a voice in the shaping of our everyday lives if we will be so bold as to claim it. Though my reflection on the global economy issues from my Christian perspective, I was introduced to the phenomenon by a host of people who have in recent years taken exception to it. These include voices from the labor movement in America, from secular activist groups, from university students, from scholars and philosophers. Among these people have stood many Christians who have had their eyes open enough to see that our role in the globalized economy brings up profound moral questions for followers of Jesus. They have gotten my attention.

The challenge to global economics, or neoliberal economics as it is also called, is being levied by a collection of groups as diverse as the patterns of hand-woven oriental rugs. It should go without saying that I do not agree with every opinion represented among them, and neither will you. But my moral consciousness has been stirred by what I have learned from some of the voices within this "global justice movement" of how neoliberal economics shapes the lives of different people around the globe. Unfortunately, those voices are rarely heard. They are not widely broadcast in the commercial media. Therefore, I intend in this book to pass on to my readers some of the information I've gleaned from these activists and writers, so that my readers might be spurred on to further ethical reflection around the issue of global economics. This book will not analyze the global justice movement,[2] but will help readers to better understand the trends against which the movement is reacting.

The current economic arrangements overseen by the international financial institutions (the World Trade Organization, International Monetary Fund, and World Bank) severely compromise the social, political, and spiritual wellbeing of humankind. I want to state that unequivocally and at the outset. But I want to make another thing clear from the beginning: I do not assert that international trade or the market economy ought to be abolished. The global economy needs radical rearranging if life is to be sustained on this planet, and if trade is to be fair, but trade itself does not constitute the problem. The way global trade is currently arranged, and the extent to which it is practiced, constitutes a gargantuan problem. Still, this book is not a treatise on how the global economy ought to be reconfigured, though I do at times express my ideas for the shape of its reconfiguration. Rather, the intent of this book is first to inform readers about the global economy, and then to explore the question of how to live as Christians in light of it.

One of the many writers who has focused in recent years on global economics posed the following question to his readers: "If capitalism is now truly global, what are the global social obligations that accompany it?"[3] In the latter part of this book I will reflect on essentially the same question, but from a Christian perspective. What are our global moral obligations as Christians in light of the globalization of economics? Jesus summed up our moral obligations: To love the Lord God with all one's heart, soul, and mind, and to love one's neighbor as oneself (Mt 22:34-40). How does this look in the global village? How do I love God with all my being while living in a materialistic culture? How do I love God with all my mind in a fact-bending, media-saturated culture? And, to ask a question less often posed by Christians: How do I relate in love to my "neighbors" residing on the other side of the globe who make the products before me on the store shelves? I have a relationship with those neighbors not only when my life directly intersects their lives, but insofar as my lifestyle alters the shape of theirs. This book will show that, indeed, my American lifestyle impacts the lives of people all around the world. So does yours. Our global neighbors are many, and we are told to love them. Still, it is my impression that, for all of our connectedness to people around the world, the majority of us do not reflect on the morality of our global relationships. We live globally but think ethically only as far as we can see, hear, and touch. As consumers deeply enmeshed in the global economy, far more is required of us—which is what this book sets out to demonstrate. First, however, we must understand what the global economy is.

What is the "global economy"?

The term "global economy" denotes the rapid expansion of trade
across borders, facilitated by advances in communication technology
and by the broad removal of trade tariffs and subsidies, as well as by
the increasing mobility of capital. Trade tariffs and subsidies are not
eliminated across the board, however. Many industrialized nations
continue to subsidize certain industries, such as agriculture, and impose
tariffs on key imports while demanding that developing countries remove
all such trade barriers. As recently as March 2002, the US imposed
tariffs of up to 30% on a range of steel imports. "Free trade" is the
term used widely to describe the intent of the global economic system,
but the system is clearly not free. Writer Michael Jacobs of the UK's
Guardian newspaper tells it plainly:

> Multinational corporations, finance capitalists, and Northern
> Governments justify themselves in terms of free trade, but
> what they actually promote are their own interests, which is
> not the same thing at all. In trade the industrialized world
> imposes liberalisation on developing countries while
> protecting its own markets in agriculture and textiles through
> tariff barriers. IMF aid conditions force Southern countries
> to abolish food subsidies—while the EU dumps its own
> subsidised food surpluses on their markets, crushing local
> farmers. The IMF forces Southern countries to deregulate
> their capital markets, while crisis-struck banks and hedge
> funds in the US are bailed out with billions of dollars.[4]

"Free trade" is a misnomer we will avoid in this book, since the term
implies that all parties involved in such trade are equally free. The
global economy is about "liberalized" trade, but it apportions to different players varying degrees of liberality.

The global economy, at least in the view of global justice
campaigners, also encompasses the *consequences* of liberalized trade,
whether they be social, cultural, political, or environmental. The term
"global economy" describes the current state of world affairs in which

the economies of nearly every country are networked with other economies around the globe,[5] and in which cultures throughout the world are becoming increasingly dominated by Western influences.

The globalization of economies involves more than the opening up of trade between nations. Global trading across borders is hardly new. It has transpired for centuries and increased exponentially during the 19th century, only to recede during the middle of the 20th century, and reemerge with gusto in the 1970s.[6] What is unique about the present-day phenomenon known as global economics is this: the increasing sovereignty of transnational corporations, the existence of so-called international financial institutions dictating the rules of the game while consistently representing the interests of corporations over the interests of citizens around the globe[7], and the denigration of cultural distinctiveness and "delocalization"[8] occurring worldwide.

Global trade in our day has become less a matter of trade between nations, and more a matter of trade between transnational corporations (TNCs). TNCs now account for about a third of global output and two-thirds of global trade. A full *quarter* of all world trade takes place *within* TNCs.[9] Consider the following: the 200 biggest corporations in the world control 28% of the world's economic activity.[10] Yet while the TNCs conduct business all around the world and exchange vast sums of money, the revenues they leave behind in developing countries are relatively meager, and disproportionately go to a small percentage of the national population, often elites associated with TNCs. In post-NAFTA Mexico, for example, where neoliberal policies heavily favor corporations producing for export, 80% of all exports come from only 300 large companies, even though there are 40,000 export companies in Mexico.[11] So, while big corporations in Mexico have benefited from neoliberalism, the majority of Mexicans have suffered. In the years since NAFTA's inception, poverty has increased in Mexico, and the average Mexican has experienced a 40% drop in purchasing power.[12] As in other parts of the world, in Mexico, the global economy clearly prospers the few at the expense of the many. This inherent inequality of the global economy results from the policies of the international financial institutions (IFIs). Global trade in the late 19th century was likewise marked by dominance of the few by the many, a state of affairs which was enforced by colonial militaries. In more recent years, international financial institutions (IFIs) such as the International Monetary Fund, World Bank, and World Trade Organization have provided the muscle to protect corporate dominance. What are these institutions, and where did they come from?

The World Bank and the International Monetary Fund (IMF) were both established after World War II at a momentous meeting in Bretton Woods, New Hampshire. The World Bank, originally charged with financing the rebuilding of post-war Europe, became the primary source of funding for development projects in developing countries, and the primary decision-making body determining how that development would take place. However, after the debt crisis of the early 1980s (See "The Debt Crisis," later in this chapter), the World Bank's power dramatically increased. The Bank began to attach strict conditions to recipients of World Bank loans, conditions which required countries to reform their economic policies according to the neoliberal economic model espoused by the World Bank (See section on *Structural Adjustments* later in this chapter). The Bank is and always has been based in Washington, DC. It comprises member countries who make decisions via a voting process, but different members receive different voting "shares". Wealthier nations hold a greater share of the vote. The US, for example, holds over 17% of the vote in the World Bank, while China holds less than 3%.

The IMF has a power structure similar to the World Bank, with voting power based on the amount of money a country has contributed to the Fund. The IMF is also headquartered in Washington, DC, and the US holds about 17% of the vote. Facilitating global trade figures prominently in the work of the IMF. The Fund also oversees currency exchange rates, and issues loans to keep trade active. Like the World Bank, the IMF began attaching far-reaching conditions to its loans during the early 1980s, conditions of a decidedly neoliberal flavor which favored large corporations and export-driven economies.

Unlike the aforementioned IFIs, the World Trade Organization (WTO) is not a lending institution, and is relatively young. It was created in 1995, though its roots are in the General Agreement on Tariffs and Trade (GATT) formed in the 1940s. Charged with the governance of global trade among all WTO members, the WTO holds enormous sway. It constitutes a worldwide legislative and judicial body made up of unelected trade representatives[13] who are often corporate lawyers, and who are granted the power to subordinate the legislative and judicial authority of individual nations. The WTO mandate is, basically, to ensure the free flow of goods and capital between nations. More specifically, WTO officials are charged with overseeing and enforcing member nations' adherence to the "annexed agreements" of the WTO, the general agreements which have been ratified by the member countries. If the officials of one member nation find that a particular law of another member nation is inconsistent with the annexed agreements and constitutes a trade barrier, they can challenge that law in a closed hearing before a review panel of WTO lawyers, and eventually have that law eliminated.[14] That this is an affront to democracy appears to be immaterial. National laws about safety, such as auto safety requirements, or laws to protect health, such as bans on toxic substances, environmental protections, or limits on carcinogenic food additives, can all be challenged by corporations and changed by trade officials.[15] In many cases, just the threat of a legal challenge by the WTO will force a developing country to change its laws, since poor countries cannot afford to defend themselves before trade tribunals, or to suffer trade sanctions if they lose. Such was the case with Guatemala, whose UNICEF-supported law banning misleading marketing of baby formula was challenged by the US-based Gerber corporation, who threatened to take action in the WTO. Formula use had had devastating effects on infant mortality in the Central American country, and the law had reversed this trend. Nonetheless, after the challenge from Gerber, Guatemala had no choice but to rescind the law.[16]

The regulatory arrangements implemented by the IMF, World Bank, and WTO keep capital investment highly mobile and trade and labor inexpensive. These arrangements make it possible for TNCs to profit quite disproportionately on the global economic scale. John Gray provides a helpful summary of the process:

> [Transnational corporations] are able to divide the process of production into discrete operations and locate them in different countries throughout the world. They are less

> dependent than ever before on national conditions. They
> can choose the countries whose labour markets, tax and
> regulatory regimes and infrastructures they find most
> congenial. The promise of direct inward investment, and
> the threat of its withdrawal, have significant leverage on the
> policy options of national governments. Companies can now
> limit the politics of states. There are few historical precedents
> for this kind of private power.[17]

The global economy, under the oversight of the IFIs, grants corporations enormous financial leverage over governments.

But the leverage IFIs have over nations extends to the *political/legal* realm as well. This leverage is exerted not only through the WTO, but through terms set by the international financial institutions. These terms, called "structural adjustments" (See "Structural Adjustments" later in this chapter),[18] can also require developing countries to change or disregard their laws, in this case to qualify for loans. In other words, laws democratically implemented within countries can be overridden by unelected officials in far away international banks. Any law considered to be a barrier to neoliberal reforms can be called into question. For example, the Ecuadorian Constitution requires Ecuador's government to provide education and health services to its citizens. But Ecuador's Structural Adjustment Program overrode the Ecuadorian Constitution, dramatically reducing social services. The government could no longer meet this constitutional requirement. Like Ecuador, many developing countries have been forced to hand over democracy in exchange for trade and foreign investment.

The abdicating of democracy and national sovereignty to IFIs and TNCs certainly distinguishes the global economics of our day from earlier manifestations of global trade. Another feature of the global economy is the abdicating of culture. The global economy has resulted in the diminishing salience of distinct world cultures, and the amalgamation of people all around the world into one mega, global pop culture. Benjamin Barber coined the term "McWorld" to denote this trend. McWorld is visible wherever people from diverse nationalities and creeds around the world sport the same handful of American clothing labels (Levis, Nike, etc.), spend time each day watching the top American TV networks (CNN, MTV, etc.), drink Coca Cola, and dine at American fast food restaurants. It is a world where language and worldviews still separate, but Hollywood movies and global brands forge ubiquitous common bonds between strangers. It is a world where people are growing increasingly isolated from the local communities with whom they once identified. The impetus for the deculturization of nations, or their reculturization into McWorld, is the proliferation of global media, predominantly American, with its global podium from which to proclaim its Western gospel: the supposedly good news of consumerism, leisure, and self-actualization. As Barber points out, the evangelists of this lifestyle have not set out with the intentions of destroying any foreign culture that happens into its path. Rather it is a "politics of inadvertence and unintended consequences in which the seemingly innocuous market quest for fun, creativity, and profits puts whole cultures in harm's way and undermines autonomy in individuals and nations alike."[19] Neither, however, do the purveyors of global Western pop culture appear to regret the damage being done. Globalization of the economy is as popular as ever with these McWorld colonialists, who take pride in the extent of their reach. The unfortunate result of the deculturization happening around the world is delocalization, where more and more people feel less and less of a connection to a particular community or place.

The globalization of economics is a multi-faceted thing. It has clearly "grown" economies and contributed to the wealth of many involved. Unfortunately, these profits have, for the most part, further fattened the already well-fed, while hurting the world's poor. But whether or not one views global economics positively will depend on the angle from which one looks at it. If one is mainly concerned about the size of economies, which are measured in terms of gross national product (GNP), then the global economy will win one's allegiance. If one is concerned with the wellbeing of *all* Earth's citizens, and with the wellbeing of God's good earth itself, global economics will fare less well.

It has frequently been pointed out that GNP is not a true measure of "progress," since GNP measures all legal money exchange—no matter what the nature of the exchange—as an indication of growth and progress. Consequently, money poured into drug treatment programs, toxic waste processing, criminal justice and prisons, auto accident claims, sale of military and domestic weapons, and abortion are all counted as indications of growth, and factored into a nation's GNP. So an increase in a country's need for drug treatment, prisons, and home security systems actually indicates progress! Moreover, the very costly cleanup of disasters such as the terrorist attacks on the World Trade Center or the Exxon Valdez oil spill are reckoned as good for the economy because they prompt the exchange of large sums of money. The GNP has no regard for environmental costs since the more environmentally taxing ways of doing things tend to contribute more to the economy. As economist David Korten puts it: "driving a mile in a car contributes more to GNP than riding a mile on a bicycle. Turning on an air conditioner adds more than opening a window. Relying on processed packaged food adds more than using natural foods purchased in bulk in reusable containers."[20] Clearly GNP is flawed as a mechanism for measuring progress and growth.[21]

One last point deserves mention before moving beyond "definitions" of the global economy. It has been suggested that the global economy may, to some degree, lessen the frequency of international warfare. One study has shown that high-level trade between countries may inhibit them from responding to conflicts with each other using military force.[22] If this proves to be the case in our day, then global economics will have that going for it. However, the globalization of economics has coincided with an increase in civil warfare within nations, perhaps a consequence of the growing inequality in wealth resulting from neoliberalism, and of the globalization of the arms trade.[23] Furthermore, the hegemony of the US in the global economy has been a factor in the spread of anti-Americanism which fuels international terrorism. Therefore, it would be difficult to argue that global trade has fostered more peaceful relationships between people. The latter decades of the 20th century were some of the most war-torn, and the conflicts of those decades appear to only be deepening.

Key Tenets of Neoliberal Economics

What we now call the "global economy" is the outworking of a broad economic worldview known as *neoliberalism*. Neoliberalism came to be instituted on a global scale during the administration of US President Ronald Reagan in the 1980s.[24] According to neoliberalism, economics should be governed by a few central tenets, all of which move in a "liberalizing" direction, or the direction of less governmental oversight and regulation (hence, the title "neoliberal"). Neoliberal economics has become the economic model favored by most Western economists. The term "neoliberal economics" is used interchangeably with "global economics" at times in this book.

Neoliberal theory contends that markets which are freed from governmental intervention will bring economic wellbeing to most people. Neoliberalism holds that the private sector can create jobs and economic wealth, which will trickle down to all sectors of society, if economic forces are allowed to run their course without regulations and barriers. According to neoliberal theory, trade is the best vehicle to bring about economic growth, and should likewise be unhampered by all governmental interference. All obstacles to the flow of goods within and between countries should be eliminated, and public services should be privatized, because competition itself will weed out inefficiencies and problems.

According to supporters of neoliberalism, competition should be used to greatest effect in global trade. Countries are encouraged to compete by providing whatever products or services they can provide most effectively and efficiently. These products or services are known as a country's "comparative advantage." A country should focus on exporting the things that fit their comparative advantage, and importing things they cannot produce effectively or efficiently. The comparative advantage of a country like the United States or Britain will include a highly skilled workforce and strong technological industry. The comparative advantage of an country like Costa Rica will include a tropical climate ideal for producing, for example, exotic fruits, as well as a workforce willing to work for very low wages. A cheap labor pool is reckoned as the core comparative advantage of many developing countries, especially in places like Vietnam, or China. According to neoliberal theory, a country should play to this comparative advantage in order to maximize their gains in the global economy. Eventually, as each country focuses on their strengths, the playing field will begin to level out and wealth will accumulate in everyone's hands.

This seems to make a lot of sense on paper. However, in our world of globalized economics the playing field has not leveled in any way. In fact, it appears very unlikely that the wealth accumulated in the global economy will end up benefiting everyone involved, as neoliberalism purports it will, because money is gravitating into the hands of fewer and fewer people. According to the World Bank, in 1993 the richest one percent of the world's population owned the equivalent of the combined wealth of the poorest 57 percent.[25] This inequality has only magnified. UN statistics reveal that the 15 richest individuals in the world are now worth more than the combined GDP (gross domestic product) of the whole of sub-Saharan Africa.[26] Moreover, in the four years leading up to 1999, "The world's 200 richest people more than doubled their net worth . . . to more than $1 trillion or an average $5 billion each."[27] The combined wealth of those 200 individuals was in 1999 equal to the combined annual income of the world's poorest 2.5 billion people.[28] These inequities do not only exist between industrialized nations and developing nations, but exist *within* industrialized nations as well. Median family income in the US has dropped since the 70's, though families now work more hours and must cope with severe cutbacks in social services,[29] while the number of multi-billionaires in the US keeps growing. In the three years leading up to 1999, "the wealth of the Forbes 400 richest Americans grew by an average of $940 million each. . . . That's an average increase of $1,287,671 per day."[30]

There are probably many reasons for the inequities of the global economy. One reason is simply human greed, and the lack of any international governing institutions charged with protecting people from the greed of individuals and corporations in the arena of global economics. Since there exist no regulatory institutions putting the brakes on corporations' ability to exploit people or lands for profit, people and lands get exploited. That is the real-world outcome of the radically liberalized economy envisioned by neoliberal theory. But another reason for the inequities of the global economy is that the game began with such vast inequalities between players. A game starting out with extremely unequal, or mismatched, players will amount to nothing but a farce. Nonetheless, this is exactly how the game of global economics is played. An economist friend of mine uses as an illustration the game Monopoly, which simulates a good, unregulated, liberalized economic system. What would you think, he might ask, if two players were beginning a round of Monopoly and one player started with $16,549, while the other player started with $1?[31] Of course, most of us would think it was ridiculous! The game would be a joke. You can bet that debt would figure into the game pretty quickly. The playing field would not only remain uneven, but would become increasingly so. This fatuous Monopoly game is a good picture of how the global economy works. Neoliberal theory does not account for such disabling inequities at the outset.

Neoliberal economics hurts the poor in a number of ways: by cutting social services and education, by pitting poor, agriculture-producing countries against one another, and by encouraging the stagnation of wages and repression of workers. When a country's comparative advantage is cheap labor, unions and talk of worker's rights will be anathema. Stomping these things out will be to the benefit of factory owners and government officials who profit from the export of cheap labor, and who want to maximize their country's comparative advantage.

Moreover, in the real world of neoliberal economics, the tenets of openness and deregulation are imposed upon poor countries while rich nations follow whatever rules are to their benefit. Countries like the US, Britain, Japan and some European Union countries continue to subsidize key industries and impose some import tariffs, while coercing developing nations, through the vehicle of the IFIs, into removing trade barriers across the board. Even the former-director of the WTO, Mike Moore, has lamented the level of hypocrisy by America and the EU with regard to trade. "Sometimes I feel like joining the kids [protesters] outside," he remarked in 2000, referring to anti-WTO protests. "When they say the system's unfair, they're not always wrong."[32]

Incidentally, it is ironic that *neoliberalism, of which a key tenet is greater freedom from governmental oversight and regulation, has given rise to the most powerful and far-reaching regulatory institutions the world has ever known: the IMF, World Bank, and WTO.* The agreement creating the WTO is itself 22,500 pages in length![33]

Finally, it should be noted that, in the real world, neoliberal theory translates to environmental suicide. Though the environmental consequences of global economics do not figure prominently in this book due to space constraints, I encourage readers to explore the subject further.[34] One consequence of implementing neoliberal theory, which says the best way to promote growth is through global trade, is that now most foods and products people consume arrive to them after traveling thousands of miles via trucks, trains, barges, and airplanes which spew pollution, gradually poisoning our air, water, and land, and consume huge sums of energy. The local production of goods is vastly more environmentally sustainable than the kind of production envisioned by the neoliberal model. Even if global trade were not costly in "humanitarian" terms, it would need to be dramatically curtailed for its environmental costs alone. But humanitarian and environmental concerns are never truly separable.

Export Processing Zones: Backbone of the Global Economy

Export Processing Zones (EPZs) are surely one of the most intriguing features of the neoliberal economy. "Export Processing Zone" is the name given multi-factory compounds in developing countries. These conglomerations of factories constitute mini McWorld villages, microcosms of the global economy, and are often the size of small towns. They are completely fenced in and heavily guarded. In some cases, workers actually live within the zone. One EPZ may contain dozens of different, privately-owned factories producing everything from designer clothing, to calculators, to plastic candle holders. The large majority of products produced in EPZs end up in the hands of Western consumers.

The privately-owned factories within EPZs produce products for transnational corporations (TNCs) on a contract basis. Transnationals strictly forbid these factories from associating themselves in any overt way with the transnational. If a factory produces clothing solely for Abercrombie and Fitch, for example, it is, nevertheless, *not* an Abercrombie and Fitch factory. The transnational's logo will not be displayed on the factory exterior, and if asked about working conditions in their factories, a company spokesperson may be quick to retort that the company *has* no factories. Factories manufacturing goods for TNCs are not owned by the companies for whom they produce; again, they function strictly on a contract basis. The EPZs are nameless, invisible places where corporate accountability does not exist, and faceless human beings manufacture the very goods a company sells, but are not considered company employees.

Trade agreements provide transnational corporations with remarkable incentives to use EPZs. TNCs can contract the manufacturing of their goods to EPZs without paying any import or export taxes to the country of origin,[35] and often without honoring the country's labor laws. For example, a factory in an EPZ in the Philippines can pay workers less than the (already-low) legal minimum wage for the Philippines because the factory is producing for export.[36] Even more advantageous for the TNCs is the readiness of local militaries to put down labor unrest within the zones.

The typical work day in EPZs, where most workers are young women, can run anywhere from 12 hours (for example, in El Salvador or Indonesia) to 16 hours (for example, in China).[37] Women are regularly sexually harassed. Bathroom breaks are kept to a minimum (in some cases, to two a day), and bathrooms are beyond filthy. Wages fall below the amount needed to meet one's basic needs, let alone that of a small family. The water available to workers on a limited basis is usually hazardous to their health. Managers routinely subject female workers to pregnancy tests, and dismiss those who are found pregnant. Workers are harassed and often physically assaulted if they do not meet ever-demanding production quotas. Where toxic chemicals are used, protective equipment is insufficient. Workers must march in and out of factories in military-fashion. Talking during work is forbidden. Attempts at union organization can get a worker imprisoned or killed.[38] These conditions are not the exception in export processing zones, they are the norm. What I have just described is a typical sweatshop in the developing world. It constitutes the backbone on which our global economy is built. Sweatshops advance western consumerism, and promote gross accumulations of wealth by corporate executives.

The trickle-down effect of neoliberal theory gets turned on its head in EPZs. Since corporations contribute very little either through taxes or wages to the economies of poor countries where they "invest," and since urban problems (such as pollution, traffic, and health epidemics) in areas with EPZs snowball the longer EPZs are around, there is no trickling down of wealth. In fact, the reality in developing countries where EPZs reside reveals more of a "trickle-up" effect. Corporations make a killing from the arrangement, while living costs rise for the average residents in the developing nation, and infrastructure crumbles. The unfathomable profits of corporations who use EPZs is shared only with the factory-owning elite class (who are often from a third-party country), and the handful of local government officials whose vocal support is desperately needed to keep EPZs as accommodating to corporations as possible.

Invisible Injustice

Far removed from the view of labor rights activists, Vietnamese workers arrived on the US territory of American Samoa in February of 1999.[39] They had been issued a three-year contract with a Vietnamese recruitment agency and the owner of the Korean-owned Daewoosa factory in Samoa costing the workers between $4,000 and $8,000 for recruitment, immigration, and airfare expenses. The apparel factory would produce clothing for a number of US labels, including privately-owned labels for Target, Wal-Mart, J. C. Penney, and a label for Sears, clothing which would proudly don the words "Made in the USA." Promised an income of $408 to $416 a month net pay for sewing clothing, as well as free food and lodging, the workers expected to pay off their contracts and then earn a decent income to send home to their families.

Instead, the experience at the Daewoosa factory proved hellish for the workers, most of whom were Vietnamese young women. Nearly every possible abuse was inflicted upon them. Their home on Samoa was a barbed-wire-encircled factory compound, their sleeping quarters in over-crowded barracks where two women would often share a bunk 36 inches wide. Those who failed to return to the barracks by the 10 p.m. curfew were beaten. Cockroaches and rats infested the workers' living quarters, and feces would back up through the shower drains as a result of inadequate plumbing.

Malnutrition soon plagued workers, who were usually fed "a watery broth of rice and cabbage," according to a US Dept. of Labor report, but sometimes went without food as a punishment for complaints. Though the original contract stated that food and lodging would be provided for free, in June of 2000, Daewoosa began to charge workers $200 a month for the starvation diet and prison-like lodging. This was by no means the first sign that workers were being cheated. From mid-February to the end of March 1999, the Vietnamese workers at the factory went without pay (though Samoan workers were paid promptly). This pattern surfaced repeatedly. When workers from Vietnam dared to strike, the factory was placed on lockdown and food withheld. After June 2000, it is estimated the "guest workers" at Daewoosa earned about $195.16 per month, when they were paid, since deductions were taken for room and board, Social Security, and a Samoan withholding tax.[40] Most of the workers thus found it would be impossible to pay off their contracts by the end of the three-year contract period.

The indignities inflicted upon the workers at Daewoosa did not end there. Female factory workers reported to local missionaries that the owner of Daewoosa frequently visited the barracks to watch them shower and dress. The same local missionaries visited the factory in May of 1999 and, from outside the gates of the factory, witnessed factory guards kicking and hitting Vietnamese girls. A crowd of girls ran up to the gate, crying and begging the missionaries for help. But soon after the girls were threatened with imprisonment by both the factory owner and a local police officer, the missionaries left. They felt powerless against the injustice they witnessed.

Because American Samoa is a territory of the United States, the Daewoosa factory functioned under the watchful eye of the Occupational Safety and Health Administration (OSHA) and the US Department of Labor (DOL). This cannot be said for thousands of sweatshops around the world. Yet the penalties enacted upon Daewoosa by the DOL were ignored, and the DOL lacked the resources to monitor the Samoan factory, or hold its owner accountable. It was not until after the

nightmare of November 28, 2000 that clothing from the factory was
finally embargoed, and the factory closed down for failure to pay back
wages. On that day, Vietnamese workers were attacked while waiting for
fabric to arrive at the factory so they could begin working. At least ten
workers were seriously wounded that day. One woman lost her left eye
after the jagged end of a PVC pipe was thrust into it. One man lost the
hearing in his left ear after being struck on his head and face with a pipe.

After the DOL placed an embargo on goods from Daewoosa, the
Korean owner of the factory withdrew all funds from the factory, leaving
it bankrupt. Though Daewoosa has been sued by the Vietnamese
workers for payment of back wages, estimated by the DOL at around
one million dollars, it is unlikely the bankrupted Daewoosa will ever
have to pay up, while most of the Vietnamese workers are still indebted
thousands of dollars to the Vietnamese recruitment agency that sent
them to Samoa. Though the J. C. Penney corporation stepped forward
to pay two month's back wages to the Daewoosa workers after being
contacted by the National Labor Committee, Wal-Mart, Target, and
Sears have not acted.[41]

Goods manufactured in US territories such as Samoa and in non-
US countries with liberalized trade status, are exempt from US import
quotas and trade tariffs. Therefore, manufacturers producing in such
places and paying the starvation wages common in developing countries
make a killing. Sales from the Daewoosa factory in 1999 are estimated
to have been $8 million. Still the factories producing the export goods
are not the biggest winners. US stores that sell the goods profit more
than amply. Their earnings are then passed on to the American
consumers who are often enabled to buy their consumables at low
prices. This may not be true for designer goods which often cost
American consumers dearly, without costing the corporation much
more to produce. But, by and large, American consumers are prospering
as a result of the whole system. Furthermore, this pattern is by no
means confined to the US. It is replicated all over the industrialized
world, where the majority of apparel corporations utilize sweatshops
and sell their products both cheaply and at enormous profit.

Exploitation has a key role to play in the global economy. If workers in places like Vietnam and El Salvador were not desperate for any kind of income, it is unlikely they would consent to working under the nightmarish conditions, and for the low wages offered in factories producing for transnational corporations. In fact, the desperate conditions in such countries, conditions precipitated by political instability, legal chaos, and lack of education, all make these places a magnetic draw for TNCs. The relative level of wages in a particular country tends to be directly proportionate to the stability and educational levels in that country. A newly industrialized nation like Singapore, with its political stability, rule of law, and strong educational system, commands higher wages for certain occupations than Britain or the United States.[42] But in countries such as Myanmar (formerly Burma), where marshal law is enforced and human rights are virtually ignored, TNCs can pay workers as little as 7¢ an hour. Parts of the world experiencing hard times are ripe for exploitation by TNCs with mobile capital to invest. This is what is meant by the now familiar phrase: "the race to the bottom." TNCs race to where a disastrous, erratic political situation makes labor cheap, environmental regulations sparse, labor and human rights laws lax, and government leaders pliable. If conditions change in a given country, and democratic forces are able to push for improvements in these areas, the TNCs simply move on to the next global sore spot. The Disney corporation modeled this behavior, moving its factories from the United States to Haiti, then, when Haitian workers strove for better working conditions and higher pay (Disney paid them around $2.40 per week), from Haiti to China, where labor conditions are especially severe.

A common response to this sort of data is that TNCs should continue their practice of setting up shop in desperate parts of the world, paying whatever they can get away with, because obviously the people need *some* sort of work. If the TNCs were not there, some argue, the plight of the workers in those countries would be even worse!

This line of thinking is important to address, and brings us around to a discussion of the *preconditions* of many global trade relationships. Such preconditions are known as "structural adjustments."

Structural Adjustments as a Feature of Neoliberal Economics

The preconditions for trade and finance set by international financial institutions usually make life harder for the poor in a given country. For developing countries to receive funds from the IMF or World Bank, to enter the WTO, or to enter into liberalized trade relationships with industrialized nations, countries are expected to cooperate with a restructuring of their economies. The structural adjustments imposed on these countries usually involve wage freezing, devaluation of currency, the lifting of trade barriers such as tariffs, fees and subsidies, cuts in social services including education and healthcare, privatization of industries and utilities, the consolidation of land holdings, and incentives to large-scale corporations producing for export. These *preconditions* of trade tend to exacerbate the desperation of poor countries at the outset, or even create desperation where it did not previously exist. Many poor families who had, for generations, been providing for themselves via small businesses and small-scale farming, find that after structural adjustments, they are put out of business.[43] As even the World Bank admits, structural adjustments have a negative impact on the poor.[44] Data from the UN reveals that areas which have undergone structural adjustment have seen significant decreases in per capita income.[45] Since the 1970's, 100 developing countries have undergone economic decline, with people in sub-Saharan Africa living on 20% less than they had 25 years ago.[46]

David Korten highlights Costa Rica as an example of the kind of decline experienced by developing countries worldwide as a result of structural adjustment. I include his summary in its entirety:

> Before the International Monetary Fund (IMF) and the World Bank restructured Costa Rica's economic policies in the name of easing its foreign debt problems, Costa Rica was widely known as a society that was more egalitarian than its neighbors. It had a strong base of small farmers and few of the large landholdings characteristic of other Latin American

societies. The policies imposed by the IMF and the World
Bank shifted the economic incentives away from small farms
producing the things that Costa Ricans eat toward large
estates producing for export. As a consequence, thousands
of small farmers have been displaced, their lands have been
consolidated into large ranches and agricultural estates
producing for export, and Costa Rica's income gap is
becoming more like that of the rest of Latin America. An
increase in crime and violence has required sharp increases in
public expenditures on police and public security. The
country is now dependent on imports to meet basic food
requirements, and the foreign debt that structural
adjustments was supposed to reduce has doubled. As
outrageous as the consequences of their policies have been,
the IMF and the World Bank point to Costa Rica as a
structural adjustment *success* story because economic growth
has increased and the country is now able to meet its growing
debt service payments.[47]

Costa Rica is exemplary only because its degrees of equality and
sustainability were relatively high prior to structural adjustment. But
the effects of economic readjustment in Costa Rica can be seen all
over the developing world. Corporations do not necessarily move in to
give jobs to people who have long had no means of survival. *Often they
move in to employ those made unemployed by the very structural adjustments
which paved the way for corporate investment.*

Prior to structural adjustment in Haiti, Haiti imported only around
7,000 tons/yr of rice, the main food staple in Haiti.[48] The food staple
was largely grown in Haiti, for Haiti. In the late 1980s, however, at the
behest of the IFIs, Haiti underwent economic reform in order to gain
special trade status with Western countries and access to financing
from international banks. As a result, Haiti lifted import tariffs on
rice. Immediately, Haitian rice farmers were unable to compete with
rice farmers in the United States, where the rice industry is heavily
subsidized.[49] Cheaper rice poured into Haiti from the US. Hundreds

of thousands of rice farmers became unemployed, and many were left with no other choice than to flock to the cities to be exploited by foreign-owned factories (sweatshops) producing largely for American markets. By 1996, Haiti was spending 100 million dollars on imported rice, importing 196,000 tons of foreign rice per year. Since then, the price of rice has continued to rise worldwide, making the Haitian food staple more and more scarce for hungry Haitians.

Structural Adjustment Programs often have detrimental effects on the environment in developing countries as well. The African country of Ghana, one of the most structurally adjusted countries in the world, furnishes an excellent example of this. Adjustment programs implemented in Ghana by the IMF and World Bank beginning in the early eighties were focused on increasing the profitability of cocoa farming in order to increase the production of cocoa for export. However, the programs resulted in a global decline in cocoa prices as output of cocoa rose. This, along with other aspects of structural adjustments, such as the cutting of public sector jobs and the removal of subsidies for small farmers, left Ghana's poorest citizens even poorer. As a "solution" to this failure, the World Bank supported a revival of the Ghanaian commercial forestry industry in the mid-eighties. This precipitated the rapid deforestation of Ghana. Ghana is now largely without trees, and both the ground and those who depend on it suffer as a result. The game, fuel, and medicines Ghanaians once reaped from the forest are now in short supply. Malnutrition has been the outcome of the World Bank forestry projects in Ghana, and Ghana's soil is rapidly eroding.[50]

The poor in developing countries suffer from structural adjustments, while a small elite class gets wealthier and producers from industrialized countries profit lavishly from exports and debt servicing. Corporations who legitimize their exploitation of the poor in developing countries by claiming the people would be worse off without them are spreading disinformation. And public ignorance allows it. But in order to understand why developing countries would submit to the rigors of structural adjustment, one must first know something about the debt crisis of the early eighties.[51]

The Debt Crisis

The story stretches back to the mid-seventies, when a worldwide recession hit developing countries like a jack hammer. At the time, most nations in the global south were agricultural producers who relied on the export of food and mined resources to northern countries for revenues. Export revenues were then used to import needed oil and manufactured products from the global north. When recession hit, prices for food and natural resources plummeted, while the costs of oil and manufactured products from northern countries rose sharply. This created unmanageable trade deficits for developing nations.

In the meantime, northern banks had become saturated with money from the prospering oil industry, and were eager to find places to invest. They found a perfect match in the nations of the global south, who were desperate for funds to finance their imports. The northern banks encouraged poor countries to take out copious low-interest loans.

But in the early 1980s, another world recession, this one even more devastating, caused prices for goods produced in developing countries to, again, fall precipitously. Feeling the need to prop up the value of the dollar, the US government hiked interest rates from 8% up to 20%, starting a trend that was mimicked by other countries. The raising of interest rates left poor nations with huge high-interest loans at a time when they were most unable to pay. More than ever, the global south was entirely at the mercy of their northern financiers.

Many developing countries turned for help to the World Bank and IMF, who were increasingly empowered and influenced by the US administration at that time, that of President Ronald Reagan. Acting on the recommendations of their supporters, the international financial institutions decided to "reschedule" the loans of poor countries if those countries would submit to a restructuring of their economies, or to Structural Adjustment Programs. Though these programs were aimed at stabilizing economies, and though they succeeded in bringing inflation under control and balancing budgets so that debt payments could be made, they did so by implementing neoliberal economic reforms, which, as already stated, had disastrous effects on the poor. However, given the circumstances poor countries were in when Structural Adjustment Programs were imposed, one can see they had little choice but to submit. The Structural Adjustment Programs did not even mitigate the debt crisis. While the debt of poor countries stood at $785 billion at the beginning of the crisis, by 1993, debts had multiplied to $1.5 trillion.[52] *Poor countries long ago paid off the original loan amounts, but continue to service the interest.* In the cases of many developing nations, the debts are simply unpayable.

Since the late 1990s, a vital international, church-based movement called "Jubilee Plus"[53] (formerly Jubilee 2000) has been pressing international banks and northern governments to excuse the debts of the world's poorest nations. The movement has made significant strides with the IFIs, and with some rich countries. Unfortunately, the commitments made by these banks and governments have, to date, not been fully acted upon.[54] In the meantime, interest on loans continues to multiply, and money that should be going to education and health care in the developing world is being paid to northern banks. But the Jubilee movement continues its important work of education on the debt crisis, as well as advocacy on behalf of the poor before world bodies. I am hopeful that debts will, eventually, be canceled as a result of their work. Interestingly, the IMF has agreed to cancel debts of "Highly Indebted Poor Countries" (HIPCs) only if the countries are carrying out neoliberal reforms. That is, if they are cooperating with their Structural Adjustment Programs.

Moral Incapacitation?

Corporations who profit disproportionately from the labor of the poor around the world should be called to task, shouldn't they? Shouldn't transnational corporations have an ethical obligation to pay living wages and provide healthy working conditions? In response to such questions, supporters of the global economic system will point out that labor and environmental standards are set not by the corporations but by the country of origin (in other words, by the developing countries where factories/sweatshops are owned and operated). Corporations are merely taking advantage of working standards that already exist in the global south. In that case, shouldn't standards such as a well-enforced minimum, living wage and requirements for healthy working environments become the *conditions* for foreign investment? If corporations were prohibited from investing in countries where labor, human rights and environmental abuse were the norm, wouldn't we begin to see these conditions changing in the developing world? Corporations obviously have a major degree of influence over governments who want their investment.[55] If corporations used this influence to pressure governments to meet higher global standards for labor and human rights and environmental protection, rather than using their influence to keep wages low and regulations slight, then the global economy would look more just. Moreover, if countries in the global south lacked the means to raise labor and environmental standards, corporations might assist them, either by advocating for or investing in development of good civic infrastructure, because it would ultimately be in their best interests to do so.

Of course, this sounds like a pipe dream. The present system simply does not work this way. Not even close. The model above would be a recognition of the value of community, interdependence, and sustainability. It would imply that ethics are a priority of the global trade system. In fact, the global economy as it is currently structured runs against the grain of ethical accountability.

There *are* individual companies that have attempted to have a positive influence on working conditions and wages in developing countries where they invest. These companies' ethical business practices have, however, been partially disabled by the broader system of exploitation and competition. Individual corporations find it hard to make a significant impact on governments when governments know there are dozens of other corporations perfectly willing to take advantage of the low wages and disempowered labor force in their countries. Furthermore, governments fear that if they improve conditions, investors will simply flee to more lax, desperate parts of the world. As the global economy is currently structured, competition disables those with good intentions.

The Gap clothing store, though no corporate Mother Teresa, attempted to improve some conditions for workers in the Salvadoran factories producing its clothing. As the New York Times concluded, though: "The lesson from Gap's experience in El Salvador is that competing interests among factory owners, government officials, American managers and middle-class consumers—all with their eyes on the lowest possible cost—make it difficult to achieve even basic standards, and even harder to maintain them."[56] After improvements implemented by Gap, workers in the Salvadoran factories now have coffee breaks, can eat lunch in an outdoor cafeteria, can use the now-unlocked bathrooms as needed, work in clean, well-ventilated factories, and can file complaints with independent monitors chosen from local unions, universities, and religious organizations. Though wages have barely risen in the last six years (from $.55/hr to $.60/hr), and though workers still work long hours with high production quotas,[57] these changes are not negligible. Nonetheless, Gap has found it extremely taxing to maintain even these improvements. The Salvadoran business sector and officials respond to Gap's independent monitors with suspicion rather than cooperation, alleging they represent left-wing, or US protectionist interests. Gap also spends great sums of money each year to pay the independent monitors, to pay managers to deal with disputes, and to pay the company's non-independent monitors.[58] Replicating the Salvadoran experiment in all 4,000 factories sourcing for Gap could cost the company around 4.5 percent of its annual profits.[59] If Gap's experiment in El Salvador demonstrates anything, it demonstrates how difficult it is for an individual corporation to force widespread change. *A global economic system warrants having global labor and human rights standards and monitors, so that each individual company does not have either the option or the burden of setting its own standards and enforcing them.*

Presently, no global institutions exist that function effectively to protect worker rights and human rights in the context of global trading. Very powerful institutions exist that protect the rights of corporations and keep liberalized trade as profitable as possible for global investors, namely the World Trade Organization, World Bank, and International Monetary Fund (the IFIs). These institutions do not, however, protect workers. Member nations of the UN are expected to adhere to the conventions of the International Labor Organization (ILO) which they, as a nation, have ratified.[60] The ILO conventions uphold some worker rights, such as the right to organize. Unfortunately, very few member nations have ratified either of the conventions dealing with freedom of association and collective bargaining. But even if more nations had signed onto those conventions it would be of little consequence. There are no effective processes for sanctioning businesses or countries who disregard the ILO standards.

There are a number of different international trade pacts, such as NAFTA, the Caribbean Basin Initiative (CBI), and the Andean Trade Partnership Agreement, as well as different unilateral trade programs such as the US Generalized System of Preferences (GSP) program, administered by the US Trade Representative. Each trade program has different mechanisms for dealing with disputes or problems. But none of the present agreements have effective means of addressing workers' concerns.[61] It should also be pointed out that neither the trade agreements, nor the ILO conventions address the problem of starvation wages. As long as a company pays the wage required by the country in which it is operating, it is deemed acceptable. Yet wage standards in the developing world, especially in countries such as China or Indonesia, are unreasonably and oppressively low.

If liberalized trade is to lead to development and equity, rather than exploitation and greater poverty, fair treatment of workers will have to become a *real* condition of trade relationships. This would require a shift from decentralized, unregulated markets, to a more accountable, regulated system of economics.[62] Activists and politicians challenging the IFIs and neoliberal economics in general are advocating for such changes. But the changes are likely to come very, very slowly. In the meantime, how are we to live as Christians *now*? That is the question I will address in the latter part of this book. It may be true that individual companies and individual persons cannot, on their own, change the system. This does not, however, excuse corporate executives or consumers from culpability for the exploitation we participate in every day. Seeking to profit from the misfortune of others is immoral according to just about any interpretation of Christian ethics. Yet Christians are as enmeshed in the global economy as everyone else, and often we profit from the exploitation of our global neighbors without realizing it, even if we have deep compassion for them. Are we simply cornered, morally incapacitated? Or, can we as Christians incarnate an alternative way of living, an alternative way of *being*, even while entwined in an abusive economic system?

The answer to this second question, I believe, is "yes." There are ways to resist moral incapacitation. Christians have always been enmeshed, to one degree or another, in systems of domination and abuse and have, from the beginning, proclaimed their good news from amidst the fray. The message of Christianity spread rapidly throughout the Mediterranean world in part because of the Pax Romana, and the fine system of Roman roads on which early Christian preachers traveled. But this did not excuse Christians from condemning the idolatry of Rome (see the book of Revelation). St. Francis received a stellar education as the son of wealthy Italian parents, but he revolted against his family's lifestyle, and used his learning to call others to lives of simplicity and self-sacrifice in service to Jesus. John Woolman, though not a slave owner himself, prospered during the boom-years of 18th-century America, a land built on the backbone of slavery. Woolman did not hesitate, however, to persuade many of his customers that slavery was morally reprehensible, and eventually, to abandon his business pursuits to spend more time advocating abolition. Elizabeth Fry was a society-born, well-educated woman of Jane Austen's England. Yet she chose to devote her life to visiting prisoners in repulsive conditions, and speaking with high-level English officials about the injustices of England's prison system. Her name is synonymous with the prison reform movement of her time.

The villagers of Le Chambon in southern France were relatively distanced from the horrors of World War II. Even during the later German occupation, when the Nazi presence in southern France and the pressures of the Vichy government were more felt, the protestant Chambonnais could have chosen to go about their business relatively unthreatened. But instead, the people of Le Chambon housed and hid thousands of Jews who had fled for their lives. In doing so, they put themselves and their families at great risk, and saved many.

These are examples of Christians whose lives, like most of our lives, blossomed in fields of oppression and exploitation. In some ways they benefited, however unintentionally, from the domination system that encircled them. Nonetheless, they did not use the fact that they were enmeshed in such a system as an excuse for inaction or complacency. Instead, they incarnated an alternative to the system, even while living in the midst of it. They incarnated the gospel, which is called "good news" precisely when it is spoken into a context of domination and despair. These Christians did not formally lead a revolt; each one of them *was* a revolt. You and I may not make history in quite the same way they did, but the Christian saints who have gone before us provide the inspiration and examples we need to envision an alternative way of living in the world, and remind us that the seeds of radical faithfulness can spring up in the most unlikely of settings. Christians who desire to be faithful to Jesus by loving God and loving their neighbors in our world which is ensnared in consumerism, exploitation, and injustice, will have to live creatively and attentively. But as we submit to the "transforming of our minds" we will begin to see a new way—a path of mercy, peace, and stewardship that leads to wholeness.

A book like this cannot initiate the process of new birth that enables truly moral living, and it certainly will not be an instruction manual on how to make moral decisions in the global economy. Moral decisions are the outworking of moral character and being. But once one has submitted oneself to God, moral character comes to be shaped in community and in dialogue, by engaging with and learning from those who also seek mercy, selflessness, and truth-telling for their lives. This book becomes a contribution to that dialogue as the voices of the merciful, selfless, and truthful are heard in its pages. I know that I, who am deeply troubled by my own complicity in our abusive economic system, have been shaped by their stories.

This book also examines the global economy in the light of biblical ethics, especially New Testament ethics. The New Testament provides us with a unique perspective from which to view the global economy, a perspective that can give direction and inspiration as we live out the Christian witness in a globalized economy. I allude to the New Testament teaching on "the powers." Besides looking at biblical teachings on wealth and its usage, we will explore the Pauline idea of the powers, focusing on how it relates to our topic. The theology of the powers, which has been admirably elucidated by such theologians as Hendrik Berkhof (1977), Walter Wink (1992) and William Stringfellow (1973), assists Christians in appreciating the cosmic and eternal significance of such earthly, visible, "created," institutions (Col 1:16) as governments, religious structures, academic institutions, and, as will be examined here, economic systems.[63] Chapter Six will focus on this theological perspective. In a world where truth-telling is scarce, we as Christians have been exhorted to name the fallen powers for what they are and remind them of their God-ordained purpose, which, according to Colossians 1:16, is service to Christ.

Stringfellow summarized our Christian vocation: to live humanly in the era of the Fall. To live humanly. And as Stringfellow prophetically states, the only life-giving, humanizing activity in a world where death is worshiped, whether in the form of greed, power-lust, military violence, or falsehood, is the activity of *confronting* and *resisting* the God-denying powers. It is the central goal of the powers to dehumanize, immobilize, and subject, in order to lull us into idolatrously pledging our allegiance to the systems and institutions of this world, to the powers themselves. In such an environment, the only humanizing response is resistance. Moreover, as a response to the powers' striving to usurp the place of God in our world and in our lives, such resistance is worship. By proclaiming the fallenness and subjectivity of the powers we see around us, we simultaneously proclaim the sovereignty of God over all.

It is my hope, then, that this book is written in a spirit of truth-telling and resistance, a spirit of worship. In Chapter Seven I tell about the shape resistance has taken in the lives of certain people I know, using the form of case studies. For many of those featured, as well as for myself, the journey on this path of resistance has only just commenced, and is far from complete. But the journey itself is liberating, as we form a clearer vision of, and move closer and closer to, a life lived in harmony with God's intentions for creation. Such a life is the only one that can truly be called "free." In our time, choosing a life that resists the dehumanizing pressures of consumerism, militarism, illusion, and self-appeasing pleasure, is to choose to move toward that which is truly human, truly reflective of the image of God, and truly free. For we were made for transcendence and for worship, and only in submission and worship to God can we move through this life unchained by the bonds of this world.

Thus, this book is titled *Free People*, a title intended as a challenge to the colossal misnomer "free trade." As one sagacious writer put it, "In the global marketplace defined as free trade, everyone is free, it seems, but the people."[64] These words resonate loudly with truth. The stories that follow weigh heavily with images of human bondage of the physical, political, and mental varieties, usually inflicted upon the poor. But looking at the global economy from a Christian perspective, one can discern a powerful spiritual bondage, a bondage more daunting as it numbs our sensitivity to God and neighbor, and to virtues such as compassion, justice, and honesty. The victims of this bondage are not counted disproportionately among the poor. These victims are mainly the well-to-do, the comfortable, who traipse through their compartmentalized lives like the emperor naked as birth. Perhaps these victims are you and I.

I have hope, though, that we can journey toward freedom. That freedom begins by telling the truth, and by acknowledging the sovereignty of God over all areas of our lives, even the economic. This seems to be something of what Jesus meant when he said, "You will know the truth, and the truth will make you free" (John 8:32).

Chapter Two

Portraits of Global Economics from the Global North

The need of a constantly expanding market for its products chases the bourgeoisie over the whole surface of the globe. It must nestle everywhere, settle everywhere, establish connexions everywhere . . . [The bourgeoisie] compels all nations, on pain of extinction, to adopt the bourgeois mode of production; it compels them to introduce what it calls civilization into their midst, i.e., to become bourgeois themselves. In one word, it creates a world after its own image.

Karl Marx[1]

Free enterprise works because, like democracy, it gives real power to the people.

[We] need to ensure that military superiority—particularly technological superiority—remains with nations (above all the United States) which can be trusted with it. We must never leave the sanction of force to those who have no scruples about its use.

Margaret Thatcher[2]

The Global Trade System;
A Thorn in the Side of Democracy

Listen to politicians, economists, or corporate executives praising neoliberal economics and you will no doubt hear them commend the model as the surest way to further freedom, or the democratization of nations. We are to believe that the more nations cooperate with the global trade system, the more likely it is that citizens in those countries will rise out of poverty, demand representation in their government, and collectively mold a strong democratic society for themselves. Advocates for neoliberalism are so committed to furthering democracy in this way, they will go to great lengths to keep "the People" from hindering them.

Apprehension about NAFTA was so acute among the populace of both the US and Mexico, and stark opposition to the policy so widespread, that public representation in the NAFTA talks was kept to a minimum. It took the negotiators of the North American Free Trade Agreement 14 months of private deliberations to draft the agreement, and after the agreement was finalized, it was not available for public perusal for over a month. Even members of Congress were ignorant of the details of NAFTA until shortly before the agreement came up for a straight yes- or no-vote (no amendments allowed) in the House. The esoteric, over-1,000-page document that was eventually made available to the public carried a price tag of $41 per copy.[3] Even if the document was translated into Spanish, it mattered little. The Mexicans most affected by the agreement could not have afforded the document, and many could not have read it. And now, six years after the conclusion of the talks, the number of Mexicans living below the poverty line has grown from 66 to 70 percent. The average Mexican has seen a 40 percent drop in purchasing power since 1994.[4]

In the realm of trade negotiations, American presidents have, in the past, been afforded special privilege to bypass democratic process and debate. It is known as "fast-track authority" or Trade Promotion Authority (TPA),[5] and allows a president to negotiate international trade deals without the threat of future amendments from members of Congress, who are the key representatives of the people and the backbone of American democracy. Once a trade agreement has been fully drafted under the fast-track process, the Congress gets to vote either for or against it in its entirety, but cannot make any changes whatsoever. This system affords enormous unilateral power to the Executive Branch of our government.

A further development in the deterioration of democracy: corporations can now take states to court. NAFTA's chapter 11 allows corporate investors to sue member nations or, more likely, states/provinces, and challenge hard-won, democratically-implemented laws which get in the way of profits. *So the will of the people as expressed in the voting booth can be overridden by the will of a foreign investor.*[6] Moreover, when corporations are awarded compensation for trade losses caused by state laws, the state's taxpayers get to foot the bill. Not only are the laws of the citizenry thrown onto the burn pile of trade inhibitors, but the citizens get to pay off the corporations who stoke the flames. To date, Canadian taxpayers could be the biggest losers in this scheme. In the first seven years of NAFTA, they paid out $11 billion in compensation to corporations. In the same period, US taxpayers paid $1.8 billion,[7] and Mexican taxpayers $294 million.[8] Though the figure for Mexico appears low by comparison, it may have the greatest impact on citizens due to Mexico's higher level of poverty.

This is all a relatively new development. Prior to NAFTA, the two international trade tribunals, one which operates under the World Bank and the other under the UN, mainly handled cases between private parties which only affected the parties in the dispute. Now, however, they constitute a forum for dealing with issues of public policy. Despite this monumental shift in their function, they continue to deliberate behind closed doors and to exclude the media and the public (even public officials) from their meetings.[9] Even more disturbing than this lack of transparency, is the fact that these tribunals are composed of trade specialists who are not barred from having a financial interest in the cases they try.[10]

Many of the features and consequences of neoliberal economics already mentioned have incited discontent around the globe. Though the collective outcry against neoliberal economics didn't reach the ears of most Americans until recent years, it has been building momentum for decades. The earliest demonstrations against global economics took place in Algeria and Egypt in the 1980s. Since then, widespread public protest against the global economic system has sprung up from the Phillipines to South Africa to Brazil. On the day NAFTA went into effect, January 1, 1994, the Zapatistas, representing the indigenous people of Chiapas, Mexico, whose land rights were rescinded as part of the agreement, actually launched an insurrection against the Mexican government that continues to this day.[11]

By 1999, the West's own global justice movement, a campaign opposed to neoliberal economics and its effects, proved to be something to reckon with. One of its greatest successes has been exposing the constraints of Western-style "democracy" and "freedom". From Seattle, Washington to Genoa, Italy, this brand of democracy has been tested by citizens of supposedly long-democratized governments, which now represent the status quo of neoliberal economics. Is western-style democracy failing miserably? In this chapter we will look at the demonstrations staged by global justice campaigners at trade and finance meetings from Seattle in 1999 to Genoa in 2001, ending with a look at the 2001 WTO meetings in Doha, Qatar. The demonstrations provide some intriguing portraits of the global economy from the perspective of the global north.

Seattle, Washington, USA, December 1999

The World Trade Organization (WTO) was established in 1995 to codify and enforce provisions of previous General Agreements on Tariffs and Trade [GATT]. Where prior trade agreements had focused on removing high tariff barriers between nations, after the "Uruguay Round" of the GATT meetings in 1986 negotiators began introducing many new and far-reaching non-tarriff provisions. It was also the Uruguay Round that resulted in the founding of the WTO in 1995.[12]

The WTO didn't see it coming. Sure, there was the buzz about activists converging on Seattle to protest their policies, but they'd seen all that before. It was business-as-usual.

What they did not expect were the numbers. Thirty thousand demonstrators showed up and in the face of mass arrests, tear-gas, and strong-arming, refused to leave. Despite the revolting image created by the media, the overwhelming majority of these protesters were completely nonviolent. Even Seattle's police chief commented that 99 percent of the demonstrators were peaceful and cooperative. In fact, with the exception of the 100-200 lamentable, media-drenched, violent anarchists[13] and non-activist opportunists, the protesters proved to be so nonaggressive and tenacious the authorities didn't know what to do with them. In the end, the trade meetings were canceled, the global justice movement made history, and the Seattle Police Department had a monumental public relations crisis on its hands. Interestingly, the meetings were not canceled due to protests. They broke down after representatives of developing countries walked out, accusing rich countries of not living up to the previous trade agreements, specifically the 1994 Uruguay Round agreement. The stated goal of the WTO ministerial meeting in Seattle was the drafting of an agreement to begin a new round of global trade talks. Needless to say, the goal was not met.

What were the goals of the Seattle WTO protesters? They were to shut down the trade meetings and get their grievances on the agendas of future ones. These goals were achieved, though the talks collapsed for reasons the protesters did not foresee. But perhaps the demonstrators' greatest victory was in exposing the nature of American "democracy". For years, activists and non-governmental organizations (NGOs) in America had been pushing for greater transparency and public involvement in the shaping of trade policy, but to no avail.[14] Many had worked tirelessly within the limits of democratic processes. When these groups took to the streets of Seattle, their numbers bolstered by a massive contingent of American young people, they were demanding the attention they had (more politely) been requesting for a long time. Among the masses of nonviolent protesters, some represented environmental concerns, some marched on behalf of workers around the world, some represented concerns about biotechnology or the outrageous costs of patented pharmaceuticals, some were taking a stand for human rights, some represented out-of-work US factory workers, and some were there because they were simply tired of corporations having so much power.

Was there a darker element among the protesters? Yes. The "Black Bloc" is the name given to violent anarchist groups who have made a showing at most major trade meetings since Seattle. These protesters, though angry at some of the same things that have angered other activists, have goals that are unabashedly violent and destructive. They destroy property, start skirmishes with police officers, set fires, and generally raise hell. They also know how to use the media. Though anarchists make up only a small percentage of the protesters at trade meetings, they get the lion's share of media attention. It is highly regrettable that their dominance of media coverage clouds the victories achieved by nonviolent protesters.

The Black Bloc also know how to make the police look bad. Unfortunately, the authorities in Seattle, as in other protest sites, did not know how to discriminate between criminal behavior and civil protest, and used the violent anarchists as an excuse to attack nonviolent protesters, fire rubber bullets into crowds, gas peaceful assemblies, set off concussion grenades, and fill jails with young idealists and weathered public servants guilty of civil disobedience for blocking streets.[15] According to a Seattle Post-Intelligencer article from the third day of the WTO protest, "Seattle Police Chief Norm Stamper said 99 percent of the demonstrators were peaceful and cooperated with authorities, and some protesters are even doing 'everything they can' to help clean up the city."[16] In the end, this made the police responses look at best disproportionate, unprepared, and desperate, and at worst, barbaric.

By the second day of demonstrations, Seattle officials had called in 200+ riot-trained National Guardsmen and 300 extra state troopers to bolster the ranks of about 1,200 Seattle police officers.[17] They had set up a 46-block protective zone around the Convention Center, the Trade Center and the hotels housing delegates. Only those with official business were permitted to enter.[18] By the second night of protests, over 500 demonstrators had been arrested[19] and some were in solitary confinement.[20]

Activists said that what started out as a struggle for workers' rights and human rights around the world ended as a struggle for the right to public protest and the right to free speech in America.[21]

Washington, DC, USA, April 2000

After the Seattle WTO protests of 1999, international finance meetings would never be the same. At the April 2000 meeting of the IMF and World Bank in Washington, DC, delegates and authorities knew better what to expect. The 30,000 people who descended on the Capitol to demonstrate against the IFIs' role in increasing poverty and suffering throughout the global south found the northwest section of the city barricaded by a wall of 10,000 police officers. This proved effective in keeping dissenters far from ear-shot or sight of the IMF and World Bank officials.

Though the protesters spent four rainy days at the lines, far from the meetings, they viewed it as a victory. For the second time, tens of thousands of protesters had converged in America to challenge the effects of the global trade system. Clearly, a vital movement had been born. Furthermore, the media attention garnered by their presence caused hundreds of millions of people around the world to ask for the first time: "What are the IMF and World Bank? And what do they do?"

Prague, Czechoslovakia, September 2000

[The protests in Prague were preceded by] a debate held on Sept. 23 at the famous Prague Castle between representatives of civil society and the leadership of the World Bank and the IMF, an event orchestrated by the Czech President Vaclav Havel. Instead of bridging the gap between the two sides, the debate widened it, since, in response to concrete demands, World Bank president James Wolfensohn and IMF managing director Horst Koehler were not prepared to go beyond platitudes and generalities.[22]

Demonstrations against the IMF and World Bank in Prague marked another important turning point in the global justice movement. They were the first pan-European protests against the neoliberal economic system. They took place in a formerly communist country. They also rapidly deteriorated into riots.[23]

The atmosphere was carnivalesque as about 15,000 protesters gathered in Peace Square in Prague. Also gathered there were 11,000 Czech police, who had been primed by the FBI and European police forces. Meetings of the World Bank were taking place in the former communist center of culture, and activists split into three groups intending to form a human chain around the center. Not long after the groups split up and headed in different directions, mayhem ensued.

One group met with armored personnel carriers, several hundred riot police, tear gas, and water cannons. Though several thousand protesters in this group backed up a dozen blocks, the aggressive "Ya Basta" activists of Italy who were leading the group crashed barriers, charged the police, and threw hundreds of water balloons. Another group tried to approach the conference center from the southwest, singing and using humor to diffuse the tension. However, when they got within 200 meters of the center they were assaulted with tear gas, water cannons, and percussion grenades. Many demonstrators engaged in scuffles with the police and hurled items at the authorities. The third group tried to get close to the center—via small, cobbled side streets, but were met by lines of riot police and military troops.

By the end of the first day of protests, Prague had seen Europe's worst riots in years. "The scale of the riots and the fact that the police had resorted to tactics not seen since the communist era shook the Czechs," according to the UK's *Guardian* newspaper.[24] After the first day of the meetings, many IMF and World Bank officials refused to go to the conference area, and the meetings were canceled. Once the violence subsided, nonviolent demonstrators engaged in peaceful protest and were subjected to mass arrests.[25]

Davos, Switzerland, February 2001

> The World Economic Forum at Davos was not created for
> controversy: it was created to bring capitalists into contact
> with politicians, media people, non-governmental people

and intellectuals, and to spark debate and action on some of the world's problems. It was a serious, heuristic exercise.]

. . . This year—as concrete blocks and razor wire surrounded the Swiss resort, and police beat rioting demonstrators diverted to Zurich—Davos, the antidote to greed, the tamer of Mammon, became, along with Seattle and Prague, another embattled emplacement of exploitation, protected from the wrath of "the anti-global people" only by clubs, tear gas and jails.[26]

The 2001 annual meetings of the World Economic Forum at the Swiss resort town of Davos were more somber than in past years. Since the upbeat 2000 meetings, America's miraculous economic growth had begun to wane and global justice protests were proving to be a real irritant. At the 2001 meetings, many important figures, including all representatives of the Bush Administration, would not be in attendance.[27]

Though trade officials coming to Davos may have been reluctant to entertain the question, was the public outcry against neoliberal economics having an effect? An agenda item at Davos 2001 would be how to address backlash against neoliberal economics. Furthermore, many representatives of non-governmental organizations (NGOs) and labor unions had been encouraged to attend. Perhaps most significant, debates from the Davos meetings would be broadcast on the internet.[28] The theme of the meetings would be: "Putting a human face on globalization."

Unfortunately, the financial elite who came to Davos were holed up in a luxury ski resort and five-star hotels in an area cordoned off by road blocks and barbed-wire fences. The hundred or so protesters who managed to cross these lines were fended off by water cannons, tear gas, and rubber bullets.[29] Activists were turned away at the Swiss border. British Socialist Alliance candidate, Weyman Bennett, was actually flown back to Britain. Even booksellers entering Switzerland with books critical of globalization, such as the bestselling *No Logo*, by Canadian author Naomi Klein, were turned back at the border. Both the booksellers and Mr. Bennett eventually did get to Davos,[30] but all in all, it was an ironic setting for a meeting aimed at humanizing global economics.

Quebec City, Canada, April 2001

> The proposed free trade area [FTAA, or Free Trade Area of
> the Americas] from Canada to Chile would encompass 800
> million people and have an economic output of $11 trillion.
> President Bush told reporters: "I'm going to be very aggressive
> about pushing a free trade agenda for the hemisphere." He
> predicted the summit would issue a strong statement that
> "nations of our hemisphere are bound together by the
> concept of a free trade agreement."[31]

Global justice protests were back on North American soil with the
Summit of the Americas in Quebec City in April 2001, a meeting
bringing together governmental and trade representatives from 34
countries of the Western Hemisphere. They would discuss expanding
NAFTA to become a Free Trade Area of the Americas by 2005, a plan
which would make the entire hemisphere a liberalized trade zone. At
the meetings, Washington bid to bump the target date up by two years.
This plan was crushed by countries such as Brazil, who have serious
reservations about the proposed FTAA.

One thing had become clear since the last major North American
demonstration for global justice (Washington, DC, April 2000): with
the battle of Prague, the ranks of violent protesters at these
demonstrations were increasing in number, and what had once been a
stand-off was beginning to look more like a war. Such was the case in
Quebec. Thousands of demonstrators, among them Black Bloc
anarchists, attempted to tear down the 10-foot-high, 4-mile-long fence
around Quebec's old city and summit venues, and threw stones and
other objects at police. This is not to say that the large majority of
protesters were not committed to nonviolent protest, however. They
were. The violent demonstrators were *dramatically* outnumbered by
the 20,000 peaceful protesters who marched through the city and
engaged in other nonviolent direct action.[32]

Again, police aggression was not reserved for the ranks of militant
activists engaged in provocation and violence. In one case, tear gas was
used to disperse a small group of Christians praying 160 yards from

the fence, after they had planted corn in remembrance of farmers in Chiapas, Mexico.[33] Canisters of gas were frequently lobbed at crowds of nonviolent protesters. The following eyewitness account by a protest medic provides a graphic picture of the weapon of tear gas:

> On the front lines on Friday we began treating people as the gassing began. We kept having to retreat more and more to avoid the clouds of gas. At one point a canister exploded right next to me. I can't begin to explain the agony of being hit head on with tear gas. First, it suffocates you. I began to walk very quickly, barely restraining panic, as I coughed and choked. I thought I would die, that any minute my asthma would kick in. Everywhere we turned there were more riot cops, more gas and no safe space to calm down and decompress. My eyes were fine, being sealed under swim goggles, but my skin was burning like fire . . .
>
> As we walked back into the chaos, we came upon a girl who had been hit by a canister of gas, which exploded all over her body. Medics were treating her by stripping off her clothing and pouring liquids all over her. The poor girl was crying and screaming, in so much pain. Around us were clouds and clouds of gas and cops advancing on all sides. The cops began shooting canisters high into the air, into the back of the crowd where we were. In that area there were only peaceful protesters; we were not up by the perimeter fence, and we were not involved in Black Bloc activities up by the front lines. Our space was full of individuals being treated for various injuries and just trying to recuperate. Nevertheless, we were being hit with dozens of canisters.[34]

Unfortunately, the US media had little to say about the police aggression meted out on nonviolent protesters. They instead fixated on the Black Bloc demonstrators attacking policemen and chainlink fences. People sitting at home watching the evening news were thus spared a realistic picture of the events, and could retire to bed feeling secure that the bastions of riot police were merely maintaining justice and order.

Genoa, Italy, July 2001

Violence set the tone for protests in Genoa. In the days before the G8 summit,[35] police confiscated car bombs and other weapons from suspects in the vicinity of Genoa, and parcel bombs were delivered to companies in Milan and Treviso.[36] A foreboding tension hung over the city.

Genoa's G8 summit, which drew over 100,000 activists,[37] proved to have the ugliest protests against neoliberal economics to date. They resulted in the first fatality of the war between protesters and authorities: the shooting of Carlo Giuliani as he attempted to throw a fuel tank at an armored police Jeep. Large numbers of anarchists and anti-fascist demonstrators came to Genoa with belligerent intentions and ended up brawling with authorities, looting stores, tossing Molotov cocktails, and attacking some journalists. In response, Italy's police force, which according to an Italian senator has a number of fascist members, used point-blank-range water cannons and clubs against violent and nonviolent protesters alike. They brutally beat numerous non-aggressive activists where they slept,[38] indiscriminately imprisoned demonstrators, and refused prisoners' access to lawyers. They are also alleged to have tortured prisoners.[39] Though the first day's violence was sparked mainly by small groups of black-clad anarchists, after the death of Giuliani, violence spread more widely among the protesters. On the whole, both the protesters and the police behaved very badly. There was a strong contingent of peaceful Europeans in Genoa calling for debt relief for poor nations, and even British Prime Minister Tony Blair acknowledged that the majority of the protesters were nonviolent.[40] Still, the numbers of violent activists had increased significantly since Seattle.

Most of the G8 delegates to Genoa lodged on luxury liners off the coast of Italy throughout the summit, while US President George W. Bush resided on an aircraft carrier. According to many in the US commercial media, the G8 leaders worked hard to address the concerns of the key pressure groups represented by the protesters. The protesters, according to this media portrayal, are ignorant and confused, and keep getting in the way of the G8 leaders' work to address global poverty, the African AIDS crisis, and disease in the developing world. After Genoa, these leaders were lauded for their statements pledging to address the concerns of the activists. However, were their pledges substantial? Consider the following:[41]

- They committed $1.3 billion toward a new Global Fund to combat HIV/AIDS, malaria and tuberculosis.
  But this is barely over one-tenth of the amount requested by UN Secretary General, Kofi Annan. Furthermore, much of the money pledged by governments for fighting disease was simply diverted from other national foreign development aid budgets. As one NGO campaigner commented "This is like robbing Peter to pay Paul."[42]
- The G8 leaders congratulated themselves on the progress they have made on debt relief for the world's most impoverished countries, and committed themselves to continuing the good work. But of the $100 billion of debt relief promised at the G8 summit of 1999, only $13.2 billion had been written off by the time of the Genoa summit of 2001. And although 23 countries had begun the process of debt relief, 20 nations were still waiting for the process to begin, while only 2 nations had completed the process. In the meantime, interest payments continue to mount exponentially, and poor countries continue to direct more money to the IMF and World Bank for debt servicing than they direct toward health and education.

The G8 statements on global warming, hunger reduction, and globalization were similarly vacuous and self-congratulatory. Tony Blair commented that their plan to combat hunger was a "kind of Marshall Plan for the future,"[43] which sounds good enough. However, the post-World War II Marshall Plan depended on massive US generosity toward struggling European nations. The parallel falls apart when one realizes that US foreign aid to address poverty has steadily declined in the past two decades, and other industrialized nations have not done much better.[44] The G8 leaders envision a scenario where hunger, disease, and poverty will be addressed via global trade agreements. Their Genoa document states: "The situation in many developing countries—especially Africa— calls for decisive global action. The most effective poverty reduction strategy is to maintain a strong, dynamic, open and growing global economy. We pledge to do that."[45] Yet they fail to explain why poverty in the developing world, and the gap between rich and poor, has increased right along with the globalized economy. In every case, the lofty statements do not reflect reality, and unfortunately, such duplicity may breed more anger and violence by those protesters hungry for violent revolution.

Cancelled Meetings/Protests in Washington, DC, September 2001

The Ruckus Society, a California-based group which trains activists in nonviolent direct action, launched an enormous effort to prepare people to engage in nonviolent disruption of the IMF/World Bank summit scheduled to take place in Washington, DC in September 2001. Expecting over 100,000 demonstrators in Washington, they hoped to ensure that the upcoming protests would not deteriorate into violence and rioting.[46] The protests, however, never took place. The IMF/World Bank summit was canceled due to the terrorist attacks of September 11.

Qatar, November 2001

The WTO ministerial meetings in Doha, Qatar seemed, in a surreal kind of way, to signal a return to the pre-Seattle trade-talk days. There was nary a problem with protesters at the meeting in the altogether non-democratic state of Qatar, in the well-armored era of post-September 11. But the illusion of retrogression was just that, an illusion. The effects of two years of global justice campaigns were evident in some significant ways: developing countries gained more of a hearing than in past meetings, and important concessions were made by industrialized nations on a number of issues.

Organizers of the 2001 WTO summit selected as the venue of the meetings Qatar, a small, oil-rich Persian Gulf state, a year prior to the November 2001 event. At the time, the site made sense as a security haven against protesters, since Qatar is a veritable police state and entrance into the country could easily be restricted by monarchical decree. But organizers did not envision the looming terrorist threat. By November 2001, the concern was far less about global justice demonstrators and far more about terrorists residing in Qatar. Prior to the summit, Osama Bin Laden, who has many sympathizers in Qatar, had threatened to kill any "infidels" setting foot on Arab soil. Therefore, security in Qatar was tighter than ever during the WTO meetings. The US Navy sent a helicopter gunship and two ships housing 2,100 marines to Doha, and US delegates were equipped with gas masks as soon as their planes touched down on Arab soil. Everyone entering the conference center were searched and all roads to the center were blocked and guarded by armed police.[47]

Through five very heated days of meetings, France stood strong against eliminating farm subsidies, and many poor countries, led by India, opposed a new round of trade talks, feeling they had not benefited from the last round. But in the end, a compromise was reached. New global trade talks would be scheduled, but with many changes to the proposed agenda for the talks. The developing countries, who were, relatively speaking, dramatically under-represented at the meetings and had expressed early on that they felt bullied into agreeing to a new round of talks,[48] ended up with some important gains. The phasing out of rich nations' agricultural subsidies, which have devastated farmers in the global south, would be up for discussion in the talks. So would the practice of "dumping", where industrialized nations sell surplus products or food to developing countries at below cost. Furthermore, a dispute over WTO patent rules and poor countries' access to medicines was favorably resolved from their point of view.[49] Finally, many of the issues that were of top concern to the US and EU, but opposed by the developing nations, were slated to be discussed in the new round of trade talks, with the developing nations excused from participation in those discussions. Included in this area were rules protecting investment, antitrust policy, and making government procurement more transparent.[50] Clearly, this was not a step back to pre-Seattle days.

What is Freedom?

When politicians and financiers state that neoliberal economics increases freedom, what do they mean? Do they mean that citizens of particular nations will have more say in the kind of government and economic system they will have? No, not if their choice involves a rejection of the global trade system. For cases where citizens refuse to accommodate the global trade system, global capitalists have supported marshal law, or waged war. Do they mean that people will have more freedom of religious and/or ideological expression? No, not if their religion compels them to opt out of consumerism and militarism, or their beliefs demands a commitment to economic justice. Do they mean that they will be free from coercive messages in entertainment and news media? Certainly not, for these are the tools on which neoliberal economics depends for its success. Do they mean that citizens will have as much influence over political representatives as do corporations and other commercial interests? No, not only because a successful election campaign requires corporate funding, but because corporate partnerships are indispensable for a government whose ultimate goal is promoting economic growth. Do they mean that citizens will be free from shouldering an unequal tax burden for financing governance and social programs while corporations are excused from these responsibilities? No, for taxation of businesses is viewed as a trade barrier. Therefore, citizens must disproportionately foot the tax bill if trade is to remain fluid and vital. You see, neoliberal economics thrives where freedom of expression, freedom of religion and ideology, freedom from coercion, freedom of equal representation in government, and freedom from unfair taxation are constrained in the interest of the economy.

What do the evangelists of global economics mean by freedom? Do they mean that citizens of particular nations will have more choice in what they buy? Absolutely! Do they mean they will be free to purchase whatever their heart desires, as long as they have the money to spend? Precisely! In a country where economic growth has become the utmost national goal, the all-important freedom will be the freedom to spend money and make money without constraints of any kind, outside of the legal constraints on things like drugs. Anything standing in the way of this freedom will be viewed as subversive and damnable, *even if that thing is democracy itself.* The global economy is not about freedom, but about shaping our values in such a way that our lives contribute to the ultimate goal of economic growth. Therefore, many great thinkers, be they in the fields of economics, humanities, politics, or theology, have in recent years argued that neoliberal economics runs counter to democracy. Such writers as Robert Kuttner, John Gray, Benjamin Barber, David Korten, Tom Sine, and Naomi Klein, and William Greider,[51] have all been keen observers of and commentators on the erosion of freedom coincident with global economics.

As Christians, what do *we* mean by freedom? What is the freedom we seek? Is the freedom we seek merely a freedom to say what we believe, to be represented within our governments, or to be unharmed by coercion and abuse? Certainly these are worthy aspirations, and I expect Christians will often find themselves alongside people of other religions and ideologies struggling for these things. But I submit that Christians seek these freedoms not for the freedoms themselves. As Christians we are motivated not by the ideal of democracy, or any other political or social ideal, but by the commandment to love. Where exclusion, injustice, coercion and abuse exist, love is not present, and we would not be loving our neighbors if we did not lovingly (which implies nonviolently) step in and try to protect them from hate in all its forms. Still, we do not love for the ideal of love itself, but because love is the mission granted to us by God. "Love the Lord your God, and love your neighbor as you love yourself." We carry out this mission in order to serve and honor and know God. We love, then, to fulfill God's purpose for us. We are told to love selflessly and sacrificially so that we will come to know something of God's love, and thus of God.

God is our motivator, and love is our mission. Not a saccharine, sentimental love, but a love that embraces the unlovely, a love that hurts. If love is our mission, then, freedom for the Christian will be the freedom to love, the freedom to act out of a Christian conviction that God loves humanity and wills that humanity act in self-giving love for one another. But it is hard to love where we cannot see. For instance, we cannot move in love to protect our neighbors from domination and abuse if we cannot even see they are abused. Therefore, Christians will highly value freedom from delusion and propaganda. We must be freed to look with open eyes and open hearts at the world. Furthermore, actively loving our neighbor is hard when we are cut off from them, or when we cannot step in and reach out to those who are oppressed and dehumanized because freedom of movement and freedom to dissent are squelched. So freedom of speech and freedom of movement will be valued by Christians. Finally, if there is no freedom of religion and ideas, then the Christian mission to love will not only be stymied, but will itself be cause for persecution and will be actively repressed. Where freedom of religion does not exist, Christians may be treated like the jailed Tibetan monks under Chinese rule who are tortured simply because they pray.

True freedom is the freedom to be all God intended for us, and such a freedom can never be gained through coercion or hate. This is the freedom we seek as Christians. But we also recognize the worth of other freedoms: the freedom of religion, freedom of speech, freedom of movement, freedom from coercion and propaganda. Even if we do not seek these freedoms for their own sake, they are worth struggling for.

I have provided some portraits in this chapter of the way dissent against global economics is handled in the global north. This is one facet of the workings of neoliberal economics in the industrialized world. Of course, many other portraits could have been chosen: for example, portraits of corporate marketing in grade schools, portraits of working families unable to make ends meet on parttime jobs devoid of benefits, portraits of US factory workers put out of work as factories relocate to the global south, portraits of a corporatized, monopolized media bent on spin and fantasy, portraits of harassment along the southern US border of the very workers on whom the US agricultural sector depends, and on and on. But these stories have been told by others.[52] I recommend you read them. Instead, let us shift our focus to portraits of the global economy from the global south.

Chapter Three

The Global Economy at Work in the Global South

> The central issue of contention is not globalization itself, nor is it the use of the market as an institution, but the inequity in the overall balance of institutional arrangements—which produces very unequal sharing of the benefits of globalization. The question is not just whether the poor, too, gain something from globalization, but whether they get a fair share and a fair opportunity. There is an urgent need for reforming institutional arrangements—in addition to national ones—in order to overcome . . . the errors . . . that tend to give the poor across the world such limited opportunities.

> Amartya Sen[1]

Neoliberalism and the War in Chiapas, Mexico

For a picture of neoliberal economics at work in the global south, one need not look far beyond the southernmost border of the US. Nonetheless, to reach the area of Mexico nearest to my own heart and mind, one needs to travel about another 1,700 miles, to the Mexican State of Chiapas. Let us begin there.

I spent two weeks in Chiapas during the summer of 2001, studying the conflict between the indigenous population and government of

Mexico, and staying in refugee camps with a group from Christian Peacemaker Teams. I left for Chiapas with little understanding of the history of the region or of the war happening there, and no idea of the extent to which neoliberal economics is tied up in it. When I arrived in Chiapas, I quickly learned neoliberalism is blazing at the core.

Of course, the indigenous struggle in Chiapas predates the global economy by hundreds of years. The oppression of the Maya of Mexico and Central America is a very long, sad tale, brightened only by the indomitable spirit and traditions of the Mayan people. However, in the last century, the communally-oriented Maya of Mexico had won some important gains. Not least among these was the addition of Article 27 to the Mexican constitution, an element of the Agrarian Reforms that came out of the Mexican Revolution in the early 20th century. Article 27 established a system for distributing land communally to landless peasants, and assured that lands populated and worked communally by peasants could not be taken from them and sold to private interests.[2] A particularly harsh blow was struck in 1993 when Mexico was pressured to rescind the land reforms guaranteed by Article 27 in order to enter into the North American Free Trade Agreement (NAFTA). Suddenly, one of the few securities the indigenous population had known was pulled out from under them.

In the months preceding NAFTA's inception, the Zapatista movement of indigenous Mexicans secretly organized an armed rebellion, citing the changes in Article 27 as one of their motivations.[3] On the morning that NAFTA went into effect, January 1, 1994, the Zapatistas descended out of the mountains of Chiapas to take Mexico, and the world, by surprise. The indigenous band, some armed with AK-47s and rifles, some with wooden cut-outs of guns, and some with large sticks, managed to seize control of the Chiapas city of San Cristobal de las Casas. After a twelve-day standoff with the military during which Zapatista supporters throughout Mexico and the world demanded that Mexico negotiate with the Zapatistas, a ceasefire was called. The San Andres peace talks began that year.

Unfortunately, another thing also happened late in 1994: the plummeting of the peso to less than half its original value. In the months that followed the peso's crash, almost 2 million Mexican jobs were lost, and the real wages of Mexicans declined by 27 percent. This economic crisis carried far-reaching consequences for the indigenous movement, which was just beginning to foster hopes for a better future as the Zapatistas represented indigenous concerns before the government in talks at San Andres. In response to the peso crisis, President Clinton unilaterally granted a $20 billion buyout package for Mexico. At the time, an advisor employed by the US Chase Manhattan bank said the Mexican leaders would need to "eliminate the Zapatistas" in order to satisfy the US investment community.[4]

It is now a widely-held view that the Mexican government, dominated by the PRI party (the Institutional Revolutionary Party), was not negotiating in good faith in talks with the Zapatistas, even though negotiators signed Table 1 (the Accords on Indigenous Rights and Culture)[5] of the San Andres Accords in 1996. Now it is known that in early 1995 the Mexican army began equipping paramilitary forces in northern Chiapas for "operations to control the population." Soon after this, they began training paramilitaries in the highland municipality of Chenalhó, where paramilitary forces became prevalent. These paramilitaries consist of indigenous, civilian men who support the PRI government, and who are armed by the military and charged with keeping down Zapatista supporters. Their principal methods include intimidation and displacement. By the year 2000, one-third of the population of Chenalhó (10,000 out of 30,000) had been displaced, fleeing their villages upon threats from paramilitaries.[6] In the Ch'ol region to the north, hundreds have been killed by paramilitaries, and thousands displaced.[7] The insidious government strategy has been far-reaching.

Mexico has acted with the support of its trading partner to the north in this effort. In the first two years after the Zapatista uprising, almost as many Mexican officers were trained at the US School of the Americas in Fort Benning, Georgia as had been in the previous 48 years put together.[8] Furthermore, between 1997 and 1999, US military aid to Mexico increased to about $112 million. In addition to this aid, between 1996 and 1998 over $360 million in licenses for direct commercial sale of defense equipment to Mexico was approved by the US State Department.[9]

While the majority of military aid to Mexico is earmarked for counter-narcotics purposes, the true intentions behind the aid are suspect. In 1996, assurance was given to the Zedillo administration that the US did not expect Mexico to use arms shipments from the US solely for anti-drug operations. Furthermore, in the period from 1996 to 1997, three times as many Mexican officers at the School of the Americas were taking courses in counter-insurgency as in anti-narcotics.[10] Despite the huge sums supposedly being poured into anti-narcotics in Mexico, there has been no reduction in the drug flow between Mexico and the US.

In December 1997, after weeks of intense threats, paramilitaries invaded a church in the community of Acteal in Chenalhó. Members of a pacifist Christian group called *Las Abejas* (the Bees), a group which refuses to affiliate with the government *or* the Zapatistas,[11] were praying in their chapel when heavily-armed paramilitaries stormed in and began shooting. The massacre lasted for over eight hours. Men with machine guns chased the women, children, and men out of the church and down through the hills, eventually murdering them all. Of the 45 dead, 21 were women, 15 were children and babies, and 9 were men. Though the police were notified of the attack before 11:30 that morning, and though a police force was stationed only 100 meters from where the massacre took place, no one from the security forces came to the scene until after 5:00 p.m. A few weeks after the killings, the perpetrators returned to plunder the empty houses of those killed.

It took months before anyone was brought to justice for the massacre at Acteal, and even today some of the perpetrators are free. None of the higher government authorities who plotted the attack have been inconvenienced with legal consequences. The governor of Chenalhó who was implicated in the massacre was forced to leave his government post in the municipality and was replaced. But lucky for him, he got a job in a Mexican embassy in the United States.

The government's response to the massacre in Acteal was to further the militarization of rural Chiapas, a militarization which had begun in 1995. After Acteal, the Army sent more security forces into Chiapas to "maintain order," so that by the end of 2000, Chiapas hosted one soldier to every 9 to 14 civilians in the conflict zone (70,000 soldiers total). Furthermore, 681 military camps had been set up, and billions of dollars had been spent on tanks, helicopters, and high caliber weapons for use by the military in Chiapas.[12] The result of this heavy militarization has been misery for the indigenous population. Villagers now live in fear. They are stopped and questioned about the Zapatistas on a regular basis. Agricultural crops have been cleared to make room for military bases. Women are intimidated by soldiers and are afraid to go about necessary chores away from their villages. Sometimes young men are recruited for paramilitary activity. More and more, impoverished women and girls are hired for prostitution by the soldiers.[13] In some cases, community leaders have turned up dead.[14] The military puts on a front of humanitarianism by offering meals and health care to the villagers,[15] but Zapatista supporters and Abejas communities refuse the services. They know that by accepting them they would be submitting to the domination of the military, and would be expected to comply with their wishes.

Human rights advocates from around the world, many from the United States, travel to Chiapas and spend time in the rural communities, forming a human shield around the indigenous people. I was privileged to meet some of these human rights workers during my two weeks in Chiapas. I only spent about five days in the refugee camps, but a couple of those were spent with the survivors of Acteal. I knelt beside them in the building where their family members are buried, and shared a drop from their ocean of sadness. The people of Acteal are a dignified, determined, and gentle people.

The indigenous Mexican population want to be citizens of Mexico; they do not seek independence or an overthrow of the government. What they demand is a say in their future. They desire a just future for the Maya, which would allow them to participate in decisions regarding the use of their land and the shape of their village economies. Table 1 of the San Andres Accords, the portion of the Accords signed by the Zapatistas and the Mexican government in 1996, guarantees the indigenous population a voice in such decisions. However, the government has not acted on the agreement, and as is now clear, never intended to. While Mexican officials were attending the San Andres peace talks and signing Table 1 of the Accords, the Mexican military was already beginning its counterinsurgency war against the indigenous population.

In response to the government's actions, supporters of the Zapatistas and the Abejas communities set up their own "autonomous communities,"[16] communities which function as if autonomous from the government of Mexico. These indigenous groups decided that if the government would not implement Table 1, they would implement it themselves in their own communities. Consequently, they refuse government services. Education promoters from the communities educate the children. Health promoters from the communities oversee health care. Democratically-appointed leaders from the communities govern all community affairs.

The autonomous communities of the Maya are communities of resistance. They are living not only in resistance to the Mexican government, but in resistance to a power that has dominated much of the world, a global economic system which threatens to encompass them too. Why do they do it? Why do they struggle against such monumental odds and face daily the threat of violence rather than integrate into the global economy? Why do they choose poverty and hardship rather than cooperating with the Mexican government and accepting handouts from the military?

The autonomous communities believe strongly that the indigenous population of Mexico have suffered and will suffer as a result of trade agreements like NAFTA, or the proposed FTAA (Free Trade Area of the Americas), or Presidente Fox's "Plan Puebla Panama."[17] They believe that such agreements profit corporations while increasing poverty among the middle and lower classes of Mexico. They believe the land they live on will be sold to corporations who will mine and sell its resources and pollute it. They believe farmers will be displaced, and *maquilas*, or sweatshops, will sprout up around the region, offering jobs to the newly-destitute—miserable jobs which barely allow them to survive. They believe their vital communities will be disrupted and broken. They believe their children will lose touch with their age-old Mayan customs. They are probably right on all counts.

Today, Mexico's indigenous movement finds itself in a period of uncertainty. The inauguration of Vicente Fox as President in

2000 raised many hopes for dialogue since Fox had promised to hear and address indigenous concerns. Furthermore, he was the first non-PRI president to be elected in over seventy years. Presidente Fox *did* act on some of his campaign promises. He closed some key military bases in Chiapas, shutting down seventy in all. He also released many Zapatista sympathizers from jail. However, little else has been done.

In order to implement Table 1 of the San Andres Accord, changes would have to be made to the Mexican constitution. Though a congressional commission (COCOPA) was appointed to work on these changes after the signing of Table 1, and though a bill was drafted in 1996, President Zedillo rejected the bill and no further action was taken. When Presidente Fox took office, he immediately put the original COCOPA bill before the new Congress for a vote. Not surprisingly, the heavily PRIista Congress did not approve of it. In the end, they reworked the COCOPA bill and gutted it of any significant concessions to the indigenous movement. The bill that was finally approved and made law actually contradicts the San Andres Accords. The Zapatistas have condemned it.

As it now stands, low-intensity war continues to be status quo in Chiapas.

The Face of Global Economics in Indonesia

For three young women who sew Nike shoes at a factory in Jakarta, capital of Indonesia, home is a 7x15 ft. concrete cell. This crowded, dilapidated space functions as bedrooms, dining room, and living room for the three, and opens onto a narrow alleyway/kitchen/laundry room shared with neighbors. To maximize space in their apartment, the women roll their tattered, musty bedding against a wall each morning, then out again each night. They work 7-15 hour shifts daily, some of them standing the entire time, but often cannot afford to both eat and pay the rent.[18] The majority of footwear workers in Indonesia are worse off, living in pillbox-sized dormitories owned by the factories. At one Indonesian factory-compound sourcing mainly for Nike, a 12x18 ft. room houses 12 people. There, the wooden platforms that serve as beds for the occupants take up most of the space, and each person has a small locker for his or her belongings.[19]

In the year 2000, the makers of Nike shoes in Indonesia made, on average, 325,000Rp (rupia), or $37, per month for 8-hr days, 6 days per week. Their bare minimum monthly living expenses included:[20]

(Cheapest) Rent	35,000Rp ($4.00)
Electricity	8,000Rp ($1.00)
Water	8,000Rp ($1.00)
Transportation	60,000Rp ($7.00)

After these necessities had been paid, only 214,000Rp ($24.00) was left for all other living expenses, including food. Even if this entire amount was allotted to food, a worker would have only 7,133Rp per day for meals, about 2,380 Rp per meal if she ate three times a day. But a simple meal of rice and vegetables costs about 2,500Rp ($0.30) in Jakarta. Therefore, makers of Nike shoes couldn't even afford to eat such a simple meal thrice daily. They would definitely not have money left over for things like soap, or medicine, or clothing.

Nike factory workers survive on debt. Yet Nike can claim: "People around the world working in Nike contract factories are paid a fair wage, which often combines cash with allowances for meals, housing, transportation, health care and even bonuses."[21] What do they mean by a health care allowance? They mean a 200,000Rp/yr ($24.00/yr) allotment, which covers about two doctor visits, plus two courses of antibiotics per year.[22] When they refer to a housing allowance, they refer to the internment-camp-style dormitories mentioned above. By meal allowance, they mean the lunch meal offered in the factories, a tiny, wholly inadequate serving of low grade rice. The transportation allowance given to Nike factory workers in the year 2000 was 1,500Rp ($0.18) per day, while transportation costs averaged about 4,000Rp ($0.48) per day. As for bonuses, workers received a 20,000Rp ($2.40) attendance bonus for the year 2000 if they did not miss a single day of work all year.[23] Nike calls this "fair," even though the company can afford to pay endorsements in the millions to sports stars like Tiger Woods, who gets $55,000 PER DAY from Nike. One year, Nike paid

Michael Jordan more for advertising their shoes than the combined earnings of all 18,000 Indonesian footwear workers involved in manufacturing Nikes that year.[24] Phil Knight, the CEO of Nike, has a net worth of over $5.8 billion,[25] making him one of the richest people in the world.

Nike also boasts about its progressiveness in the area of monitoring factory conditions where its shoes are produced. This too is an example of Nike's supreme adeptness at public relations. Factory workers who make Nike shoes in Indonesia reported that before monitors arrived, they were: 1) provided with protective masks, 2) told to clean up the entire factory, 3) briefed on the Nike "Code of Conduct"[26] and told to know it, and 4) cautioned to report that they were completely happy. All worker interviews were translated by factory managers.[27]

Figure 1 *Cost of Living and Sweatshop Wages in Indonesia in 2000*[28]

Sweatshop Wages: 325,000Rp/month ($37.00), 10,835Rp/day ($1.20)

Food Costs: (in rupia)

Small bottle of milk	1,500	($0.18)
Instant noodles (single serving)	1,000	($0.12)
1 kg oranges	4,000	($0.48)
Block of tofu	1,000	($0.12)
1 bunch spinach	500	($0.06)
Small bottle of Coca-Cola	1,200	($0.15)
1 kg butterfish	10,000	($1.20)
2 bananas	700	($0.08)
1 chicken	11,000	($1.33)

Medicine Costs: (in rupia)

Aspirin (8 ct.)	1,700	($0.24)
Acetaminophen (4 ct.)	900	($0.11)
Antacids (1 dose)	2,500	($0.29)
Antiseptic	4,000	($0.48)

Cold medicine (1 dose)	· 900	($0.10)
Children's cough medicine (1 dose)	13,100	($1.50)
Adult multivitamins (5 ct.)	3,900	($0.47)
Kid's multivitamins (1 bottle)	7,100	($0.86)

School Tuition for children (Cheapest)		
One month	25,000	($3.01)

Most of the workers in the Indonesian footwear industry are young adults, the majority women, who came to the factories from poor, rural communities. At home they helped with agriculture, or labored in home industries where work was not steady. In order to survive, they had to leave their villages and seek other employment. The factories sourcing for transnational corporations send recruiters to rural areas to recruit new workers, and when times are hard, recruiters are hard to resist. Most of the workers arrive in the city with only their documentation, clothes, and cash totaling anywhere from $1.00-$15.00. They are able to visit home only once a year, and do not make enough money to send assistance to their families.[29]

Add to the oppressive wages paid to workers the following: the coercion used to make employees work inhumane overtime shifts, the tragically inadequate protections for workers using toxic chemicals, the excessive heat and lack of drinking water workers must endure, the unreasonable quotas they must meet, the abusive, humiliating treatment of them by management, and the sometimes lethal threat to those who dare organize into unions.[30] What you get is the epitome of exploitation.

Does the desperation of Indonesia's rural poor legitimize transnational corporations' exploitation of them, or legitimize starvation wages? Some citizens of industrialized nations believe it does. Most of us simply don't know enough to have an opinion. For example, most of us do not know that for years the corrupt Indonesian government, led by the dictator Suharto, was treated as an ally by Western governments simply because he followed an economic course favoring foreign investment.[31] It mattered little that he committed atrocities against his people, or that economic gains in Indonesia went disproportionately to those associated with the Suharto family. The economy of Indonesia was growing steadily and the labor repression of Suharto's reign kept wages low for transnational corporations. The following excerpt by William Greider demonstrates how cheerleaders of global economics, including President Clinton, helped foster the illusion of Indonesia's economic success during the early and mid-nineties. I include the rather long excerpt in its entirety because of the striking picture it provides of Indonesia at its economic peak:

> Jakarta was the Potemkin village of global capitalism, the place that statesmen and business executives regularly visited to exclaim over the miracle of Indonesia's economic growth. The city's main boulevards were alive with commercial energies, lined with palms and flowering trees and with the gleaming glass office towers bearing important nameplates of global commerce, Price Waterhouse and Barclays and the Bank of Hong Kong. The swirling congestions of traffic— big German cars surrounded by armadas of Japanese motorcycles—bespoke new affluence. The rapid growth was made visible by the huge new department stores and construction projects, condominium high-rises with tropical flora draped from every balcony, elevated highways and rapid transit system abuilding.
>
> President Clinton passed through Jakarta himself in November 1994 and posed in a splendid batik shirt with other leaders assembled for a meeting of the APEC, the Asia-Pacific Economic Cooperation organization. Clinton, like others, expressed his admiration for what the New Order of President Suharto has accomplished during the general's thirty-year-reign. Indonesia has averaged 7 percent annual growth for two decades. Per capita income has tripled to $650 and was expected to triple again; absolute deprivation was reduced dramatically. Indonesia was described by the Clinton Administration as one of the the the "BEMs"—"Big Emerging Markets"—that were targeted for special attention.

US cabinet officers came through regularly to court opportunity.

In the months preceding Clinton's visit, the Indonesian military had cleaned up Jakarta much the way that Soviet authorities used to prettify their Potemkin villages in the 1920s for visits by the starry-eyed foreigners eager to confirm that Communist collectivism was working. Before the APEC delegation arrived, Jakarta's regional military command launched *Operasi Bersih*—"Operation Cleansing"—to clear the streets of beggars, thieves and prostitutes, but also troublesome political dissidents. Security troops were instructed to "watch over possible persons wishing to embarrass the country for the sake of their own group's interests." Some forty alleged criminals were shot and killed in the cleansing process.

. . . Away from the glamorous Jakarta Hilton and other first-class hotels, the city seemed less promising. Its streets were clotted with uncollected garbage and the reek of broken sewers and smoky buses . . . Jakarta and its environs had swollen to thirteen million people and groaned with dense, physical strains. Neighborhoods still had the broken-down look of perennial poverty, and at night the streets were crowded with peddlers and shadowy teenagers hustling for change, the air rancid with burning cooking oil and the kerosene lanterns that lit curbside food stalls. Guests at the luxury hotels were urged not to attempt an evening stroll, even along the best boulevards.

Despite the fabulous growth statistics, Indonesia's national economy was still itself something of a fiction. The boom existed in Jakarta, Surabaya and a couple of other Javanese cities, but not across the vast archipelago of 13,000 islands and three hundred languages. Sixty percent of the nation's money supply circulated in the Jakarta area alone.[32]

Most westerners will also not know that Indonesia's illusory global economic "miracle" of the mid-nineties has burst its bubble. Indonesia was hit very hard by the Asian economic crisis of 1997, triggered in part by IMF mismanagement. After the crash, an inexperienced team of IMF advisors went in to size up the Indonesian crisis. Their recommendations to shut down 16 banks proved disastrous, as both the World Bank and IMF have now acknowledged, but have taken no steps to ameliorate. By the end of 2001, the economy of Indonesia was on the brink of total collapse. As one of the most heavily-indebted poor countries in the world, the country is sinking under an unbearable foreign debt of over $150 billion. Before the IMF blunder in 1997, Indonesia had almost no domestic debt. It now bears a domestic debt of $80 billion.''And the policies imposed by the IMF in 1998, such as the sudden removal of subsidies on fuels like kerosene, and those proposed for the future, such as the lowering of tariffs on sugar imports into Indonesia, mercilessly burden the nation's poor.[34] The IMF has insisted that Indonesia lower tariffs on imported sugar to 25%, while IMF shareholder Japan maintains tariffs of 80% on imported sugar. The policy exemplifies the flagrant double standards posed by the IMF to benefit IMF shareholders. When Japanese sugar begins to flood the Indonesian market, where will destitute Indonesian sugar farmers end up? Perhaps Nike has an idea.

The IMF's concerns seem to be: 1) to raise the state budget so that Indonesia can make its debt payments to the IMF and World Bank, and 2) to benefit the most powerful IMF shareholders. The impact IMF policies have on the poorest citizens of Indonesia, such as sugar farmers, seems to be of little concern to the international financial institution. In the meantime, poverty in Indonesia is steadily on the rise. In 1960, the poverty level in Indonesia was at 50%. By 1997, that number had dropped to 11%. By 1999, 80% of Indonesians had fallen below the poverty line.[35]

Background information on the Indonesian economic situation reveals the fact that neoliberal economics has worsened rather than improved the plight of Indonesia's poor. Many factors contributed to their vulnerability, of course. Among those factors, however, was the opportunism of Western nations and transnational corporations during the Suharto years. Instead of making foreign investment an incentive for clean government and respect for human rights during the eighties and nineties, *Western governments turned a blind eye to flagrant governmental abuses while transnational corporations reaped billions of dollars in Indonesia.* Another major factor in the Indonesian economic crisis were the recommendations of the IMF. Citizens of industrialized nations who justify the exploitation of the Indonesian factory workers by making reference to their desperation do not realize that our own governments helped to create that desperation.

Coffee and Starvation in Central America

In Central America, coffee matters. It is the main export in countries such as Guatemala, Nicaragua, and Honduras, and pivotal to the economies of other nations, like El Salvador. People in Central America have long depended on the export of coffee for survival.

For this reason, the crash of global coffee prices, which at the end of 2001 were at an all-time low of $.49 per lb,[36] has devastated the majority of Central Americans. Acre after acre of coffee bushes stood unpicked at the end of the 2001 harvesting season since farmers would have paid more for the picking and processing than they would have earned for the coffee. The families of many coffee farmers had no money, and many of the hundreds of thousands of workers dependent on seasonal coffee harvesting, had no work. Coupled with the 2001 drought affecting much of Central America, which destroyed many subsistence crops of corn and beans, this coffee crisis devastated Guatemala, Nicaragua, Honduras, and El Salvador. Only foreign food assistance averted mass starvation during the drought. Experts predict that coffee prices may stabilize in 2004,[37] but coffee producers in Central America cannot hang on that long. Understandably, farms have been abandoned, as an exodus of people have taken to the cities to search for work and to beg.

In the early 1990s, the IMF developed a scheme to stimulate the economy of Vietnam: they would finance extensive coffee-growing projects there.[38] A few years down the road, when the Vietnamese coffee plants matured, they added more coffee to the market than the market could bear, and prices began to drop. Though prices rose during the Asian economic crisis, from 1996-97,[39] prices have sharply declined since. This is in part due to the fact that the high prices of 1996-97 prompted growers in Southeast Asia and Brazil to plant more coffee. When these plants matured, the market was so glutted that coffee prices plummeted.

Vietnam has become one of the largest coffee producers in the world, though its coffee production was minimal before the nineties.[40] This is not good news for the Central American coffee farmers who have depended on coffee exports for generations, and who must now compete in a saturated market. What were the IMF officials thinking, one might wonder?

According to the outgoing head of the National Federation of Coffee Producers (Federacafe) at the end of 2001, Vietnam is favored by transnational corporations and foreign investors as a site for coffee production because of its low production costs. Whereas minimum wage in a South American country like Colombia hovers around $4 a day, in Vietnam, rural workers earn only $.50 for a day's work.[41] This makes Vietnamese coffee cheaper for corporate coffee buyers. Could this be why the IMF has encouraged the development of the Vietnamese coffee industry with a steady flow of credit on amiable terms? I do not know the answer, but it seems a fair question. In any case, the IMF either did not foresee the effects their development strategy in Vietnam would have on Central America, or they felt the devastating consequences in Central America were not important enough to cause them to modify their strategy.

The deregulation of the coffee market since the 1989 collapse of the international pact on export quotas also factors into the equation,[42] and for this the IMF is not to blame. Nevertheless, that deregulatory action is entirely consistent with the recommendations both the IMF and World Bank have made to Central American countries. Consider the example of Nicaragua: There, the international financial institutions included deregulation of the economy as a key goal of their Structural Adjustment Program introduced in 1991, along with drastic cutting of social spending and the devaluation of currency. The Nicaraguan government has made substantial efforts in all these areas. The effects have devastated the population of Nicaragua.

In 1990, 60% of the population lived in poverty. But after the recessionary effect of structural adjustment, unemployment and underemployment increased dramatically. By 1994, 70% of Nicaraguans lived in poverty, and about 55% of workers in Nicaragua were without jobs, compared with a 20% jobless rate in 1985. Because of cuts in public sector spending, jobs in the public sector decreased 63% from 1990 to 1993. Because protective tariffs were eliminated in 1991 and the antiquated Nicaraguan industrial sector was unable to compete with foreign imports, there were 44% fewer industrial jobs than there had been in the late-eighties. Because of restrictions on credit and the privatization of agro-business, small-scale farming became scarce by 1993.[43]

With the currency devaluation of 1991, workers' purchasing power fell by 40% in a single day. But living costs continue to rise. By 1993 it was estimated that 50-60% of workers in the formal sector, and 80% of workers in the informal sector were not earning enough to adequately feed their families. Spending on healthcare was cut in half during the early nineties, which has had a profound impact on the wellbeing of Nicaragua's poor. Infant and maternal mortality rates are on the rise, as is death by preventable diseases like diarrhea and measles. Because of cuts in spending for education, teachers in Nicaragua earn less than half of a poverty-line salary, and are responsible for 60-70 students per classroom.[44]

Astoundingly, the IMF and World Bank view structural adjustment in Nicaragua as a success. Since the government pays so much less for social services, healthcare and medicine, and since it cut public sector jobs so dramatically, it is able to meet its debt payments. So instead of government revenues enriching the lives of the people of Nicaragua, they are being deposited into northern banks, into the coffers of Western governments. This defines economic success, in IFI terms. The IMF and World Bank recognize that the poor pay the price for the austere measures they devise, but they contend that the price is worth the outcome of a fully liberalized, trade-based economy, in which wealth will, they predict, "trickle down" to the masses. Unfortunately, there are no examples of structural adjustments having this effect. According to the UN's *Human Development Report*, per capita income has significantly decreased in the past twenty years in areas where adjustment programs have been applied by the IFIs,[45] and in much of the world, poverty has increased under structural adjustment. Strikingly, structural adjustment has not even alleviated the global debt crisis. While the debt of the developing world stood at $785 billion when the crisis ensued, that debt has multiplied to an inconceivable $1.5 trillion debt burden. This is because the interest on loans continue to mount even as countries make their payments.[46]

The IMF is pushing ever harder for Nicaragua's government to *further* liberalize, regardless of the effects IMF recommendations have had in Nicaragua. Nicaragua had been on the list of "Highly Indebted Poor Countries" (HIPC) being considered for debt relief as a result of the Jubilee Plus global debt relief campaign. But the debt relief program designed by the IFIs in response to the campaign is conditioned on countries following IMF structural adjustment demands. In October 2001, in the thick of drought and the crisis brought on by the coffee market crash, the IMF put a stop to the debt relief program in Nicaragua. The government of Nicaragua had refused to meet IMF demands to further slash spending, to pull money out of circulation, and to privatize public utilities.[47]

In Central American countries like Nicaragua, the coffee crisis has been an invisible killer. Unlike the graphic devastations of Hurricane Mitch and the Spring 2001 earthquakes in El Salvador, the devastation wrought by the coffee storm won little press attention. Consequently, the outpouring of development aid that followed natural disasters did not come to Central American coffee farmers and workers. They are the victims of a slow, calculated, and crushing economic system that is as ubiquitous as air, and almost as difficult to see.

The world coffee economy is worth $50 billion a year. Only oil ranks higher in the global commodities market. In the US alone, just the gourmet coffee industry commands $8 billion a year.[48] Nonetheless, sitting in a US coffee shop at the end of 2001 one would not have known there had been a crash in global coffee prices. One still forked over $3.50 to $4.00 for a 16 oz. latte, since coffee barons like Starbucks or Nestlé were by no means passing on their windfall savings to consumers. In fact, while coffee farmers the world over were slowly slipping into destitution from 1997 to 2001, Starbucks' profits tripled.

For the year 2000, Nestlé boasted stunning profits "thanks to favourable commodity prices."[49] In other words, starvation scenarios for coffee farmers translate to boom years for the transnationals. In May 2001, coffee industry executives met at the Park Lane Hotel in London for a conference that cost each attender more than some coffee-growers could earn in a 100 years.[50]

Meanwhile, Lidia Avilez, a Catholic immigration worker in Honduras, warns that peasant farmers in Central America have run out of "coping strategies."[51] As they watch the hair of their children discolor from malnutrition, and see their bellies distend, they are left with few choices. Besides the many who will leave the countryside for nearby towns where their children can root through garbage for food, many will migrate North to the United States. What kind of reception will we give them?

Family Values and Global Economics in Bangladesh

Anyone concerned about the health of families and the well-being of children should not overlook the impact of sweatshops on families, or the issue of child labor. The impact of sweatshops on children is heartbreaking beyond expression.

Bangladesh provides a good example of the many ways sweatshops directly hurt children, even aside from the impact of general poverty and malnutrition. More and more apparel destined for the US market originates in Bangladesh. Bangladesh is now the third largest apparel exporter to the US, and the fifth largest to the European Union. 1.6 million Bangladeshis are employed sewing garments, almost half of which end up on the US market.[52]

Eighty-five percent of garment workers in Bangladesh are young women, ranging in age from mid-teens to late-twenties. Many of these young women are mothers. The average work day in Dhaka's export processing zones runs from 12 to 14 hours a day, allowing women very little time with their children. Garment workers labor seven days a week. In addition to hours spent at work, some women spend hours walking considerable distances to and from factories, because the rock-bottom wages they earn do not cover the cost of transportation via bicycle, or rickshaw. As difficult as it is to imagine, garment workers in Bangladesh are regularly subjected to strings of 20-hour shifts when orders are due. Workers will work the twenty hours, then take a few hours to sleep on a scrap of cardboard on the factory floor, then return to work for another 20-hour shift. These shifts can take a woman away from home and from her children for three to four days in a row, often with no advance warning. Wages paid to garment workers in Bangladesh are far below subsistence wages (more on this below). Therefore, no mother working in the export processing zones (EPZs) can afford childcare. Children are left, often hungry and sick, to care for themselves throughout most of the day.

As you might imagine, the health of Bangladeshi garment workers is dramatically compromised. Women in sweatshops report suffering almost constantly from headaches, vomiting, fainting, diarrhea, and other illnesses.[53] Since sick days are unheard of in the EPZs, and healthcare benefits don't exist, it should come as no surprise that most garment workers are used up by the age of 30. In the meantime, children are growing up without the involvement of their mothers in their lives. Mothers working in garment factories in Bangladesh cannot afford the fees to send their children to school, therefore most of their children go unschooled. They are prime candidates for Bangladesh's manifold child labor force.

At Lim's Bangladesh, Ltd., a factory producing sportswear for Wilson and Headmaster, licensee for a number of major US universities,[54] workers average about 84.5 hours a week. Since workers are systematically cheated of overtime pay (though overtime is obligatory), they are paid for about 76 to 78 hours a week.[55] Pay scale at Lim's, as in other EPZ factories in Bangladesh, is determined by experience. Senior sewers receive 18 cents an hour, while junior sewers receive 12 cents, and helpers (young teenage girls who do jobs other than sewing) receive only 8 cents an hour for their work. At this wage, sewers are paid less than 1.5 cents for each university cap they sew, caps which retail in the US for $18.99. When asked what wage would allow them to rise out of misery into poverty, the garment workers at Lim said they would need to make 34 cents an hour (which would amount to about $70/month, for a 6-day/48-hour work week). At this more livable wage, Headmaster corporation would be paying less than 3 cents toward the direct labor cost for each university cap made. The impact this kind of wage increase would have on Headmaster would be very negligible, only about 1.2 cents per cap, less than 1/10 of one percent of the retail cost of the cap.[56] Yet such a small pay increase would allow a Bangladeshi family to avoid hunger, and to send their children to school rather than to work.

The pay scale at Lim's is comparable to that of all the factories in Bangladesh visited by a delegation of the National Labor Committee (NLC) in May 2001. The group inspected different factories producing clothing for major US universities as well as, in some cases, for Nike and Reebok. Injustices in the factories go well beyond the starvation wages, however. Garment workers in the factories need permission to use the bathroom, and bathroom visits are timed. Talking during their long hours of work is strictly prohibited. The factories are extremely overcrowded and hot. In some of the factories inspected, workers had been beaten by managers.[57] Though the transnationals contracting the factories have highly publicized "Codes of Conduct," the workers in the factories had never heard of them. In Bangladeshi EPZs, the codes are meaningless. Likewise, the conventions of the International Labor Organization proved to be an entirely new concept to the workers, none of whom would even dare to think of forming a workers' association or union.

All the workers at factories visited by the NLC earned substantially less than the minimum wage legally required in EPZs in Bangladesh. The legal wage stands at 22 cents an hour (a wage which, as we've already seen, still falls short of allowing subsistence). Bangladeshi labor laws also grant workers sick leave and healthcare, daycare centers, severance pay, protection from physical abuse, and the right to organize. Yet every one of these legal requirements had been brushed aside in the factories visited.[58] Furthermore, transnational corporations contracting with factories in Bangladesh's EPZs pay absolutely no taxes or duties. That's the beauty of the global economy, according to neoliberal logic. TNCs can exploit the poor of Bangladesh without paying a cent in property taxes, local or state taxes, income taxes, or sales taxes. Import and export duties are, likewise, nil. For TNCs, Bangladesh constitutes a global jackpot.

Transnational corporations are quick to point out that their standards absolutely prohibit the use of child labor.[59] In theory, this is true. Most developing countries also have laws prohibiting child labor. Still, these laws are not enforced in many countries, and child labor is ubiquitous in the developing world. To the chagrin of transnationals, sometimes children even show up working in EPZs. But let's assume for a moment that the codes of transnational corporations prohibiting child labor were well-enforced, and child labor was entirely wiped out of the EPZs. Transnational corporations would still be contributing heavily to the problem of child labor because they are paying rock-bottom wages to adult workers. When parents do not earn enough money to feed their families, let alone to send their children to school, children are forced to spend their days struggling to earn much-needed cash for their families. Therefore, underpaying parents is the best way to guarantee the perpetuation of child labor. No matter how lofty a corporation's "Code of Conduct," corporations are implicitly responsible for child labor if they pay starvation wages, as most TNCs do in Bangladesh.

Child labor sets in motion an insidious cycle wherever it is practiced. It works something like this: where a child is available and willing to complete a given job for a fraction of what an adult would earn for the job, that job is taken away from the adult. For this reason, child labor is directly related to levels of un- and underemployment in the developing world.[60] Where children do the work, adults are underemployed. Where parents are un—or underemployed, children cannot be sent to school. Children who do not go to school look for occupation elsewhere, and end up taking jobs that would otherwise go to adults. The cycle perpetuates itself. Furthermore, if children spend their childhood working at menial tasks instead of going to school, they will not have the skills as adults to attain subsistence—or higher-paying jobs. They will likely end up in situations where their own children must join the labor force.

Many child workers, especially in East Asia, are bonded laborers.[61] Desperately poor parents who cannot provide for their families' basic needs are often encouraged to "loan" their children to factory owners in exchange for money. Millions of bonded child laborers in East Asia work under unfathomable conditions in carpet factories, as brick makers, in the infamous fireworks factories, or as street vendors. Parents are usually promised that their children will work to pay off the parents' debts, then return home within months. But children bonded to pay off loans often end up enslaved into their adult years, as meal expenses and fines are added to the original loan amount at such a rate that the loan becomes virtually unpayable. While bonded labor is not practiced in EPZs, the misery and abject poverty experienced by the families of Bangladeshi garment workers are precisely the circumstances that force families to consider doing the unthinkable: loaning out their children.

Advocates of neoliberal economics regularly remark that every industrializing nation must go through the travail of labor oppression and child labor in the process of becoming industrialized. They are quick to point to the days of the industrial revolution when American factories employed children and working conditions were extremely harsh. They want us to believe those circumstances were part of the natural process of industrialization every country must go through, and that, if left alone, the market will eventually correct such imbalances. But this approach is entirely ahistorical. Labor repression and child labor were not corrected in industrialized countries by any normal economic processes, they were changed only through decades of bitter struggle on the part of child and labor advocates. History, and present-day reality, actually supports the argument that if left alone the market will reward those who exploit the weak. The reality is that children in places like Bangladesh are paying the hidden costs of global economics. They are forced to sacrifice their childhoods, their parents, their educations, and their health, so that folks like you and I can win big on the stock market and own closets full of clothing.

It is crucial to look at child labor as a piece of the larger puzzle. Approaches to abolishing child labor that merely remove one piece of the puzzle are ineffective and even destructive. If countries implement laws to remove children from the workforce without also implementing provisions allowing them to attend school, and without raising the wages of their parents, children are often forced into "underground" jobs more dangerous than factory work. Banished from the factories, children can end up building fireworks in underground factories, recycling the pieces of used syringes, or selling their bodies in the sex trade.

Likewise, a constructive answer to sweatshops is not as simplistic as closing down EPZs. As we have already seen, in countries worked over by Structural Adjustment Programs, jobs in EPZs can mean the difference between life and death for rural farmers put out of work, for the newly unemployed public sector workers, and for struggling families simply unable to cope in a country where the currency has been devalued and social programs stripped away. Those who advocate for the poor must advocate for fair treatment of workers in the EPZs, and for livable wages in the factories. Heaven knows, transnational corporations can afford to pay. Additionally, we should advocate for a gradual reversal of the austerity measures imposed by international financial institutions so that governments can once again invest in education, healthcare, and public sector jobs. We should advocate for increasing support for the local production of goods consumed locally, such as food staples. And we should advocate for debt relief to poor countries.

These are just a few of the ways we can promote "family values" on a global scale. The economic schemes of the IFIs and northern governments always hit poor families the hardest, and rob children of their future and hope. It's time we stop asking the children of developing countries to subsidize our habits of consumption.

I have provided four examples of global economics at work in the global south. These are just a few out of a legion of possible examples of the dominating, destructive effects of global economics in that vast region. No book could encompass all of these stories.

At this point we are left with many questions, such as: how as Christians ought we to live in light of global economics and the suffering it has brought to our global neighbors? Or, how ought we to live in light of the dominating effect "the market" seeks to have over our lives. To address these questions, our focus will now shift away from descriptions of global economics and portraits of its consequences, and toward reflections on the ethical issues global economics presents us with— issues such as how we use and think about wealth, or how we are called to respond to the weak and vulnerable, or how a power such as "Mammon" competes with God for our allegiance. Fortunately, we are not the first to grapple with these issues—far from it. In fact, God's followers have been grappling with them since before the written word. Nonetheless, in our reflections, we will begin with the written word. Specifically, we will begin with the "Christian scriptures"—the Old and New Testaments, and with what their authors had to say about the issues we face. The biblical story has significantly shaped our story, and our conceptions of God and of ethics. As we look at what the biblical authors had to say on issues of wealth and its usage, economic justice, and caring for the vulnerable, we will see that their experiences were not so unlike our own. This is not to say that they were "like" us. Rather, despite our many differences from them, we are faced with the timeless issues they faced—greed, domination, suffering. The foundational scriptures we share as Christians have a lot to say to us about these things. We will begin on that common ground.

From there, we will turn to stories of specific Christians whose lives and economic choices have been shaped by the Christian story, and by Christian community. Their stories offer answers to the question: how ought we to live as Christians in light of global economics? There are many more stories and answers; answers are all around us. We just have to get to know the right people.

On that note, let us turn to the biblical story.

Chapter Four

Biblical Economics, Part I:

Ancient and Modern,

A Contemporary Conversation

It is remarkable that, notwithstanding the universal favor
with which the New Testament is outwardly received, and
even the bigotry with which it is defended, there is no
hospitality shown to, there is no appreciation of, the order
of truth with which it deals. I know of no book that has so
few readers. There is none so truly strange, and heretical,
and unpopular. To Christians, no less than Greeks and Jews,
it is foolishness and a stumbling-block.

Henry David Thoreau[1]

The Bible and Economics

Why would Thoreau write such a thing? Surely Christians in his
day read the New Testament regularly, as do many Christians today.
Why would he say, "no book has so few readers"? His words strike
many Christians as offensive! But Thoreau's words are intentionally
provocative. In the passage cited, Thoreau ruminates on the religious
arrogance of his Christian contemporaries. He suggests that despite

their self-assuredness, his Christian friends would writhe upon listening to certain portions of scripture. Thoreau continues:

> There are, indeed, severe things in [the New Testament] which no man should read aloud more than once. "Seek first the kingdom of heaven." "Lay not up for yourselves treasures on earth." "If thou wilt be perfect, go and sell that thou hast, and give to the poor, and thou shalt have treasure in heaven." "For what is a man profited, if he shall gain the whole world, and lose his own soul? Or what shall a man give in exchange for his soul?" Think of this, Yankees! . . . Think of repeating these things to a New England audience! . . . Who, without cant, can hear them, and not go out of the meeting-house? They never *were* read, they never *were* heard. Let but one of these sentences be rightly read, from any pulpit in the land, and there would not be left one stone of that meeting-house upon another.[2]

Like many Christians in our own contexts, Thoreau's aristocratic contemporaries had no patience for Jesus' teachings on wealth. They had no appreciation for the radical truths the Bible proffers on the subject; indeed, they would not even read them, or hear them. The truths were too challenging to absorb. They were a stumbling-block.

The Bible, when read responsibly, has always leveled life-altering challenges to its readers. It is therefore best avoided by those with an interest in protecting the status quo, whether from a liberal or conservative perspective. An honest reading of the Bible is uniquely dangerous to those with a vested interest in maintaining things, especially their own lives, as they are. This is nowhere more true than in the area of economics. The Old Testament writers frequently align faithfulness to Yahweh with economic justice and provision for those vulnerable to destitution. The New Testament builds extensively on this foundation. *Jesus had more to say about wealth and its usage than any other single topic.* Yet Jesus' teaching on money, or for that matter, any of the New Testament teachings on money, rarely seem to impinge on the financial decisions of American Christians. This alone confirms the pertinence of Thoreau's acrid assessment to our times. In this chapter we will look at wealth and its usage in the Old Testament, and in the following chapter we will look at Jesus' teachings on the matter. From there, we move on to Pauline reflections. One thing becomes clear through such study: for all the diversity within the Hebrew/Christian Bible, the call to use resources justly is integral to the biblical story. The fact that the call is so pervasive in the Bible increases the bitterness of the indictment that we have largely failed to heed that call.

With this chapter, our focus shifts away from explanations and pictures of the global economy to Christian responses to the global economy. The remainder of this book focuses on discerning answers to the question: how does one live as a Christian in light of the global economy? Or stated another way, what are our global moral obligations in light of the globalization of economics? I will begin by looking at what biblical authors have to say about wealth (meaning material possessions),[3] and how it should be used. As a Christian, I am especially concerned to know what Jesus had to say about it, and what Jesus' life and ministry mean for how I live my life and use my wealth. I am convinced that the Bible is the place to begin in seeking direction on Christian ethical decision making. This is not because I view the Bible as an "answer book" for ethical quandaries. One does not just look up a verse or verses "answering" a given moral question, in part because one is likely to get a variety of answers for many questions. But I believe that we Christians should hold our lives up to the light of the biblical story. The stories of the Israelite people and the early followers of Jesus form a grand narrative that has shaped our stories. Their lives and experiences reveal God's movements and intentions, and teach us many lessons. Usually, the lessons are bigger than isolated segments of scripture would suggest. Only after we have looked at the topic of wealth and its usage in both the Old and New Testaments will discussion turn to the way the biblical story sheds light on how we should live in our world of globalized economics.

Due to space constraints, I will necessarily discuss biblical economics in a rather summary fashion. In this chapter on the Old

Testament, I will look at biblical economics in the Pentateuch, in the histories of the kings, and in some of the prophets, rather than isolating a few key books or passages.

Furthermore, I will treat the Bible not as a homogenous collection of spiritual books, but rather as a collection of distinct perspectives all reflecting on the revelation of God, and interpreting it in many different ways. Together these voices tell a marvelous story. They are of the nature of a symphony, rather than a droning unison. They display point and counterpoint, dissonance and resonance, and at the end a grand resolution.

Third, I will seek to accomplish a culturally sensitive reading of the biblical texts, and will begin both my treatment of the Old Testament and of the New with a discussion of socio-cultural context. Though I have already employed the term "biblical economics" in this chapter, the term is admittedly inadequate for the cultural context of the Bible. The ancients did not have a system of "economics" per se, meaning a distinct system occupied with the analysis of social and economic interaction. Though our word "economy" derives from the Greek word *oikonomía*, even the Greeks did not mean by that word what we mean by "economy."[4] Nonetheless, the ancients did have definite ideas about wealth and its usage. However, these ideas were not separated into a system characterized as "economic," but commingled with ideas about religion, politics, and family. Most of the Old Testament reflects a period when society could be separated into only two distinct social systems, the kinship system and the political system. In a tribal society, which is marked by the lack of a centralized power (or political) structure, there only existed a kinship system. We will have to think along these lines when interpreting certain portions of biblical text, specifically those that presuppose the monarchy. But for the most part, the Bible speaks out of a context where people were tied both to a kinship system and a political system. Within this context, religion and economics were not separate social systems, but were embedded in the systems of kinship and politics. Thus, one can speak of kinship religion and political religion, or kinship economics and political economics. In kinship religion, religious practices are part of the kinship system and are overtly conceptualized and controlled within families, while in political religion a political hierarchy controls and dictates the religion of the *polis*, or political unit. Ideas and behavior of an economic nature were likewise embedded within kinship and political systems. Consequently, there is no simple way to talk about "economics" in the Bible, and one must realize at the beginning of an investigation like this that we do not think about economics as the ancients did. We must be prepared to do the work of cultural translation if we are to learn from them.

Another problem with the term "biblical economics" is how it implies that the Bible offers one set of ideas about wealth and its usage. In fact, there are many different ideas of an economic nature represented in scripture. The political-economic views associated with David and Solomon, for example, differ widely from those of the prophet Amos. As with every other issue, the Bible does not present the reader with unanimity. Nonetheless, when all the biblical writers are heard, one sees that some central ideas about wealth and its usage surface repeatedly throughout scripture. I submit that these central ideas constitute what one might, for lack of a better term, call "biblical economics." I will use the term to talk about these ideas.

I dare say that economics, religion, and politics are not as separate today as we would like to believe. Though we can now speak of economic systems as distinct social systems, economic systems still do not function independently. They are very much dependent on religious and political assumptions and movements. Still, the way that economics, religion, and politics interact today, and the way they interacted in ancient times are not the same. In ancient times, economic ideas and practices were *overtly* conceptualized and controlled by politico-religious hierarchies and kinship groups.[5] Today, on the other hand, at least in market-based economies, political powers exercise more of an implicit *influence* over the economic system, and kinship systems have far less of an impact on it. In fact, the modern family seems to be shaped and influenced by the economic system, rather than the other way around. Finally, in today's intersection of social systems, the religious system often serves merely to legitimate an economic system over which it exerts little direct control. That is to say that in market-based economies, religion is often used to explain and justify a people's economic behavior, which, one must acknowledge, is what allows economic systems to become entrenched. With that said, let us turn our attention to the Old Testament, listening first to what anthropologists can teach us about the biblical world.

The Agrarian Society[6]

Societies in the Middle East shifted from horticultural societies to what anthropologists term "agrarian" societies five to six thousand years ago, at least a millennium before the period of Abraham.[7] "Agrarian societies" is an abstract model used to denote societies in all times and places who share the following features. Most of the stories we read in the Bible occur within the context of an agrarian society, and an understanding of that context is necessary for an adequate interpretation of the biblical texts. Economic practices and ideas about wealth in agrarian societies differed dramatically from the economic practices and ideas characteristic of our own societies. When biblical authors write about economic exchange, about the rich and the poor, or about wealth, these things do not carry the same meanings for those authors that they do for us. Meaning derives from one's social context. Therefore, before looking into biblical economics, we must learn some basic information about agrarian societies, and in studying the Bible, keep that information in mind. Doing so will facilitate better understanding.

Agrarian societies came about because of significant advancements in tools and technology which precipitated dramatic shifts in agriculture.[8] The invention of the plow and the harnessing of animal power for agricultural and military purposes, advancements in metalworking, and broader usage of the sail and the wheel, all played a key role in the process. Because of the use of new tools and technology for agricultural purposes, agricultural production rose sharply. People grew more food than was needed for themselves and their families, making surplus food available to support others, people who were thus freed from agricultural work to fulfill other occupations. Therefore, the food surplus gave rise to a non-agricultural class, a class we will henceforth refer to as the "elite class." Those whose lot was agricultural production will be referred to by the term "peasant class." Peasants represented about ninety percent of the agrarian population.

In agrarian societies, the agricultural surplus ended up in the hands of the very wealthy elite class, who were a staid feature of such societies. Though elites constituted only two to three percent of the population, the society revolved around them. They were the political leaders (usually grouped around a monarch), military elites, priests, and scribes. Elites resided in the administrative and religious centers, the preindustrial cities, which, by modern standards, were rather small. Nonetheless, the cities were hubs of monumental influence and importance, and the wealth (or surplus) of all the outer-lying areas under their control gravitated in their direction. The elite class, being the government leaders and religious aristocracy, exacted taxes and tithes to keep revenue flowing their way. Many of the urban elites were also large landholders who resided in the cities as absentee landlords.

Also calling the cities home was a "retainer class" composed of artisans, merchants, day-laborers, and those of specialized skills. Socially marginal urbanites, such as beggars and slaves, lived in the cities as well. These two groups of non-elite urbanites made up roughly seven to eight percent of the population, and, with the exception of the beggars, functioned to serve the needs of the urban elites. Though the lot of some retainers, in particular that of merchants, was sometimes significantly more felicitous than that of peasants, the retainer class did not constitute a middle class. The daily lives of most retainers were as hard as those of peasants. Since retainers existed for the sole purpose of meeting the needs of elites, they were a dependent class. They carried little influence, and in relation to the peasant class, were small in numbers. Many urban craftsmen worked in guilds and occupied the same sector of a city, as the preindustrial city was a highly segregated place. The elites were safeguarded from the rest of the urban population by walls and sacred spaces, and would send their agents or slaves out to do business with their "inferiors."

Writing developed and spread widely along with agrarian societies and helped further the elite classes, who held something of a monopoly on literacy. They were the ones who produced the laws and most of the literature that came out of agrarian societies. The literature we read from ancient Egypt or Babylon and, for the most part, Israel, largely represents elite class interests and elite class interpretations of reality. Hebrew prophetic literature stands as a striking exception to this pattern. Some prophets, such as Isaiah and Ezekiel, were of elite birth and were called to speak and write against the waywardness of their elite contemporaries. Other prophets of non-elite status had their prophecies recorded and preserved by influential friends among the Israelite elite class (one example being Jeremiah with his scribe Baruch). But for the most part, ancient literature that was deeply critical of the elite classes is rare. In the amount of self-critical material it includes, the Hebrew Bible stands apart.

Religion and state were well-integrated in agrarian societies, not because the political leaders were especially devout, but because they knew the importance of gaining religious support for the state. In fact, in agrarian societies, religious leaders were so closely linked to the political leaders that national religions were the norm. The religious elite and political elite functioned almost inseparably, with political language and ceremony always carrying a decidedly religious tone, and religion always being used to legitimate the actions of the state. "God" was invoked as the director of political affairs; so much so, that in some cases, such as in ancient Egypt, the supreme leader was actually deemed to be an incarnation of the supreme god.

Military advancements played a monumental role in the rise of agrarian societies, and in the accompanying rise of large empires. Urban-based rulers relied on relatively advanced weapons, and on cavalries, chariots, and standing armies to impose their will. The greater their military force, the greater their power. Conquests of more and more territory became possible for rulers, who began to envision empires, and to realize those visions. The constant struggles for power resulting from these technological advancements made agrarian societies uniquely conflictual. There was constant vying for power between states, and in states where succession to the throne was not a clear process, there were constant power struggles within.[9]

It is in this sociological context that the biblical stories are set. While the primordial history of Genesis 1-11 reflects on periods prior to agrarian societies, the stories of the patriarchs through the Apocalypse of John can be read against this general framework. For the most part, the patriarchs were semi-nomadic agriculturalists who came into contact with urban centers of influence only sporadically. During the period of time in which the Hebrew people were wanderers without connections to a state, they avoided some of the limitations placed on non-elites in agrarian societies, notwithstanding, of course, the period when they ended up on the wrong side of the equation as slaves in Egypt. In any case, throughout *most* of the pre-Davidic period, the kin-group was the only social system of importance to the Hebrews,[10] and both economics and religion were conceptualized and overseen by kin-groups. After the time of David, however, when Israelite land was consolidated and the Hebrew people could be said to have a state, economics came to be embedded in a political system. Throughout the post-Davidic period, Israelite life would have been marked by the class structure of agrarian societies outlined above. One cannot fully understand what the Bible says about "economics" without knowledge of the role social class played in the biblical world.

Ideas on Wealth and its Usage in the Old Testament

Ideas on Wealth as Expressed in the Genesis Narratives. According to the creation stories narrated in the Hebrew Bible, God intends the fruit of the Earth to provide for the needs of God's creatures. In the first creation story (Genesis 1:1-2:4a), God creates plants prior to the creation of man and woman, and after the creation of humans, God "gives" every seed-bearing plant and tree to them for food. To the animals he gives "every green plant." In the second story (2:4b-2:25), God creates the first human, Adam, right away, "when no plant of the field was yet in the earth," then God plants the garden and puts Adam in it, giving him fruits from the garden to eat, and placing him as steward over its resources. In both of the stories, it is apparent that God created a world which would provide for the needs of both humans and animals. The stories also show that God charged human beings with taking care of the creation. The commands God gives the first man and woman to "subdue it" and "have dominion over it" (1:28) have sometimes been interpreted as license to use up and exploit the earth's resources, but this interpretation is inconsistent with the respect the story exudes for God's creation. God calls the created order "good," and "hallows" it (2:3). The Earth is sacred because God made it and it belongs to God. The early Hebrews who provided us with these creation narratives would not think of exploiting that which is sacred. In the second story, man is told to "till" the Earth and "keep" it (2:15), words which together indicate maintenance and wise use rather than exploitation. The creation narratives provide us with a picture of the ancient Hebrews' foundational beliefs about the created world and about God. They show us a God who cares deeply about the created order, and about providing for the needs of both humans and animals through creation. They also speak to the role God gave to human beings in maintaining creation, for if creation is not maintained, God's purposes of providing for needs through creation cannot be fulfilled.

At Genesis 12, the focus shifts from the human family to a focus on a particular family, that of Abram. This family's story occupies the rest of Genesis, and sets the stage for much more. In the stories about Abram's family, the key idea about wealth and its usage is that God must be trusted to supply one's needs and those of one's family. The stories about Abram and his offspring, down to Joseph, exhibit their share of abundance and want. Some times are good; some times are bad, materially speaking. But at all times, the patriarchs are challenged to trust the Lord despite their circumstances. Furthermore, generosity toward one's kin-group is portrayed as especially honorable by the writers of these stories, as is evident in the portrayal of Abram's generosity in allowing Lot to choose the more promising land to settle (Gen 13), and in the portrayal of Joseph's entirely undeserved generosity toward his back-stabbing brothers who had treated him not like kin, but like an enemy (47:11-20, 50:15-21). Greed toward one's kin-group is especially dishonorable. This is nowhere better portrayed than in Laban's acquisitive scheming against Jacob, both in the marrying off of his daughters (29:15-30), and in his attempts to cheat Jacob out of fair remittance for his work (30:25-36). But such dishonorable behavior also surfaces in Jacob's conniving to wrest the birthright from Esau. In a sense, Jacob and Laban were a perfect match.

Ideas on Wealth as Expressed in the Exodus and Pentateuch. The story of the Exodus and the law codes of the Pentateuch address the issue of wealth and its usage more directly, and it is there that one begins to see how the standards of the God of the Hebrews went far beyond cultural norms. God expected more from them than did their culture, and they were to meet God's expectations out of honor to God, who had rescued them from slavery. The Exodus became the foundational story of the Hebrew people, and the basis of their covenant with Yahweh. They were given the Ten Commandments, which define the Hebrews' relationship to God and to one another, precisely *because* God had led them out of slavery in Egypt (Exodus 20: 1-2). Because God had rescued them, they were to be a particular kind of people, as outlined in the Ten Commandments (Ex 20:3-17). The constitutional event of rescue in the Exodus reveals some remarkable things about the God of the Hebrews. Unlike the gods of Mesopotamia and Egypt, this God chose the lowliest rabble of society, a dishonored people, as were the *hapiru* slaves in Egypt (the people from whom came the Hebrews), rather than the most powerful and honorable members of society. This God was not the patron of the elites, but of the lowly. According to the foundational story of the Hebrews, their God was compassionate, and acted on behalf of an oppressed group of people, a people stripped of the honor they once held. Allusions to these characteristics of God surface repeatedly with Hebrew mandates on the treatment of the most vulnerable members of society. Since God had shown mercy to them, the Hebrew people were to act mercifully toward those in dire need.

The covenant God makes with the Hebrew people (via Moses) at Mt. Sinai differs from God's covenant with Abraham in that God attaches to the Mosaic covenant both a basis for the covenant and conditions for its continuance. As stated above, it is based on God's actions in the Exodus. The conditions and promises of the covenant are thus: "If you obey my voice and keep my covenant, you shall be my treasured possession out of all the peoples. Indeed, the whole earth is mine, but you shall be for me a priestly kingdom and a holy nation" (Ex

19:5-6). The Hebrew people believed that the laws God had given to them were to be followed *so that* they might serve as mediators to God and as people reflecting God's holiness. This was the role God intended for them. Out of the many laws the Hebrew people connected with this Mosaic covenant, there were some far-reaching laws about wealth and its usage.[11]

The Hebrews assumed that the whole earth belonged to God, an assumption that likely influenced the way they thought about property. It is not that they did not have a concept of ownership, they certainly did. But they believed that God's desire to meet the needs of God's creatures was always of primary concern, and must be honored. Whether or not one owned something was of little consequence if God wanted it to be used by someone else. God was to have authority over how the Hebrews used their possessions. God's authority over how the chosen people used wealth, and God's desires for a just use of wealth, are evident in several of the laws included in the Pentateuch (the books of Genesis through Deuteronomy).

Among the laws of the Pentateuch is the law on gleaning. This law would have meant more to the Hebrew people settled in the land and actively engaged in agriculture than to the Hebrew people wandering about with Moses. In any case, the law states that the Hebrew people were to leave a portion of their agricultural produce unharvested and available for gleaning by the poor and the alien. "When you reap the harvest of your land, you shall not reap to the very edges of your field, or gather the gleaning of your harvest. You shall not strip your vineyard bare, or gather the fallen grapes of your vineyard; you shall leave them for the poor and the alien: I am the Lord your God" (Leviticus 19:9-10, 23:22). The tag "I am the Lord your God," attached to many of the Hebrew laws, is significant. If God is Lord over the Hebrews and all they own, then it will not seem exceptional for them to leave a portion of their fields to provide for God's creatures who otherwise have no provision. After all, what the Hebrews "own" ultimately belongs to God. Lev 25:23 states this belief most succinctly: "The land shall not be sold in perpetuity, for the land is mine; with me you are but aliens and tenants." Furthermore, the practice of leaving food for those without food harmonizes with the Hebrew assumptions about God as expressed in their stories of creation. The Hebrew people believed that God desired for, and had provided the resources for all of God's creatures' needs to be met. The Hebrews' usage of wealth needed to be consistent with God's intentions in this regard if they were to serve as mediators to God and reflect God's holiness.

In agrarian societies, where the majority of the population were subsistence farmers, the "poor" were those who could not subsist, who could not provide for the basic needs of themselves and/or their families. These were the most vulnerable members of society. Included among them were those who had no family, specifically widows and orphans, who are often used in the Hebrew scriptures to epitomize need. The Hebrews are not only instructed to provide for the most vulnerable among them, however, they are also instructed to reach out to aliens, to strangers. This is quite an exceptional injunction within a kin-group-based, agrarian society where out-group[12] members would normally be viewed suspiciously, as presumed enemies. Because of this norm, aliens are in a particularly vulnerable position in kin-group-based societies. But the Hebrew people are not to treat aliens as enemies, or to oppress them; rather they are to see that their needs are met, to treat them as fellow citizens, and to love them as they would want to be loved themselves (Lev 19:33-34). Such hospitality would certainly have looked radical in the ancient near-eastern context. The Hebrew people had been aliens in a foreign land themselves, therefore, they are to treat aliens as they would have liked to be treated by the Egyptians. Again, such far-reaching things are commanded them because they belong to God (19:34), and God desires that the resources harvested from the created world be shared with those who are vulnerable to destitution.

Another group of Pentateuchal laws addressing provision for the vulnerable are the laws regarding the Sabbath Year and the Jubilee. Both laws speak to the time when the Hebrew people are settled in the land. While some form of the Sabbath Year law is mentioned in Exodus (23:10-11), in Leviticus (25: 1-7) and in Deuteronomy (15:1-18), the Jubilee legislation appears only in Leviticus (25: 8-55). Details differ widely in the different accounts of the Sabbath Year legislation, as will be discussed below, but together they demonstrate important convictions on behalf of the Hebrew people about God's desires for how they use their wealth. Similar convictions are expressed in the Jubilee legislation, even if the Jubilee was less popular a concept than the Sabbath Year.

Every seventh year was to be deemed a Sabbath Year by the Hebrews. In Exodus and Leviticus, the focus of this Sabbath is on leaving one's land unharvested. The people were not to gather in crops, and were to leave their trees and vineyards unpruned. The motivations behind this agricultural Sabbath are a bit different in the two accounts, however, with the focus in Exodus being clearly on God's provision for those in need (23:11), and the focus in Leviticus being on allowing the land to rest (25:4). In Exodus, the crops are left alone so that the poor and the wild animals are free to gather from everyone's fields, vineyards, and orchards, but this motivation is not mentioned in Leviticus. According to the Leviticus tradition, owners are free to gather from their unattended fields food for their own families, slaves, and animals to eat for the season. They are merely prohibited from sowing, pruning, and harvesting a surplus (Lev 25:5-7).

Because the Exodus tradition is more radical than that of Leviticus, it is quite likely to be more original. One can more easily imagine people adapting the law reflected in Exodus to be less radical and demanding than imagine that people took the law reflected in Leviticus and adapted it to be more extreme. The Hebrew people probably adapted the Sabbath Year law of Exodus so that they could use the food from their unattended fields to feed their own families rather than leaving it for the poor, and such an adaptation is likely reflected in Leviticus. In any case, the Sabbath Year law once again demonstrates that the Hebrew people assumed that their wealth belonged to God (Lev 25:23), and that God could command them to use it in particular ways. The earlier Exodus tradition depicts God's desire that a (significant) portion of the yield of their crops be made available to those who do not have crops of their own.

In Deuteronomy, the Sabbath Year aligns with legislation on the forgiveness of debts (Deuteronomy 15:1-18). This is a very different kind of Sabbath than the agricultural Sabbath of Exodus and Leviticus. According to this law, every seventh year the Hebrew people are to forgive the debts accrued by members of their community, and to release all Hebrew slaves. In effect, the releasing of Hebrew slaves constituted another form of debt forgiveness. The circumstances under which a Hebrew man or woman would have become a slave of a fellow community member would normally have been circumstances of indebtedness (II Kings 4: 1, Amos 2:6-8). The scenario would look something like this: a person who was unable to make payment on a debt owed to a neighbor would "pay off" the debt by becoming the slave of that neighbor, or by selling a family member into slavery. Alternatively, it was possible for someone to become the slave of a neighbor as restitution for a theft (Ex 22:3). In either case, this version of the Sabbath Year law would give the indebted person a fresh start, a new chance. Unlike the law on gleaning, which legislates a countercultural treatment of aliens, the Deuteronomic Sabbath Year legislation on forgiveness of debts applies only to in-group members. A person would not be required to remit the debts of foreigners, or to set non-Hebrew slaves free. This exclusion of munificence to neighbors is socially predictable behavior for agrarian societies. It doesn't, however, convey the same spirit as that conveyed in other passages, such as the following from Leviticus: "When the alien resides with you in your land, you shall not oppress the alien. The alien who resides with you shall be to you as the citizen among you; you shall love the alien as yourself, for you were aliens in the land of Egypt: I am the Lord your God" (19:34-35). Nevertheless, the Sabbath Year tradition reflected in Deuteronomy suggests that God desired the Hebrew people to extend grace liberally to their neighbors so that imbalances in society might regularly be set right. By forgiving debts every seven years and granting a new start to those who had become enslaved, the Hebrews would be limiting the extent to which certain members of the community could dominate and take advantage of others.

The Jubilee legislation in Leviticus includes features of the Sabbath Year legislation in Exodus, Leviticus, and Deuteronomy, though it legislates for broad release of Hebrew bonded laborers, forgiveness of debts among the Hebrew people, and rest for the land on a fifty-year, rather than a seven-year, cycle. Upon the Jubilee year, every family was to return to their property (Lev 25:10b). The law, therefore, addresses situations of destitution or indebtedness, where families have been forced to sell off family lands out of financial necessity. The legislation aims to correct societal imbalances which lead to the consolidation of land into the hands of an elite class. The Jubilee law speaks to the time when the Hebrew people are settled in the land, and serves to preserve the equitable allocation of land to the various Hebrew tribes described in Joshua 13-19. The Hebrew people believed that their land had been provided to them by God, that God desired that the land be distributed equitably among the tribes, and that it be held by families. By practicing the Jubilee, the Hebrews were ensuring that God's intentions for the land were honored. Unfortunately, as becomes apparent during the monarchical period, the Jubilee law was not popular among the Israelite ruling class. Nonetheless, the ideals behind the legislation are consonant with those mentioned above.

Legislation on tithing features mostly in Deuteronomy. For our purposes, it is interesting to note what the many tithing laws convey the Hebrews' beliefs about wealth and how it should be used. Because they believed that what they had belonged to God, they made their wealth available to be used in the ways they felt God desired. In this sense, tithing was a way of honoring God. But tithing also provided for various needs according to God's desires. For example, it provided for the needs of the Levites, and for the rituals of worship. Beyond this, however, tithing was used by God to provide for the needs of the destitute (14:28, 26:12-13). Every third year, the full tithe, which in an agricultural society took the form of produce, was to be stored and used for feeding those who otherwise had no source of food, namely the orphans, widows, and resident aliens, along with the Levites. This amount of food would have gone a long way toward providing subsistence for these vulnerable members of society.

A number of the laws in the Pentateuch specifically call for compassionate treatment of the poor. While these laws do not instruct the Hebrew people on the usage of wealth, they do place limits on how wealth can be gained. For example, in Exodus 22:25, the Hebrews are prohibited from charging interest on loans to the poor. "You shall not deal with them as a creditor," says the passage. This passage would suggest that gaining wealth at the expense of the destitute is inconsistent with God's desires (cf. Lev 25:35-36). Furthermore, limits are placed on the taking of collateral from the poor. If someone loans money to a poor man and takes his cloak as pledge, he must return the cloak at sunset, in case the man has nothing else to shield himself from the cold night (Ex 22:26-27; cf. Deut 24:12-13). This passage accents the compassionate nature of God: " . . . for [the cloak] may be your neighbor's only clothing to use as cover; in what else shall that person sleep? And if your neighbor cries out to me, I will listen, for I am compassionate." The Hebrews are to regard the poor with compassion because God is compassionate, and if God's people are to serve as mediators to God, and to reflect God's holiness, they too must be compassionate.

Finally, the Pentateuch features several laws that prohibit the Hebrews from abusing the weak and vulnerable members of their society. Such laws include protections for the destitute members of the community, such as widows and orphans (Ex 22:22-24; Deut 24:17), and the deaf and the blind (Lev 19:14), as well as protection for aliens, or non-community members (Ex 22:21, 23:9; Lev 19:34; Num 35:15; Deut 1:16-17, 10:19, 24:17). The Hebrews are commanded not to show favoritism in the courts, either to the rich or the poor (Lev 19:15), for God's desire is for fairness. Unlike human judges, who are prone to favoritism toward those who can reciprocate most liberally, God is a fair judge who will not be bribed. As Deut 10:17-19 states: "For the Lord your God is God of gods and Lord of lords, the great God, mighty and awesome, who is not partial and takes no bribe, who executes justice for the orphan and the widow, and who loves the strangers, providing them food and clothing. You shall also love the stranger, for you were strangers in the land of Egypt."

The laws of the Pentateuch reveal many things about God and how God desires human wealth to be used. To summarize, the following general beliefs about God and wealth are evident: 1) The wealth of God's people belongs to God, and God desires to use it for certain purposes. 2) Among those purposes is to ensure that the needs of the destitute are met. 3) God is compassionate and desires that God's people act compassionately toward "the poor." (Included in that category are vulnerable members of society as mentioned above). 4) God's people are not to profit at the expense of the poor. 5) As evident in the legislation

about forgiveness of debts, God desires, at least within the community
of God's people, that those who have become economically enslaved be
given a new start so that economic domination will not be manifested
among God's people. On that note, let us turn to look at economic
ideas during the Israelite monarchy.

Ideas on Wealth During the Israelite Monarchy. It is not until the
dawning of the kingship of David that one can really begin to speak of
"Israel" as a state, or of "Israelites," meaning those sharing a common
nationhood. Consequently, I have used the term "Hebrew" as opposed
to "Israelite" up to this point. This is helpful for distinguishing between
the tribal (or kin-based) confederacy that predated the monarchy of
David, and the centralized nation after David. Before David, the Hebrew
tribes did not have claim to a unified land, or a state, not even during
the reign of Saul. But with David's conquest and consolidation of an
expanse of land in Palestine parallel to the Mediterranean Sea and
stretching from the Red Sea almost to Kadesh, and with his efforts to
establish a centralized form of government, the state of Israel was born.
Little can be known with any certainty about the period between the
Exodus and the monarchy, or about the way wealth was used by the
Hebrew people during that time. One assumes that many of the laws
found in the Pentateuch reflect the ideals of this period regarding wealth
and its usage, and to some degree, reflect how those ideals were realized
in the lives of the Hebrews. But it is likely that at least some of the
Pentateuch speaks to the ideals and aspirations of a later period, that of
the Pentateuch's editors, and I will not spend time sorting out the
differences here. For our purposes, it is helpful to recognize the Hebrew/
Israelite ideals enshrined in the Pentateuch regarding wealth and its
usage. They will help us to think about the monarchy, and shifts in
economic practices during that stage of biblical history. They will also
help us to understand the message of the prophets.

Before discussing the period of the Israelite monarchy, I want to
acknowledge the ambiguous portrayal of the monarchy in the Hebrew
scriptures. Preserved in those scriptures are some very diverse views
about kingship within Israel. On the one hand is a view which deems

the monarchy to be God-directed and (as long as the king behaves) divinely blessed. Most of I, II Kings and I, II Chronicles reflects this perspective. On the other hand is a view which deems the monarchy to be a betrayal of God's leadership, a view most clearly stated in 1 Sam 8:4-22 and 12:12-25. When interpreting what is written about the kings, one must keep this diversity of perspective in mind. One reason it is important to do so is because of the confusion which can result from a one-sided reading of the kings. If one simply accepts the view that the kings were intended as God's representatives on earth, what will one think of the fact that even the best of the kings, such as David and Solomon, disregarded much of what Hebrew tradition had to say on wealth and its usage, not to mention other things? One might just assume this disregard was okay with God, and feel free to likewise disregard the early Hebrew economic ideals in thinking about one's own economic decisions. One might just choose to model one's economic life after Solomon, rather than letting one's economic choices be influenced by the economic principles gleaned from the Pentateuch and other portions of scripture. After all, it is written of Solomon: "I [God] will give you a wise and discerning mind; no one like you shall arise after you. I give you also what you have not asked, both riches and honor all your life; no other king will compare with you" (1 Kgs 3:12-13). According to this reading, Solomon is a model of wisdom, uniquely blessed by God, both with wisdom and riches. One problem remains, however: this is not the whole story given in scripture. One must look at the whole story if one is to properly understand Solomon and assess his qualification to serve as a role model for how one thinks about wealth. It would be a mistake to pattern one's economic choices after those of Solomon. As will be discussed below, Solomon's use of wealth is not consistent with the central biblical ideas on the subject, and Solomon's economic choices resulted in many significant failures. A more appropriate way to look at kingship in the Old Testament is to acknowledge the critical way in which kingship is treated in portions of scripture, and to read what is written about the kings in light of that balancing perspective. In the end, one will be less likely to pattern one's life after any of the kings' lives.

Sociological models can assist us in picturing life in Israel following the establishment of a monarchy and the transition to statehood. Of specific interest here is the sociological model of agrarian societies, which is quite useful for filling in the blanks left by the biblical text. The historical books of the Old Testament tell us much about the comings and goings of the elite class (the kings, military leaders and religious officials), during the period of the monarchy, but tell us little about what life was like for the large majority of the Israelite population who subsisted as agriculturalists, and who labored to support the elite class. Some hints are provided, such as brief references to Solomon's use of Israelite peasants for conscripted labor on his magnificent building projects (1 Kgs 13:17), or references to peasants associated with Elijah and Elisha (1 Kgs 17:8-24; 2 Kgs 4:1-37, 8:1-6). But for the most part, one has to look outside of the historical books for much information on non-elites in the Old Testament. Even there, much is left unsaid.

As stated earlier, agrarian societies are marked by sharp distinctions between social classes. After the Hebrew people had been settled in the land for a time, one begins to see the emergence of an elite class among them. The trend may have been advanced by Saul's gathering of soldiers around himself, which eventually became something of a standing army, or a military elite. During the reign of David, however, an elite class is very visible in Israelite society. Even before he became king, first of Judah, then of Judah and Israel together, David had his own military troops and ruled over a large territory which has been granted to him by the Philistine king (1 Sam 27:5-7); he thus had great power and wealth. But he became far more rich and powerful during his reign. Soon after becoming monarch of both Judah and Israel, David established the capital of Israel (meaning, the united kingdom) at Jerusalem and moved the Ark of the Covenant to that seat of power. At this point, the governmental/religious power of Israel became centralized in one location, and under one man. From then on, Israel was to be governed by a conspicuous elite class, composed of David and his politico-religious administration (see II Sam 8:15-18; 20:23-26).

Much of David's wealth came from the Canaanite populations he conquered and annexed into Israel, and the regular tribute they were required to pay to David, their patron-king. The booty acquired during his campaigns also bolstered his coffers. Additionally, David acquired many slaves from conquered lands (e.g. II Sam 8:6-8, 14), negotiated some very lucrative treaties with various kings, most notably with the king of Tyre (II Sam 5:11f.), and established patron-client relationships with others (e.g. II Sam 8:9-10). Subsequent kings of Israel would gain wealth in these same ways, but none would compare with David as a conqueror of foreign lands.

Another source of wealth of the Israelite kings deserves mention: as in other agrarian societies, in Israel the wealth of the peasants was funneled in the direction of the elites. Though the biblical text does not mention a system of taxation under David, it is likely that the massive census he undertook was aimed at facilitating the institution of such a system. By the reign of Solomon, it is clear that the burden placed on the peasant class was immense, both in the forms of taxation and conscripted labor. A good portion of Solomon's wealth resulted from trade, which will be discussed below. But the burden he placed on non-elite Israelites also contributed greatly to his wealth. Not only that, but it had dire consequences for the nation.

In Samuel 8:11-17, when the elders of Israel approach Samuel demanding a king, the old prophet paints a brilliant picture for them of what a king will do to the nation. The passage provides a fine description of the role of kings in agrarian societies. Samuel states that the king will take their sons and put them to work in his military, or in his fields. He will take their daughters and make them servants in his palaces. He will take the best of their fields and vineyards, and a tenth of the produce of their remaining lands, and he will take for himself the best of their cattle and slaves. In short, Samuel tells the Israelite elders: your king will act just like a king.

The biblical histories of the monarchy do not provide a wealth of information about the lives of Israelite peasants. How the elites used their wealth and what kind of impact it had on the majority of the Israelites was not, for the most part, a pressing concern to the scribes who produced the monarchical histories. Nevertheless, the narratives about Solomon *do* provide some information on the impact of Solomon's economic policies on the larger Israelite society. The economic prosperity of Solomon's reign was one of its defining characteristics, but it also seems to have precipitated the division of the kingdom.

By capitalizing on Israel's location on major near East trade routes and charging taxes and duties on overland trade (I Kgs 10:15), by engaging in sea trade himself (I Kgs 9:26-28; 10: 11, 22), and by trading in things like horses and chariots (I Kgs 10:28-29), Solomon amassed for himself enough wealth to wow people near and far (I Kgs 10:7). But Solomon's prosperity could not keep pace with his opulent tastes, elaborate establishment, and grand building schemes. During Solomon's reign, new lands were not added to the empire as they had been in David's time, so the amount of money coming from tributes had not increased. Trade was the main source of income from outside of Israel, and it was not enough. Solomon had to rely on the Israelite people to provide what outside sources could not.

Solomon dismantled old tribal arrangements to divide Israel into twelve administrative districts for the purpose of collecting taxes from the people, to provide "food for the king and his household" (I Kgs 4:7). Mind you, the needs of his household were not meager. According to I Kgs 4:22f., Solomon's household required for one day (apart from non-perishables): thirty cors of choice flour (about 185 bushels or 6.6 kiloliters), sixty cors of meal (about 375 bushels or 13.2 kiloliters), ten fat oxen, twenty pasture-fed cattle, one hundred sheep, besides deer, gazelles, roebucks, and fatted fowl. Each of the twelve districts was responsible to provide for the needs of the king's courts for one month out of the year. William Albright estimated that each of these districts would have averaged only about 100,000 people,[13] which means that the economic strain on these villagers would have been enormous. As Samuel had predicted, the best of the kingdom was being funneled into the king's coffers. It was a typical "agrarian" arrangement, and amply confirmed Samuel's prescience about kingship. Besides erecting a taxation system to provide for elite class needs, Solomon also conscripted Israelite peasants to help build his magnificent palaces and to staff his massive army (I Kgs 5:13-18; see also I Kgs 4:6; 12:18). For freeborn Israelites to be forced to leave their homes and fields for periods of time to help the king harvest trees and quarry stone for his palaces must have been intolerable, and likely precipitated both poverty and indebtedness for many peasants who hadn't family members to look after their fields and families in their absence. As a kingly move, the institution of conscripted labor must have been fueled by a mixture of blinding hubris and fiscal desperation. That Solomon was financially desperate is evident in the fact that he resorted to giving away Israelite territory in payment for his "loans" (I Kgs 9:10-14).

Despite the laudatory words used to describe Solomon's reign and the well-being of the Israelite people in I Kings and I Chronicles, there is ample reason to doubt that Solomon's economic choices were either pleasing to God or successful for Israel. For one thing, Solomon's actions were just what God had warned the Israelites about through the prophet Samuel when they demanded a king in Samuel 8:4-22. According to that thread of scripture, God saw their demand for a king as a betrayal of God's own leadership. In light of this, it is interesting to note that Solomon, praised for building the temple of the Lord, spent almost twice as much time building his own luxurious palace as he had spent on the temple (cf. I Kgs 6:38 and 7:1)! Second, Solomon's actions did not bring success to Israel. They precipitated such deep divisions among the Israelite people that the kingdom was torn asunder. By the time Solomon died, the tribes of the north were so disaffected with the harsh economic policies of Solomon that they sought, under the leadership of Jeroboam, to distance themselves from the Davidic dynasty. Therefore, they issued an ultimatum to Solomon's son, Rehoboam, saying, "Your father made our yoke heavy. Now therefore lighten the hard service of your father and we will serve you" (I Kgs 12:3-4). But Rehoboam's myopic young advisors told him to play hardball. Not surprisingly, he ended up losing the northern kingdom of Israel. The economic prosperity of the Solomon years was bought at the price of the unified kingdom, and ended up causing David's family to lose control of most of the country.

All this is to say that with the rise of the monarchy in Israel, class distinctions between elites and non-elites in Israel became extreme. There is little reason, moreover, to doubt that the typical agrarian arrangements evident during Solomon's reign did not persist throughout the reigns of subsequent Israelite monarchs. As already stated, the monarchical histories do not speak much of non-elite concerns, such as taxation, forced labor, and the like. Still, the extensive needs of subsequent kings and their elaborate courts evident in the histories would have required a substantial siphoning of resources from the villages.

During the reign of Solomon, wealth in Israel came to be concentrated in the hands of the elite class, and was used to support the lifestyle of the elites and the government establishment they comprised. Was this arrangement consistent with the beliefs about God and wealth expressed in the Pentateuch? In a way, it is hard to say, since the monarchical histories tell us so little of the story. But the level of outrage among the people of the north about the "heavy yoke" placed on them by Solomon at least hints at a notable degree of economic injustice. Were the needs of the destitute going unmet? Were the vulnerable members of society being oppressed, or were they being treated with compassion? Were people profiting at the expense of the poor? Were measures being taken to ensure that economic enslavement and domination were not being practiced among God's people? The historical narratives about the kings *suggest* answers to these questions, but do not provide quite enough information to allow one to answer them convincingly. One must look to the prophetic books to help fill out the picture.

Ideas on Wealth in the Prophets. Amos. The first of the classical prophets, Amos, did not arise until about two centuries after the death of Solomon. We do not, therefore, have prophetic commentary on the immediate after-effects of Solomon's policies. However, the prophecies of Amos show us that the two hundred years after Solomon did not see a reversal of the class disparities made salient during his reign. By the mid-eighth century BCE the world still, predictably, revolved around the Israelite elite class. Unlike the writers of the kingly histories though, the prophets do not just tell us about elite class dealings. The prophets were astute observers of the broader society and provide valuable glimpses into the lives of the peasant class, that invisible majority in agrarian societies.

Amos ministered in the northern kingdom, Israel, around the middle of the eighth century. During the prior century, the fortunes of

Israel had waned. Internal strife, warring with Judah, and repeated threats from neighboring countries resulted in tumultuous times for the northern kingdom. But circumstances during the eighth century provided some reprieve from all this. Enemies like Assyria were too preoccupied elsewhere to cause much trouble for Israel. Israel was at peace with Judah, and Israel benefited from the military leadership of Jeroboam II. During this period, Israel regained control of lands lost since the reign of Solomon, lands encompassing major Near East trade routes. The result of all these factors was a period of unparalleled prosperity for some in Israel. Archaeologists have uncovered evidence of the opulent wealth of the period in the form of ornate buildings in Samaria.

The view of this period provided by archaeology and historical literature is a view from above, however; it is the view of the elites. This is not to say that the historical literature contains no criticism of Israelite society in the eighth century. It does. But the criticism offered in the monarchical histories, written by religio-governmental elites, focuses on the religious syncretism of the period, the idol worship practiced within Israel. It has little to say of the corresponding economic idolatry and immorality. Amos, along with later prophets, provides a different picture, a view from below, if you will. It is a view that sees acute economic injustice and ethical deterioration among the elites, in addition to the worship of idols.

Amos himself was a peasant. He lived on the edges of the Judean wilderness where he sheep-herded, and tended an orchard (1:1, 7:14). He was not a member of a prophetic guild (7:14), but prophesied out of an undeniable sense that God had called him to do so (7:15). God had called him to leave his home and go north into Israel to speak against her excesses. Amos' prophetic oracles are mainly addressed to Samaria and Bethel, the two key urban centers and centers of elite power in Israel, and his oracles largely focus on the wealthy. One can assume it took enormous courage for Amos, a modest sheep-herder from the backwoods of Judea, to obey God in going to the core of the Israelite power structure. Amos rails against them: "(6) Thus says the Lord, for three transgressions of Israel, and for four, I will not revoke the punishment; because they sell the righteous for silver, and the needy for a pair of sandals—(7) they who trample the head of the poor into the dust of the earth, and push the afflicted out of the way; father and son go in to the same girl, so that my holy name is profaned; (8) they lay themselves down beside every altar on garments taken in pledge; and in the house of their God they drink wine bought with fines they imposed" (2:6-8).

Several injustices are exposed in this first denunciation of Israel in the book of Amos. It alludes to the practice of elites enslaving people who cannot pay on their debts (v.6). Verse 7a suggests that the rights of the oppressed are "pushed out of the way" in the courts (cf. 5:12). Verse 7b may simply refer to sexual immorality, but it is probably a reference to the sexual submission of household slave girls. Verse 8a speaks of a blatant disregard for the law (Ex 22:26-27; cf. Deut 24:12-13) which states that one cannot keep overnight a poor man's cloak as pledge on a debt, since he may have nothing else to keep himself warm at night. 8b alludes to fines imposed by the temple elites, which allow the temple officials to live in luxury.

This set of verses paints a picture of a society where indebtedness has become epidemic and the needs of the poor are openly disregarded by those in power who live in luxury at the expense of the vulnerable. Indebtedness of the poor was common in agrarian societies. Whenever taxes and tithes imposed by the elites could not be paid by peasants, either because of circumstances like drought or crop failure, elites would loan out money, often at steep interest. Then, when another bad year came along and loan payments could not be made, they would either dispossess creditors of their land, or "buy" debtors or their family member as payments for debts. It was a system which allowed land to be consolidated into the hands of the few, resulting in the large landholdings characteristic of agrarian societies, and bolstering the slave holdings of the elite class.

According to Amos, these typical agrarian practices had become entrenched in Israel by the middle of the eighth century. They had probably been so since the reign of Solomon. Apparently, there was not much regard among Israelite elites for the Hebrew laws on the usage of wealth and treatment of the poor which, if obeyed, would have helped the Israelites to avoid the abuses and disparities typical of agrarian societies. The unjust practices mentioned above are just what the legislation preserved in the Pentateuch seems to have been aimed at curbing. If the Sabbath Year laws, the Jubilee law, the laws on gleaning, and those against usury and abuse of the poor had been followed, these practices would not have become prevalent in Israelite society. But clearly, faithfulness to the ways of Yahweh was not characteristic of Israel at this time.

According to Amos, the prosperity enjoyed by elites in Israel was gained at the expense of the poor. Amos excoriates the wealthy women of Samaria for oppressing the poor and crushing the needy (4:1), and he accuses his listeners of trampling the poor, of taking grain from the poor so they themselves can live in fancy houses, and of using the legal system to oppress the weak (5:11-12; also 8:4-6). Amos describes the Israelites as people who hate the just arbiter and the one who speaks the truth (5:10). Based on these words, one might think that the Israelite elites had absolutely given themselves over to material pleasures, and tossed aside all semblance of devotion to God. But outwardly they were quite devout! They observed all the religious festivities, and solemn assemblies (5:21). They observed the Sabbath (8:5), and diligently made offerings to God (5:22). They would lift their voices in praise to God, giving to God melodious offerings of song (5:23), but according to Amos, all such worship was emptiness. No, it was worse than emptiness, it evoked God's hatred and loathing (5:21). It was a betrayal. What God really desired was that "justice roll down like waters, and righteousness like an ever-flowing stream" (5:24). This desire of God had been articulated in the law of Moses, but Israel's elite leadership had cast aside the economic principles preserved in that tradition and adopted instead the economic practices of the world surrounding them. Their service to God had become an outward means of legitimation, merely justifying the social order they had created. They outwardly honored the Lord's day while inwardly longing for it to end so they could continue cheating the poor and getting rich off of their misery (8:5-6).

Because Israel was too far gone to listen to Amos, Amos predicted that a terrible fate would befall them. God promised to turn their "feasts into mourning," and all their "songs into lamentation" (8:10). Indeed, Amos is likely the first prophet to predict the destruction of Israel (ch 5; 7:11), which came in 721 BCE at the hands of the Assyrians.

Isaiah and Micah. The first thirty-nine chapters of the book of Isaiah are generally attributed to the prophet described in Isa 1:1, for whom the book is named. Later chapters of the book reflect a later period, and are generally attributed to a later prophet, but I will not bother to go into the debate here. I will simply use the name Isaiah to refer to the prophet behind chapters 1-39. The prophet Micah was a contemporary of Isaiah, who was called to the prophetic ministry in 742 BCE. Both men prophesied into the reign of Hezekiah, who became king in 715 BCE (Isa 1:1; Mic 1:1). Though the prophecies of Isaiah and Micah share some common themes, the two men came from radically different backgrounds. Isaiah seems to have had roots in the Judean elite class. Chapters 7 and 38-39 of Isaiah portray Isaiah having a conference with the king, which was likely a luxury reserved for those either of elite status, or with elite connections (cf. 37:21). Micah, on the other hand, came from a humble village in southwestern Judah. Both prophets devote much of their career to railing against economic injustices perpetrated by the Judean elite class, however. Isaiah may have had connections Micah did not have, but he did not water down his message to avoid jeopardizing those connections.

The careers of Isaiah and Micah overlapped the end of Amos' career, and reflected many of his same concerns, though Isaiah and Micah ministered in the southern kingdom of Judah. Like Israel, Judah had experienced a rare bout of relative peace and strength during the mid-eighth century, and was economically flourishing. During the reign of King Ahaz (735-715), however, Judah's fortunes dramatically altered. In order to gain Judah protection against an Israelite-Aramean alliance which Ahaz refused to join, Ahaz sought an alliance with Assyria (a move Isaiah warned him against, Isa 7:18-25, 8:5-8). Sure enough,

Assyria responded by crushing the Israelite-Aramean alliance, and eventually destroying Israel altogether. But by striking up a pact with Assyria, Ahaz basically sold Judah's soul. Judah became a client-kingdom of Assyria, not only forced to pay heavy tribute to the Assyrian king, but compelled to incorporate Assyrian gods into worship. Ahaz's move precipitated deterioration, including socio-economic deterioration, in the southern kingdom. It is against this context that Isaiah and Micah prophesy. Judah had lost vast tracts of territory to the Israelite-Aramean alliance. Coupled with Judah's onerous tribute obligation to Assyria, this made for hard times for Judeans during the late eighth century. But according to Isaiah and Micah, the poor disproportionately bore the strain.

Even though there existed in Judean society prior to Ahaz a wealthy elite, after Ahaz's compromises, the elites were apparently working feverishly to consolidate Judah's remaining wealth into their hands (Isa 5:8). The poor had no recourse against such actions since the legal system was manipulated to advance the interests of elite rulers (Isa 1:23; 5:23). Therefore, Isaiah warns that God has leveled a lawsuit against "the elders and princes of the people," or the Judean elite, and God will execute justice on behalf of the poor (Isa 3:13-4:1).

Isaiah employs venomous words to describe the rulers of Judah. In his view, they are murderers! They are no better than thieves (1:21,23). What do they do to deserve such accusations? Instead of doing justice, they dole out privilege to the highest bidder, and leave the orphans and widows defenseless (1:23; 5:23). They seize the possessions of the poor and crush them, so that they themselves can live in luxury, decked out in the hottest fashions of the day (3:14-15, 18-23). They steal land from the peasants, so that the land of Judah ends up in fewer and fewer hands. Their beautiful, sprawling homes sit on vast tracts of land, while the poor have nowhere to live (5:8). But the elites of Judah are too busy drinking and celebrating to see the judgment coming their way (5:11-13, 22). Isaiah also prophesies against the wealthy citizens of Israel in the north, confirming Amos' portrait of Israel's inequities (1:16-17; 10:1-4).

The prophecies of Micah ring an even more shrill note than those of Isaiah. While Isaiah seems to leave room for Judah's repentance and protection from disaster (33:14-16), Micah sees the utter desolation of Judah as inevitable. He writes:

> Alas for those who devise wickedness and evil deeds on their beds! When the morning dawns, they perform it, because it is in their power. They covet fields, and seize them; houses, and take them away; they oppress householder and house, people and their inheritance. Therefore thus says the Lord: Now, I am devising against this family an evil from which they cannot remove their necks. . . . Is the Lord's patience exhausted? Are these his doings? Do not my words do good to one who walks uprightly? But you rise up against my people as an enemy; you strip the robe from the peaceful, from those who pass by trustingly with no thought of war. The women of my people you drive out from their pleasant houses; from their young children you take away my glory forever. Arise and go; for this is no place to rest, because of uncleanness that destroys with a grievous destruction (2:1-3a, 7b-10).

Micah uses some of the most gruesome language found in the prophets in 3:1-4, where he vividly compares the elite's oppression of the poor to cannibalism, saying that just as the elites ignored the cries of their slain victims, God would ignore their cries on the day of punishment. Repeatedly, Micah describes the leaders of Jerusalem as justice-haters, who have no scruples and will stop at nothing to earn a bribe (3:2, 9-11; 7:3). The courts are rendered useless by them. They are men of violence and deceit who use "scant measures" and "dishonest weights" (6:10-11) to rob the poor. Micah denounces the wealthy citizens of Judah with the passion of one who has lived among the poor and heard their wearying sobs. He reminds the rich that they are without excuse. God had shown them long ago what was required of them. God had given them the law, which commanded justice, and mercy, and humility before God (6:8). And they had ignored it.

Fortunately, both Isaiah and Micah speak of restoration, in addition to speaking of corruption and doom. Both speak of a future kingdom in which God would rule the world in peace, through a promised redeemer whose reign would be marked by fairness, and gentleness, and defense of the poor (Isa 11; 26:1-6). During this time, God's spirit would be poured out, and those who were oppressed would triumph, while oppressors would be shamed (26:5-6). It would be a reign of justice, and of peace (Isa 2:2-4, 9:6-7, 16:5; Mic 4:1-40).

Jeremiah. Since the reign of David, an elaborate national theology had developed in the southern kingdom of Judah that viewed the Davidic monarchy as never-ending. This view was based on Nathan's oracle to David which promised, according to the tradition preserved in 2 Samuel, that David's house and kingdom would be "made sure forever," and the Davidic throne would "be established forever" (2 Sam 7:16; cf. 1 Chr 17:14). It was, understandably, a very popular notion in Judah, and was so tightly woven into Judah's self-understanding that the idea survived her very close call with Assyria in the eighth century. In fact, after the Judean people had survived that, their overconfidence in the perpetuity of the Davidic monarchy was more entrenched than ever. No matter what, God would not allow the line of Davidic rulers to be cut off.

Judah's arrogance reached a climax in the days of Jeremiah, who ministered during the period of 627-587/6 BCE, in the years leading up to the Babylonian Exile. As hard as it was for him to fulfill at times, Jeremiah's mission was to relentlessly denounce Judah's arrogance. Jeremiah stood with two feet firmly rooted in the traditions of the Mosaic covenant which had long been neglected by Judeans (11:9-13), who preferred to rest in God's promises to David. Jeremiah's task was to call his people back to the reciprocal relationship their ancestors had established with Yahweh at Sinai, and to prepare Israel's faith to survive even the fall of the nation (see chs.32-33). According to Jeremiah, the promises of God to David were utterly revoked, since the kings of Judah and the people under their leadership had completely disregarded the obligations God had placed on them as a people (21:11-22:30). Judah was doomed to disaster as a result (4:19-27; 8:14-17; 21:3-10).

Of the accusations Jeremiah levels against the Judean kings, accusations of economic injustice figure prominently. In the message to the Davidic line cited above (21:11-22:30), Jeremiah cries:

> (12:12) Oh house of David! Thus says the Lord: Execute justice in the morning and deliver from the hand of the oppressor anyone who has been robbed . . . (22:3) Thus says the Lord: Act with justice and righteousness . . . and do no wrong or violence to the alien, the orphan, and the widow, or shed innocent blood in this place . . . (13-14a) Woe to him who builds his house by unrighteousness, and his upper rooms by injustice; who makes his neighbors work for nothing, and does not give them their wages; who says, "I will build myself a spacious house with large upper rooms." . . . (17) But your eyes and heart are only on your dishonest gain, for shedding innocent blood, and for practicing oppression and violence.

Jeremiah's portrayal of the Judean elites shows that the group had changed little in the two hundred years since Isaiah and Micah. Generally speaking, they were still deaf to the cries of the poor, and to Yahweh's commands to meet the needs of the destitute (see also 5:26-28; 7:5-7). In the use of their wealth, they were still behaving like typical agrarian elites instead of like the people of God, called to be mediators to God, and to model God's compassion and holiness to the world. But the elites are not the only ones participating in injustice. Apparently, a wide swath of the society, "from the least to the greatest" is "greedy for unjust gain" (6:13). The people of Judah had fallen far below God's intentions for them to be a blessing to the nations (Gen 12:3).

The prophet Ezekiel, whose career followed that of Jeremiah, corroborates this picture. Writing during the Exile, he explains the precipitating factors of Judah's demise. In Ezekiel 7:20, he attributes their moral decline to their wealth, which he names as "the stumbling block to their iniquity." In 16:46-50, Ezekiel compares the sins of Jerusalem to those of Samaria and Sodom, saying: "This was the guilt of your sister Sodom: she and her daughters had pride, excess of food, and prosperous ease, but did not aid the poor and needy. They were haughty, and did abominable things before me" (v.49-50a). Finally, in a detailed description of Jerusalem in chapter 22, Ezekiel reveals a society utterly permeated with injustice. Along with the sins of idol-worship and disregard for the covenant, he lists the sins of "extortion" and "oppression." Moreover, in Ezekiel 22 the "people of the land," or peasants, are implicated right along with the elites:

> (6-7) The princes of Israel in you, everyone according to his power, have been bent on shedding blood. Father and mother are treated with contempt in you; the alien residing within you suffers extortion; the orphan and the widow are wronged in you . . . (13) See, I strike my hands together at the dishonest gain you have made, and at the blood that has been shed within you . . . (29) The people of the land have practiced extortion and committed robbery; they have oppressed the poor and needy, and have extorted from the alien without redress . . . (31) Therefore I have poured out my indignation upon them; I have consumed them with the fire of my wrath; I have returned their conduct upon their heads, says the Lord God.

Ezekiel had witnessed the economic oppression infecting all of Judean society and, like Jeremiah, knew the consequences of it.

It should be mentioned that in Jeremiah's indictment against "the kings" in 21:12-22:30, he takes pains to single out Josiah as exceptional. Of Josiah he writes, "Did not [Josiah] eat and drink and do justice and righteousness? Then it was well with him. He judged the cause of the poor and needy; then it was well. Is not this to know me?" (Jer 22:15-16). But Josiah is the exception that proves the rule. If Josiah was a picture of one who knows God, then clearly the majority of the kings were absolute strangers to Yahweh. According to Jeremiah, they could expect to be treated as such.

The sins of Judah were, as usual, of a religious nature as well as a socio-economic nature. Idol-worship and economic oppression were typically wedded in Israel's experience. Jeremiah famously employs the language of adultery to describe Judah's relationships with foreign gods, portraying Judah's prolific worship of idols as the ultimate dishonor to God. Still, cleaning up the temple and tearing down the apostate shrines, as Josiah's reforms had done, was not enough to appease God and win God's blessing (6:19-21; 7:1-4; 14:1-11). Josiah's heart had undergone a true transformation, but there was little he could do to reform the hearts of his people. As the career of Jeremiah trudges on, it is clear that Josiah's reforms, however well-intended, had only effected an outward purging of Judean society. Inwardly, the people remained as faithless as ever, since faithlessness is really a condition of the heart (4:3-4). For this reason, Jeremiah castigated the Judeans for thinking the reforms would save them. But after Josiah's ignominious death, they lost confidence in God's ability to protect them anyway. They struck up a fatuous alliance with the vacillating Egypt, and ended up conquered by Babylon. Gradually, the most powerful and promising of Judah's citizens were murdered or carted off to exile, confirming the veracity of Jeremiah's portents of doom. For the most part, only Judean peasants remained in the homeland, which was reduced to a province of Babylon.

Conclusion

The Hebrew traditions preserved in the Pentateuch attest to some radical ideals regarding wealth and its usage. These ideals of the Hebrew people were the outworking of their essential beliefs about God: beliefs about God's oneness, about God's claim on their lives and all they owned, about God's purposes for them as a chosen people, and about God's nature. The laws of the Pentateuch can be understood as interpretations of God's revelation to them, and of the implications of that revelation.

The Hebrews were early monotheists. Though it took them a while to refine their monotheism, they believed relatively early that their allegiance was due to only one God, and that was Yahweh. Yahweh was not just their Patron-God in the way that every people group had a patron god or goddess, rather Yahweh was the *only* legitimate divine patron. They also believed that of all the people on the earth, this supreme God had singled them out for a specific purpose, to be a "priestly kingdom and a holy nation" (Ex 19:6). They were to be the means through which God would be revealed to the entire world.

Also crucial to their understanding of God was the fact that God had rescued them. They believed that when their forebears were a bunch of dejected slaves in Egypt, God had reached out to them and shattered the yoke enslaving them. God had even appeared to their leader, Moses, revealing God's intentions to them, and calling them to a covenantal relationship. They believed they were God's "possession" (Ex 19:5), and all they had was from God, and could be used by God. The Hebrews believed their God to be full of compassion, and merciful to the oppressed. Furthermore, God had ordered creation with the intent of meeting the physical needs of all creatures. The Hebrews were called to act compassionately as well, and to use their wealth to meet needs.

These remarkable beliefs about God shaped the ethical ideals of the Hebrew people. Their lives were to be ordered around these foundational precepts, and thus, were to look very different from the lives of the nations around them. Unlike other peoples, they had a unique calling to be mediators to God and to reveal God's holiness to the world. The prescriptions regarding how the Hebrew people are to view and use wealth come out of this unique self-understanding. The way God's chosen people handled wealth needed to be remarkably different from the way wealth was handled in what we have called "agrarian societies".

In our study of the theme of wealth in the Pentateuch, the kingly histories, and the prophets, we have traced the following movement: from the ideals enshrined in the Pentateuchal laws, to the ethical deterioration of Israelite society under the kings, to the Israelite prophets urging of their neighbors back to faithfulness to the ideals of the Pentateuch. It is in some ways a tragic story, given the outcome for the kingdoms of Israel and Judah. But the prophets seem to have had the last word, and in that way, the story is far from tragic. The hope and vision provided by the prophets, that is a hope for a union with God outside of the homeland, and a vision of a world under God's reign, allowed the faith of the Hebrew people to survive. And it allowed their remarkable beliefs about God and ethics to continue to shape the lives of the faithful.

The foundational beliefs and ideals expressed in the Hebrew scriptures are integral to the religious beliefs of people the world over. In this study on Christian ethics, I note that the story of the Old Testament is part of the Christian story, and I note the role that the ethics of the Hebrew people played in shaping Christian ethics. One cannot either understand the ministry of Jesus or the "new law" given by Jesus to his followers without an understanding of the revelation of God to the Israelites. In many ways, Jesus reasserted God's long-ago claim on the lives of God's people, and the imperatives that accompanied God's claim on their lives. Jesus' teachings on wealth can only be understood in light of this claim, and in light of God's purposes for Israel, which, in the tradition of the prophets, Jesus and his followers redefined. Jesus' teachings build on the traditions of the Pentateuch and the prophets, and transcend them. It is to those teachings we now turn.

Chapter Five

Biblical Economics, Part II:

Jesus' Teaching on Wealth and its Usage

Having succeeded in spiritualizing the good news
announced by the Lucan Jesus to the destitute, the European
scholarly establishment should not be too surprised that
during the last 150 years the working classes have abandoned
the leading Christian denominations in the West in their
droves.

Philip Esler[1]

The Socio-Economic Context of First-Century Palestine

Before exploring what Jesus had to say about wealth and its usage, I
want to first look at the socio-economic context of Palestine in the first
century CE, since understanding what Jesus and his earliest followers
thought about wealth requires that we have some understanding of
what wealth symbolized within their unique situation. What form did
wealth (which is to say material goods) take in Jesus' day? How was
wealth attained by first-century Palestineans? What purposes did wealth
serve for them?

Economically speaking, Roman Palestine was eons removed from our world. It had no open markets or middle class. In Palestine, money (coinage) functioned altogether differently than it does in the twenty-first century. For first-century elites, it primarily constituted a means of holding and displaying honor, the central social value in Mediterranean society,[2] though they also used money as a medium of exchange in urban markets. For peasants in first-century Palestine, money was little more than a necessary means of paying certain taxes, tithes, and debts.[3] Goods and services needed by peasants were generally procured by trading other goods and services.

Entrepreneurs and innovation were scarce in first-century Palestine, since workers had little incentive to increase production. Most of the surplus produced by farmers, fishermen, or artisans flowed to the ruling elite through copious extractions. Opportunities for peasants to invest some of their surplus before such extractions did not exist. Neither did banks. The "national treasury" resided in the temple, and was overseen by elite bureaucrats and their retainers. As one can see, there was much that distinguished the economic landscape of first-century Palestine from our own lay of the land, where hundreds of new inventions are introduced each day and money is exchanged like oxygen. Readers who have not read the sections on "The Bible and Economics" and "The Agrarian Society" in Chapter Four should do so before reading this chapter. First-century Palestine can be characterized as an agrarian society and bears the features of such societies as described in Chapter Four.

There were some unique factors at play in the Palestine of Jesus' day, however, catalysts that served to heighten the tensions and inequalities endemic to all agrarian societies. One factor with pronounced repercussions for life in first-century Palestine was the skyrocketing of the Herodian family to importance in the previous century. The Herods dramatically escalated economic trends that had earlier beginnings. For example, the movement toward a more market-based economy in Palestine received a felicitous boost when Herod the Great built the port city of Caesarea Maritima. Herod, the Rome-appointed ruler of Palestine from 37 to 4 BCE, and his progeny did much to stimulate Palestinian trade.

Unfortunately, though not surprisingly, the period of Herodian rule in Palestine also saw a marked increase in the degree of socio-economic imbalance between elites and peasants in the region. Taxation played a key role in this development. Few periods of history saw Palestineans more buckled under the weight of taxation than the early first century CE. During that time, most regions of Palestine were compelled to pay taxes to the Roman Emperor, to their Herodian rulers, as well as to the temple (in the form of tithes).[4] The overall burden proved almost unbearable. It sparked social upheaval, and eventually, a costly revolt (66-70 CE). The peasants, who constituted most of the population of agrarian Palestine, didn't distinguish much between the taxes due to the government and the tithes due to the temple. Not only were the effects of the two the same, namely destitution, but the political and religious leadership were so closely linked in Palestine as to be almost inseparable.

The temple, which stood at the center of Palestinean politics, was tightly interwoven with the Roman political system through a web of patronage, intermarriage, and nepotism. High priests in the temple were appointed by the Roman prefects and the Herodians, who were conspicuous clients of Rome. According to the first-century Palestinean historian Josephus, the office of high priest essentially went to the highest bidder.[5]

According to the model of agrarian societies, the small elite class (2-5%) in a given territory might hold half of that territory's goods in their clutches.[6] That this was true in Roman Palestine is confirmed by extant evidence from the period.[7] One scholar estimates that Herod the Great alone owned one-half to two-thirds of the land in his kingdom.[8] An intricate system of taxes, tolls, and tithes devised under Herod and bolstered by military might, allowed the Herodians and other Palestinean elites to funnel the resources of Palestine into their pockets. Herod the Great took 25-33% of Palestinean grain as tax, and 50% of the produce of Palestinean fruit trees.[9] On top of this, his administration collected: one denarius (two week's sustenance for one person[10]) per year from every male, market taxes (in the cities), transit tolls, port taxes on shipping (which went directly to Rome), and rent on city-controlled resources, which included everything from roads to the harbors and breakwaters used for fishing.[11] These revenues were gathered by tax and toll collectors who came from ruling-class families, and who often tacked on a bit extra for themselves.[12] These tax collectors were also known to line their pockets with the bribes of those hoping to stay in the rulers' good graces.[13]

Out of the copious revenues he gathered, Herod the Great would then pay regular tribute to Rome, which one scholar estimates to have been one-tenth to one-fourth of the produce of Palestine.[14] The taxation systems adopted by subsequent rulers seem to have been similar to this. Harold Hoehner, in his study on Herod Antipas, suggests that Antipas, like his father, held the majority of the land in his realm.[15] In Jesus' day, when the region of Judea[16] was governed by a Rome-appointed governor, Rome administered tax collection there, while Herod Antipas oversaw collection in Galilee and Perea, and Herod Philip in the regions northeast of Galilee. But whether administered by one of the Herodians or by Rome, the system of taxation was onerous.[17]

On top of the taxes collected by the local rulers, citizens of Palestine were also expected to pay a number of "taxes" to the temple.[18] These extractions can be understood as taxation since they were essentially involuntarily, and were used to support the affluent lifestyle of the temple elite. Those who chose not to pay tithes were deemed religiously unclean and socially ostracized, and were believed to be a barrier to God's blessing on the land.[19] For obvious reasons, only the desperately poor did not tithe.

The combined effect of these taxes, tolls, and tithes crushed Palestinean peasant families, and led to the increased consolidation of Palestinean land into the hands of the elite class.[20] The loss of land by peasants was deeply painful for at least two reasons. One, because land was the source of wealth in agrarian societies.[21] And two, because Israelite tradition bespoke God's desire that land be divided equitably amongst families. The inequality of property holdings in Palestine was an affront to Israelite peasants, who could no longer keep a hold on their patrimonial lands.

Elites generally accumulated land by loaning out money to peasants who were unable to pay their taxes.[22] When the peasants found themselves unable to make payments on their debts, as peasants often did, they lost their fields and became tenants on lands belonging to their creditors.[23] This was the main payoff for elites who loaned out money. While they could not rely on subsistence farmers to pay interest, they could be relatively certain they would default on loans and be forced to forfeit their property.[24] As a result of the cycle of debt and dispossession, Palestinean peasants tended to pay rent for the ground on which they lived and worked, on top of their other burdens.

To call the cumulative effect of the taxes, tithes, rents, and debts oppressive would be an understatement. After the extractions from their produce, a peasant agriculturalist family was left with very little on which to live.[25] Ultimately, the situation was intolerable. Indeed, history has shown that in agrarian societies, peasants rarely speak out or revolt until their situation becomes unbearable;[26] their situation becomes unbearable when they are no longer able to subsist.[27] In first-century Palestine, the situation had sunk to this depth and, as we will see below, rebellion, in the form of banditry, began to make its appearance on the trade routes criss-crossing Palestine.

As mentioned earlier, the extreme imbalances in Palestine can in part be attributed to the acquisitiveness of the Herodian family. When Herod the Great died in 4 BCE, a delegation set out from Judea to complain to Caesar Augustus about conditions in Palestine. According to Josephus, himself an elite, Herod had "reduced the entire country to helpless poverty." Little real change transpired after Herod's death, especially in the region of Galilee, to which our attention now turns. Herod Antipas, who ruled the provinces of Galilee and Perea from 4 BCE to 39 CE, may have been as ambitious and avaricious as his father.[28] A "lover of luxury," according to Josephus,[29] Antipas commanded lavish building projects in Galilee, funded by the taxes of his subjects. Though Herod Antipas stimulated the Galilean economy in many ways, his economic program profited the few at the expense of the many.[30] His rule provides the backdrop for Jesus' Galilee-centered ministry. What did Antipas' Galilee look like?

Herodian Economics in Galilee

Galilee of the first century was a uniquely rich land. Agriculture flourished in lower Galilee and was respectable up north, and the region's fishing industry thrived. During his reign, Antipas maintained an economic system that ensured dominance over Galilee's resources by the ruling class.

Jesus' ministry centered around fishing communities. His earliest disciples were fishermen, his house was situated in the important fishing hub of Capernaum (Mk 2:1, 3:19; Mt 4:13, 13:1; Lk), and his travels in Galilee carried him almost exclusively to fishing towns and villages. Jesus' views on wealth and the relationships between rich and poor must have been notably affected by what he witnessed in the fishing communities.

The main thing to note about the fishing industry in Galilee during the first century is its multi-tiered nature. Common fishermen held a relatively low place on its ladder. Profits from fish caught in Galilean seas were shared with a number of different players, with a majority of the profit being paid in taxes to Antipas, out of which tribute was given to Caesar. A breakdown of the Galilean fishing economy reveals the many rungs of the system. Sharing the profits gleaned from the waterways of Galilee were the Roman emperors, Herod Antipas, tax and toll administrators, tax collectors, fishing cooperatives, secondary laborers, farmers and artisans who produced items like nets and baskets used in fishing, or salt and oil used in processing, fish-processors, merchants, and finally, carters and shippers.[31]

While those closest to Jesus seem to have been fishermen, the large majority of Galilean peasants would have spent their lives cultivating the rich soil of the region, rather than the sea. According to Josephus, Galilee was "entirely under cultivation" and produced "crops from one end to the other."[32] Some scholars estimate that 80-90% of those living in Galilee at the time of Jesus were regularly involved in agricultural work.[33] The many agricultural metaphors Jesus employed in his teaching indicate that the crowds who flocked to see and hear Jesus, and to receive his healing, likely understood the agrarian life.

Circumstances in the Roman Empire during Jesus' day that led to an enormous demand for grain imports to Rome, made land in Galilee a highly valuable resource. As has already been mentioned, Herod the Great imposed astronomical taxes to ensure that he got hold of most of the output of grain in the region. Out of this store he gave grain in tribute to Rome. This kind of extraction persisted with Antipas.[34]

As was the case throughout Palestine, much of the land of Galilee was consolidated into large landholdings held by absentee landowners.[35] These landowners prospered as a result of the good market since they could afford to devote the majority of their land to growing specialized crops for sale, unlike small subsistence farmers. Elite landowners were not untouched by over-taxation, but were protected from its devastating effects because they owned such large tracts of land, and grew crops which yielded great profits.

Unrest and Banditry in First-Century Galilee

Coinciding with the consolidation of land in elite hands and the extensive taxation seen in Jesus' day was the dispossession of many peasants. Debt was a fact of life for Galilean peasants. But some peasants in Galilee became *desperately* poor, or no longer able to subsist, due to mounting indebtedness and the loss of their family lands to elites. Some young men in this situation turned to social banditry. Hanson and Oakman offer the following definition of bandits:

> Social bandits are peasants who have been repressed and separated from their land and village. This is usually the result if they have been excessively taxed and forced to sell their land, have had their land confiscated by elites, or have broken a law enforced by the elites. They lash out by organizing into bands that raid and steal to survive, usually from the local and imperial elites (like Robin Hood of English legend).[36]

Bandits were perceived by other peasants not as common looters but often as heroes taking a stand for justice and challenging the perpetrators of injustice, even if they acted in self-interest doing so. Social banditry was commonplace in first-century Galilee, and in fact, throughout Palestine. Eventually this widespread banditry evolved into a full-scale peasant revolt against the Judean elite class, a revolt that precipitated the destruction of Jerusalem by Rome in 70 CE.

Though Jesus was clearly not a bandit, it is interesting that at points in the Gospel, elites seem to associate Jesus with bandits. This suggests that he was perceived as a challenge to their power and their ostentatious lifestyles, as were bandits. Incidentally, in his account of John the Baptist, Josephus suggests it was John's critique of the lifestyle of the rich which precipitated his execution.[37] This tradition, divergent in significant ways from the Gospel accounts, associates John the Baptist with the protest of the peasants. Perhaps Jesus, who was closely aligned with John the Baptist, was similarly understood by elites. In Mark 14:48, Jesus asks the temple guards, "Have you come out with swords and clubs to arrest me as though I were a bandit?" Moreover, Jesus uttered sayings about Roman taxation and about the temple which would have been perceived as threats by elites (Mk 12:13-17=Mt 22:15-22=Lk 20:20-26; Mt 12:5-8; Mk 14:58 =Mt 26:61).[38] Finally, and most significantly, Jesus was executed using a form of execution typically reserved for bandits and political revolutionaries, namely crucifixion. He was crucified between two bandits, and at his trial another bandit, Barabbas, was released in Jesus' place. These elements of the Gospels suggest that Palestinean elites saw Jesus, despite his nonviolence, as posing a threat like that of bandits, a threat to the social order which ensured their prosperity. Interestingly, in his action against the temple, Jesus turns the tables and accuses the elites of making the temple a "cave of bandits" (Mk 11:17; Mt 21:13; Lk 19:46).

Jesus ministered during a time of acute socio-economic upheaval and imbalance. In this setting, he chose to direct most of his teaching and healing to peasants like himself, indeed to many who were worse off than himself. Many of Jesus' Galilean followers, and those in the crowds who came to sit at his feet and hear a message, were deeply in debt, pressed by their elite rulers to the brink of absolute poverty, and religiously marginalized because of their inability to keep up with tithes to the temple. What did Jesus speak into this setting on the subject of wealth and its usage? What does it imply for us?

Wealth and its Usage in the Life and Teaching of Jesus

There are many places one could begin in looking at Jesus' sayings on wealth and its usage. The material is abundant.[39] Due to the constraints of this chapter, I will focus on the Beatitudes, miscellaneous parables and teachings, and the concept of the kingdom of God. The kingdom of God cannot be bracketed in the way this breakdown implies, since it was central to all Jesus taught and did. Yet for the sake of organization, I will treat it separately.

The Beatitudes. Matthew and Luke probably culled this group of Jesus' sayings, which appear differently in the two gospels, from a written source that predated the Gospels, a hypothetical source scholars call "Q".[40] But while the Beatitudes take different forms in Matthew and Luke, I will not deal with the differences much here. I will come back to them in a section on Luke-Acts below. Here the question I want to ask is: what do the Beatitudes seem to be saying in general?

"Honorable are the poor," Jesus begins the Beatitudes, making a statement as jarring in his context and it is in ours. The best translation of the Beatitudes begins with this phrase: "Honorable are," since this comes nearer to the meaning of the Greek than the common translation "Blessed are." In the sayings, Jesus contrasts the things that bring honor in God's kingdom with the things that bring honor in human society. According to the Beatitudes, God honors the beggars[41] (Lk 6:20b), or as Matthew says it, the impoverished in spirit (Mt 5:3). God honors the mourners, the humbled, and those who hunger (Lk 6:21b; Mt 5:4-6 has "those who hunger after righteousness"). God deems honorable those who are merciful, pure in heart, and who work to build peace (Mt 5:7-9). Finally, God honors those who are persecuted and reviled on account of Christ (Mt 5:10-11; Lk 6:22). All who do and are these things hold places of honor in the kingdom of God, and are promised remarkable blessings in that kingdom. They will inherit the earth! They will see God, and be God's children! The kingdom of God will belong to them! (Mt 5:3-10). The high honor status of an elite in Palestinean society, graced as he was with birth into an esteemed family, brought promises of great blessing. He could expect a life of luxury and leisure, a seat among society's finest, and the best of everything, from food to teachers to spouses. Yet no one could offer him the kinds of blessings Jesus promised to those who chose the kingdom.

The Beatitudes proclaim words of reassurance and encouragement to Jesus' peasant followers, who, already hard-pressed, have been challenged by Jesus to abandon what little social security they have left in order to follow him. In these sayings Jesus promises them rewards in God's kingdom. At other points in the gospels, however, Jesus assures them that the way will be very costly (Mk 8:34-38=Mt 10:37-39=Lk 9:23-26; Lk 14:26-27, 21:12-19). Jesus' followers know that they risk rejection by their families, and alienation within their social networks, such as synagogues and occupational guilds.

The economic consequences of breaking social ties, especially family ties, within the society of first-century Palestine would have been severe. Peasants, though they usually could not afford to reside as large extended families, depended on the willing hands of all their immediate family members in order to make ends meet. Moreover, individual families were economically dependent on the social networks they cultivated, and on ties of patronage, within their communities. Yet the severing of these crucial familial and non-familial ties were often an inevitable consequence of following Jesus. Jesus warned of family rejection in the bluntest possible terms, saying: "For I have come to set a man against his father, and a daughter against her mother, and daughter-in-law against her mother-in-law; and one's foes will be members of one's own household" (Mt 10:35-36). He was not expressing anti-family sentiment. Throughout his ministry Jesus calls disciples to join the family of God, and to relate to one another as family. But in this passage Jesus speaks hyperbolically about the inevitable consequences many will face for choosing to join God's family. It may result in expulsion from one's biological family.

In the Beatitudes, Jesus seems to have in mind the costs of following him.[42] It may very well make the stomachs and pockets of his peasant disciples emptier. Despite Matthew's emphasis on poverty "in spirit" and hunger "for righteousness," which were likely emphases added to the original Q sayings,[43] the word used for "poor" in both Matthew and Luke, *ptochos*, means destitute and beggarly. Besides making them poor and hungry, following Jesus will cause them mourning, and cause them to be "humbled." These too can be understood as consequences of the loss of family ties. Few things were greater cause for mourning in ancient Mediterranean culture than the rejection of someone by his or her own family. Likewise, nothing would result in one's being humbled more than a loss of family honor. Meekness in this saying likely refers to the canceling of social honor one would suffer in being disassociated from the honor of one's family.

In Matthew's version of the Beatitudes, Jesus also refers to the merciful, the pure in heart, and the peacemakers. Followers of Jesus who faced rejection by their families and other social networks would have been in a prime position to practice mercy, to forego vengeance in favor of "purity of heart", and to work at building peace. According to the Beatitudes, those who respond to the costs of discipleship in these ways are honored in God's kingdom. Though they are persecuted and reviled, they reflect the character of God and are thus God's children. To them, the kingdom of heaven belongs (Mt 5:10-12; Lk 6:22-23).

The costs of discipleship are likely in view in the Beatitudes, and no one sitting on a patch of grass in rural Galilee listening to Jesus would have failed to recognize the economic costs which factored into the equation. In these sayings, Jesus offers encouragement to the disciples he is addressing. Though the Beatitudes are often read as a general expression of the values of the kingdom, and though they do articulate those values, Jesus is specifically addressing his peasant followers who *are* destitute, and hungry, and persecuted. Their lot likely worsened as a result of their choice to follow him. Jesus speaks to the very real-life concerns of these followers. He addresses them in the Beatitudes by publicly lauding them. "You are highly honored in God's kingdom!" he tells them. "You are God's very children, who will inherit the kingdom and the earth!"

In the Beatitudes, Jesus reassures his followers that their sacrifices of economic wellbeing and status in this life brings them honor in God's kingdom, and blessings in the life to come. This is not to refute the graciousness of Jesus' summons to the kingdom of God, or to say that salvation is earned. However, the Beatitudes *do* demonstrate that an honorable response to God's gracious invitation will involve sacrifice and devotion. God's grace elicits a response that is total and life-changing.

In the Beatitudes Jesus emphasizes relief in the hereafter for his poor followers. But this is not Jesus' last word on the subject. Elsewhere, Jesus articulates a vision of a kind of human interrelating that takes away the occasion for destitution. He calls his followers to a new kind of "economics," a house-keeping (the literal meaning of the Greek word "economics," *oikonomía*) by which needs are met within the family of God.[44]

Parables and Miscellaneous Teachings on Wealth and Its Usage. Several of Jesus' parables and other sayings touch on the subject of wealth and its usage. Some general themes can be gleaned from them, for example, in those teachings, 1) self-sufficiency is renounced; 2) radical generosity is commended; 3) the forgiveness of debts is commended; and 4) the standards of the kingdom of God are shown to upset norms of economics.[45] In this section, we explore each of these themes.

Self-sufficiency is renounced. Self-sufficiency was a core value in the societies of the ancient Mediterranean. This does not mean, however, that people in that time and place were individualistic. They were integrally connected to their families and communities and defined themselves in terms of these interdependent relationships.[46] They were very dependent on others for survival. Still, people desired to be the lesser dependent party in particular relationships, since to be in the position of less dependence (for example, to be the patron in a patron-client relationship) was to be in the position of greater power. The proverb: "It is better to give than to receive" speaks to this cultural truism. Of course, elites were in a better position to give, because they owned far more. They shared "gifts" with their "clients" who became socially dependent on them, and in so doing boosted their own honor. Most elites in first-century Palestine owned large enough estates that they were protected from many of the vagaries affecting small farmers, and had many workers beholden to them. This allowed them a certain level of self-sufficiency. On the other hand, tenant farmers in first-century Palestine, the majority of the peasants, were exploited by the elite class and were utterly dependent on them for the little sustenance they had. Their dream, consequently, was for a life of self-sufficiency wherein they were free from the claims of others on their lives and work.[47]

Jesus turns the value of self-sufficiency on its head and teaches that, in the kingdom of God, total dependency on God is valued. This is expressed especially well when Jesus elevates the flitting birds of the air and the resplendent lilies of the field as exemplary of a proper attitude toward possessions (Mt 6:25-34=Lk 12:22-31). Rather than worrying about the next day, they trust God to provide what they need (See also Mt 7:7-11=Lk 11:9-13; Lk 12:32-34). Jesus encouraged his disciples to do likewise. When he sends his disciples out to neighboring villages, he tells them to carry no provisions for the journey, but to trust that their needs will be met (Mt 10:9-10=Lk 9:2-5). In this same way, the rich young man who was told by Jesus to sell all he had and give to the poor is challenged to completely depend on God's provision for his physical needs (Mt 19:16-30; Lk 18:18-30; Mk 10:17-22). This proved to be more than he could do. Jesus enjoined his disciples to adopt an attitude of utter dependence, despite the fact that in their socio-cultural context such an attitude was despised. People in their society would have coveted the position of Jesus' parabolic "rich fool," who builds new barns to store all his surplus then lives sumptuously, without a care for the needs of others (Lk 12:16-21). This man is the epitome of self-sufficiency. Yet, according to Jesus, he is a fool who thinks only of himself. He serves the god of Mammon (Mt 6:24; Lk 16:13).

Jesus did not leave his disciples clueless, however, as to how God would provide for those who left themselves at God's mercy. Just as Jesus envisioned the needs of his traveling disciples being met by sympathetic households (Mt 10:11-15=Lk 9:4-5), Jesus envisioned his followers' needs being met by one another. Jesus called his followers to become a part of God's family, a boundless kinship in which the needs of all family members were to be met by God through the cooperation and generosity of all God's children. We will talk more about this below. But this new kind of kinship and community to which Jesus called his followers was the antidote to self-sufficiency.

Generosity is commended. Jesus could encourage his followers to depend on God's provision for them through one another because generosity was central to the life to which they were called. Jesus elevates generosity in many places; for example, in the parable of the Good Samaritan (Lk 10:30-37), in his praise of Zacchaeus who generously recompenses those he has defrauded (Lk 19:8-9), in his story about the sheep and the goats in which those who are generous toward the needy inherit the kingdom (Mt 25:31-46), and in his instructions to his disciples to "sell [their] possessions, and give alms" (Lk 12:33).

The value of generosity is also commended by Jesus via the negative portrayal of less-than-generous characters. Notable among these is the rich man of Luke 16:19-31 whose callousness toward the wretched beggar Lazarus lands him in Hades. Additionally, the brother in Jesus' parable of the prodigal son, with his begrudging self-righteousness, exemplifies a lack of generosity in responding to his father's gracious reception of his brother (Lk 15:25-32). He is of the same ilk as the unmerciful servant in Mt 18:23-35 who, upon receiving a generous forgiveness of debt by his master, turns around and withholds mercy toward his own debtor, meting out punishment with an iron fist.

In ancient Mediterranean culture, it was common to give goods or pay favors to non-family members in order to gain something from them in the future. But a person would give to his or her close family without expecting a return. Jesus desires the generosity of his followers toward others to be like that of kin. He teaches his disciples to lend money without expecting reciprocation (Mt 5:38-42=Lk 6:29-30; Mt 5:44=Lk 6:27). As Douglas Oakman writes, Jesus' intent in encouraging generosity is not to obligate others, as was common in his culture, but "to announce the destruction of the old order and the ushering in of the new."[48] Whereas people in first-century Palestine would give to others in order to hedge their bets, Jesus encouraged a generosity commensurate with the kingdom values of selflessness, justice, and love. It was a generosity due not only to friends and neighbors, but to enemies (Mt 5:44=Lk 6:27). In certain parables, Jesus paints pictures of generosity that go far beyond social expectations. These include the parable of the prodigal son (Lk 15:11-32), that of the Good Samaritan

(Lk 10:30-37), and that of the lost sheep (Lk 15:3-7), in which the shepherd risks everything to rescue a single wayward beast.

The radical generosity Jesus commends has its basis in God's generosity. Jesus expects his disciples to give liberally because God has given liberally to them (Mt 10:8). Furthermore, Jesus desires his followers to practice radical generosity believing that God will continue to provide for all their needs. If one trusts God for one's daily provisions, as do the "birds of the air," it is unnecessary to hoard possessions, or to give only to those who can reciprocate. God's generosity toward God's children frees us to give abundantly.

Still, it was a presumptuous demand for Jesus to make: telling destitute and nearly-destitute peasants to live in a spirit of absolute generosity. He wasn't merely asking them to give out of their excess. His followers and listeners had little conception of excess. He challenged them to put their very survival on the line, and to see risk-taking generosity as an inexorable characteristic of their life as Jesus' disciples. Being generous with the little wealth they had required a stalwart faith in God's provision, and in the vision of God's family as Jesus had articulated it. If they were going to risk losing their kinship ties and thus their economic security by following Jesus, they would need to have a firm confidence that their new family, the family of God, would help care for their needs as had blood relations. *This is what Jesus had in mind.*

Forgiveness of debts is commended. Jesus envisioned the forgiveness of debts as another manifestation of the generosity his followers would extend to others. This too was based on God's gracious actions on their behalf. As God had shown them mercy, they were to extend mercy by forgiving debts owed to them. In the Lord's Prayer, Jesus includes the petition "forgive our debts," which surely referred to the actual canceling of monetary debt. The Greek word used in the Matthean version of the prayer, *opheileemata*, has the meaning of actual debts.[49] Instead of *opheileemata*, Luke used the word *hamartias*, which can be translated "offenses" or "sins." But Luke's version is likely an adaptation of the tradition. Jesus was teaching the prayer to deeply-indebted peasants, to whom monetary debt was all too relevant. Therefore, it seems likely that the original wording of Jesus' prayer included "debts" rather than "sins," and that Jesus' poor followers understood Jesus' petition as a request from God to help them out of their crushing indebtedness. This does not discount the need to ask God to "forgive us our sins."

The petition, "forgive us our debts," assumes that the petitioners have forgiven their own debtors: " . . . as we also have forgiven our debtors" (Mt 6:12). The preservation of the Sabbath Year and Jubilee traditions in the Hebrew scriptures affirms that the Hebrew people believed God desired the forgiveness of debts. If carried out consistently, these laws would have corrected the economic imbalances which develop in human society and would have preserved the egalitarian, tribal ideal of the early Hebrews in Palestine. If lands that had been lost in debt were periodically returned to their original owners, land and wealth could not be monopolized by the few, and an elite class would not develop. The Sabbath Year and Jubilee legislation constituted a corrective to the exploitation so endemic in agrarian societies. Jesus revives the tradition of the Jubilee, in essence, by proclaiming the forgiveness of debt as an effect of the kingdom of God. God does not desire for the domination of any human beings by others. Since debts were and are a key vehicle for domination, Jesus calls for his followers to respond to the kingdom by canceling debts.

The standards of the Kingdom of God upset norms of justice and economics. Finally, Jesus' parables and other teachings frequently turn economic norms on their head.[50] Several seem to applaud very "uneconomic" actions. The widow who gives her last mite is praised (Mk 12:41-44=Lk 21:1-4), for example, while the hearer can't help but ask, "What would happen if everyone gave away their means of subsistence? Isn't the widow's action economically unwise? How will she eat?" In her profligacy, the widow is an example of the extravagant faith characteristic of the kingdom. Likewise, in several other parables profligate actions are portrayed glowingly. For example, the woman who loses a denarius[51] in Luke 15:8-10, searches through the night for the coin, burning valuable lamp oil in the process, and throws a (no-doubt-costly) neighborhood celebration when the coin is found, yet she is an example of someone who recognizes worth! Her actions are the height of prodigality since she spends more on lamp oil and feasting than the worth of the lost denarius, but she recognizes what really matters: her friends and community. The parables of the treasure in the field (Mt 13:44) and the pearl of great price (13:45-46), in which all else is sacrificed for the thing of worth that is found, also showcase uneconomic actions. The farmer and the merchant in these parables give up their very means of subsistence in order to buy the field and the pearl, respectively. Yet who can eat a pearl? The characters aren't exactly financially savvy. Neither is the woman who symbolically prepares Jesus for burial by emptying a bottle of costly perfume over his feet (Mt 26:6-13=Mk 14:3-9). "What waste!" her onlookers exclaim. Yet Jesus exalts her.

The intent of the aforementioned passages seems to be to get audiences thinking about value. The parables direct their attention to something of great value, the kingdom, the long term benefits of which far outweigh its short-term costs. In each of the parables, what appears economically foolish in the short-term leads to long-term blessing in the kingdom of God. In the kingdom, writes Oakman, "uneconomic actions may, under the care of God, lead to a different kind of community and different kind of economics."[52] All of the displays of uneconomic action mentioned above reveal a deep faith and hope on the part of the actor that his or her actions will "pay off." Jesus' teachings commend this kind of faith, a faith that defies economic norms in pursuit of values greater than economic wellbeing.

Kingdom of God. Before wrapping up this section on Jesus' teachings regarding wealth, it is important to look at the concept of the kingdom of God in Jesus' life and teachings, since the kingdom of God was at the center of all Jesus taught and did. The kingdom has a significant bearing on how we understand and apply Jesus' teachings on wealth and its usage. Few would refute the claim that the kingdom of God (or the "kingdom of heaven," the preferred terminology in Matthew) is a central theme within the recorded teachings of Jesus. Yet there is ample disagreement about what Jesus intended as the *timing* of the kingdom. Jesus characterized the kingdom of God as having come in his ministry, as in Mt 10:7, 12:28, and 21:31, 43, Mk 1:15, Lk 9:27, 10:9-11, 11:20, 17:21, and 21:31-32, yet also characterized it as a more distant, otherworldly reality, as in Mt 7:21, Mk 14:25, and Lk 13:29. Throughout the centuries, Christians have tended to fixate on either the presentness or the futureness of the kingdom, emphasizing one at the expense of the other. But the kingdom Jesus proclaimed and inaugurated is a "both/and" scenario, not an "either/or." It is both made present and near in Jesus' ministry, and incomplete until a future day.[53]

It is a fact that the majority of Jesus' recorded sayings about the kingdom emphasize its presentness. Apparently, the kingdom of God exists as a process. It is present *now*, but in an emerging form, just as a tree is present in seedling form long before it towers conspicuously above the garden. As the kingdom emerges, followers of Jesus are to live in expectation of its full realization. We are to live as though it has fully emerged. In so doing, we make real in the present what will ultimately come to pass, God's divine will reigning throughout all creation. The vision of God's reign as articulated by Jesus is one of the most exciting things I can imagine. It is also one of the most frequently misunderstood and neglected of concepts, which has some very unfortunate consequences. For one thing, the kingdom of God properly understood as an emerging reality, both present and yet incomplete, makes sense of Jesus' ethical teachings. Jesus' teachings appear fatuous and unrealistic when taken out of the context of the dawning kingdom. Those who over-emphasize the futureness of the kingdom of God have tended to dismiss Jesus' ethical teachings as inapplicable in our era: since the kingdom of God has not emerged, the ethics of the kingdom should not dictate our actions. Those who hold this view see Jesus' ethic as an ethic intended for the age to come, when the reign of God is realized.

Yet how can this be so? Did not Jesus intend kingdom ethics to govern actions in a world where there exists anger, and enmity, and deception, and greed? Did he say "love your enemies" (Mt 5:44), but intend it for an age in which there would be no enemies? Did he say "sell your possessions, and give alms" (Lk 12:33), but intend it for an age in which there would be no poverty? No. Jesus called people to rigorous standards knowing the harsh realities of the world in which we live, and knowing that the way of the kingdom would cause hardship in this world for his followers. But he knew God's kingdom was emerging and growing, and that those who walked in the way of the kingdom would prevail because God would prevail. This is why holding the present and future aspects of the kingdom in tension is so imperative for Christians. Hope in the *future* fullness of the kingdom allows us to live out the way of the kingdom *now*. One cannot live out the strict ethic Jesus commends without a vital faith that one day God will reign over all things, and will restore all of creation to wholeness. It is this hope in the fully-realized justice of the one day fully-realized kingdom which makes Jesus' way possible. In this life we can face death and persecution and deprivation resulting from our faithfulness to the way of the kingdom, only because we have utter confidence that God's kingdom is emerging, and growing, and will one day order all things.

The cross and resurrection constitute the culmination of Jesus' inauguration of the kingdom. It was through the cross that the kingdoms of the world were exposed as impersonators of the kingdom of God.[54] By being exposed, they were defeated, and this not through violence and force, but through self-sacrifice and love. The resurrection was the vindication of God's way, the way of the kingdom to which we are invited. It was the vindication of an overcoming love, and the forgiveness, rather than the annihilation, of enemies. It was how God chose to triumph over evil. The cross stands as the symbol to us of God's way of overcoming, challenging us to choose its arduous road while simultaneously pointing us to the beauty and levitating hope of Easter morning.

Jesus' directions to his disciples on wealth, like his directions on things like nonviolence and truth-telling, look extremely difficult to carry out, and they are. But they are instructions for a people called to take up their crosses and be disciples, or followers. Living out the values of the kingdom in our economic relationships with others is part of how we cooperate in God's work of exposing that which is fallen and evil in our world. By walking in the way of the kingdom we become like a city on a hill, a point of reference and hope in a dark, scary world, and a light by which people can better see what is true and real. And by ordering our lives in accordance with God's active presence in the world, we make God's reign more visible and accessible. By our love, and our generosity, and our forgiveness of our enemies, God's kingdom grows.

The kingdom of God is the motivation and the goal of Jesus' ethics, including his teachings about wealth. He did not lay down a new law to be absolutized, but called people to join a new community and to order their lives around a new reality, the kingdom of God emerging all around them. Jesus was not an ascetic who shunned all earthly goods and pleasures. On occasion he even attended lavish meals and parties (Lk 5:29; Jn 2:1-12). Jesus seemed intent to live in accordance with God's active reign, but not to adhere to principles for the sake of principles. Jesus was both movable and obedient, which is always a good combination.

Conclusion. When viewed in light of its context in the world of first-century Palestine, Jesus' teachings dance. Jesus was largely addressing crowds of peasants pressed to the breaking point by exploitation. Among these were many poor workers in the fish industry, as well as a large contingent of agricultural workers. They all lived in a region of the Middle East abounding in resources, where the land was fecund and the waters teemed with fish. Yet for all of this richness, they were barely subsisting, dispossessed of their family lands, and deeply in debt. Jesus called them to order their lives around a new reality, the reality of God's kingdom present among them. They were called to turn their backs on the value systems that oppressed and constrained them, and by which they oppressed others, and to become members of God's family, who take care of one another and manifest a completely different set of values. For some of Jesus' disciples, this meant a total departure from the kinship and economic structures ordering their lives. It meant a decision to drop their nets and "Follow!" For others of Jesus' followers, such as the women who supported the traveling disciples (Lk 8:3), it meant an entirely new perspective on possessions, and the purposes for which they were to be used. But for all those who became followers of Jesus, it meant that the values of their culture could no longer determine their actions.

Implications of Jesus' Teachings on Wealth and its Usage

What do Jesus' sayings, addressed to audiences altogether different from us, imply for our actions? In particular, what do they imply about the way you and I conceive of and use our wealth? Every Christian is in a unique economic situation and must seek the guidance of the Spirit in discerning specific actions to take in obedience to Christ. Nonetheless, some general things certainly can be said regarding Jesus' teachings about wealth and its usage and what those teachings imply for us. Let us look at some of the implications of the passages studied above.

Firstly, the Beatitudes. The Beatitudes remind us that though the way of the kingdom is costly, God blesses those who make the sacrifices inherent in obedience. Because our socio-cultural context is so different from that of the first-century Palestineans to whom Jesus spoke, the social and economic costs of following Jesus will not look exactly the same for us as they did for his original audience. For one thing, being rejected by one's family does not bear the same economic consequences in my socio-cultural setting as it did in first-century Palestine. But choosing the way of the kingdom is no less costly for me.

Followers of Jesus who resist participation in the dehumanizing and oppressive structures of our economic system will inevitably experience economic consequences. We will experience economic "losses" because of placing the values of justice, honesty, and generosity above the values of profit and growth. We will place limits on the ways in which we attain wealth by refusing to do work that exploits and manipulates people. This may mean a refusal to work for businesses and corporations which abuse workers, or contract with sweatshops, or fail to take heed of the environment, or which legitimate the abuses of our economic system. For many it will mean giving away a significant portion of what we earn to assist those unable to earn a decent living themselves. These sorts of actions will be costly, *both economically and socially*.

Still, one must acknowledge that in our economic context, it is increasingly difficult for concerned individuals to find work that does not in one way or another support the abuses mentioned above. Simply working in a grocery store, for example, forces one to participate in an economic system which manipulates people into buying what they do not need, which takes advantage of disenfranchised farmers overseas and migrant laborers at home, and which deposits astronomical amounts of chemical pollution and garbage upon the earth. In such a predicament, the best some of us can do is to *limit* the amount of our participation in the system. A Christian looking for work in a grocery store could do this by choosing an employer which respects labor unions, for example, while refusing to work for those which put profits above people. He could also strive to impact the system from within by, for example, discussing fair trade or the importance of supporting local small farmers with the managers and buyers at his store, and introducing them to outlets for products like fair trade coffee. Yet ultimately, advocating for kingdom values from within our economic system will be risky.

Another action we can take to resist participation in the dehumanizing and oppressive structures of our economic system, is to limit the amount of wealth we work to acquire. As we are shaped by the values of the kingdom rather than the values of our culture, we will be less concerned about the amount of our paychecks. Instead of devoting ourselves to earning as much as possible, we will devote ourselves to caring for each other as God intended, and to fulfilling our God-given vocations. This will mean spending more time with our families and communities, and serving those in need among us. As we seek to live out God's vocation for us, our choices of work will be directed by God and by vocation, not by a lust for money. All in all, we will choose to live with less, and to give more.

Chapter Seven tells the stories of individuals who have taken steps to bring their economic lives more in line with the kingdom of God. Their steps may appear minor when held up to the sacrifices of Jesus' first-century peasant followers, whose very sustenance was on the line. Nonetheless, their actions reflect the priorities of God's kingdom as articulated in the Beatitudes. Jesus assures us that such actions will be rewarded. The values of the world: wealth, luxury, and power, all offer temporary rewards. Yet compared with the rewards promised to those who choose the demanding way of God's kingdom, these rewards appear myopic and misguided.

Moving on, Jesus' parables and teachings enjoin his followers to renounce the god of self-sufficiency, to practice radical generosity, to forgive debts, and to live according to the kingdom of God even when the values of the kingdom conflict with the economic norms of their society. All of these teachings carry implications for our lives as followers of Jesus in the twenty-first century. Self-sufficiency is as much an idol in Western cultures as it was in Jesus' culture. In our world, it is called "financial security." Like the rich fool in Jesus' parable, we build our barns of multiple savings accounts and retirement plans to store away our surplus. Just as it did in Jesus' day, the value of self-sufficiency inhibits our dependence on God and one another. Jesus had little patience for it, and we should take this as a rebuke of our habits, and as a stark challenge.

Also challenging to us is Jesus' commendation of generosity. As followers of Jesus, our lives ought to be characterized by radical generosity based on faith in God's provision. As stated earlier, Jesus called people to become members of God's family where the needs of all God's children would be met by one another (Mk 3:31-35=Mt 12:46-50=Lk 8:19-21; Mt 25:31-46). Generosity is, thus, to be an indispensable response to God's generosity toward us. Jesus directed his teaching largely toward peasants, and called them to a life of radical generosity, even though most of his followers already lived on the brink of total deprivation. Would Jesus have demanded anything less than absolute generosity if his audience had been the wealthy? Generosity is to be a characteristic of the emerging kingdom of God, and all those who order their lives according to the way of the kingdom are called to radical generosity. Yet I know that my life is certainly not characterized by a generosity that would be called radical. When I compare my life with the lives of people around the world, I see that it is not analogous to that of Galilean peasants. I am far more wealthy than they. In the global scheme of things, my life is more analogous to that of the elites of Jesus' day. And if Jesus expected absolute generosity of his peasant followers, who had so little to give, how much more is expected of me?

In my context, it is hard not to notice that Christians rarely take care of one another the way Jesus envisioned. I am struck by the fact that the kind of generosity Jesus commended, and the familial kinds of relationships that were to characterize Jesus' followers, are mutually dependent. One cannot exist without the other. Yet in our culture, the relationships between believers are rarely characterized as family-like. As a consequence, we rarely practice radical generosity toward one another. How can Christians make their possessions available to God and others, trusting God to care for their needs, when the community God intended to use as the source of that care has shirked this responsibility (or starved itself of this blessing)? Have we as American Christians, by our self-sufficiency and our unwillingness to practice radical generosity toward one another, failed to heed Jesus' call to be the family of God?

We can take steps to change. We can work to build communities of believers who live out God's vision of the kingdom in our economic relationships with one another. This will require a huge shift in the way we relate to each other, but huge shifts are generally comprised of many small steps. We can take those steps. Additionally, we can give generously to those in the world who everyday go without clean water, or a bed to sleep in, or who go to bed hungry. We can give some of our resources or *all* of our resources, depending how God directs us, in order to care for such needs. In doing so we will be fulfilling our intended role as God's instruments to meet the needs of our brothers and sisters. If we find that the needs of those in our local Christian communities are already well provided for, we can make our resources available to Christians in poorer parts of our country, or our world, thus responding to them as Jesus envisioned, as family. I would not encourage anyone to give solely to other Christians. But Jesus did call us into a unique kind of relationship with fellow believers, and as we give generously to *all* people in need, we should not lose sight of our unique obligations to our Christian family.

According to Jesus' teachings on wealth and its usage, Christians should not be involved in dominating people through indebtedness. Jesus told his followers to forgive debts. As with the Jubilee tradition, this kind of debt forgiveness was intended to correct societal imbalances, and was consistent with the kingdom values of justice, mercy, and self-sacrifice for the sake of others. This aspect of Jesus' teaching has profound implications for our economic lives, since debts are an ubiquitous feature of our economic system. Do Jesus' teachings on debt apply to us? Does the meaning of those teachings translate into the language of our economic system? If we look honestly at debt in our society, we can see that there are many places where debt is used to dominate. Corporations encourage an almost maniacal reliance on debt, or "financing," to allow people to buy more and more of their products. Many people around the world, including many Americans, are deeply indebted because of the overuse of credit for things they do not truly need. According to Jesus, Christians should have no part in the dominating of others through debt, or in becoming so dominated. This is a profound challenge to Jesus' followers in our day.

On the other hand, debt is also used in our context for purposes that are apparently positive. In many cases, debt is the only thing that allows families to buy a home, or to send their children to college. Is this the kind of debt Jesus had in mind? What about relief organizations who give "micro-loans," often without interest, to people struggling in poor countries, loans which allow them to start up sustainable businesses? Are these debts inconsistent with the kingdom of God? In such cases, we must keep in mind the values of the kingdom as Jesus articulated them, and seek to discern the intentions of Jesus' teaching. Was Jesus intending to abolish all lending as an absolute principle? Or was Jesus intending to build a community of people who related to others in a way that did not involve domination? He intended the latter. Therefore, in assessing whether to be involved in the lending or taking out of particular loans, we should ask ourselves: does this promote the domination of someone by others, or does this promote the liberation of someone? If giving or taking a loan results in domination, even if it is non-personal, such as domination by materialism, we should not be involved in it. On the other hand, loans which make adequate housing available to families, for example, without placing life-draining demands on them, can be liberating. It is my conviction that families should have, as Habitat for Humanity defines it, "simple, decent housing." Having a safe, reliable place to go home to can free parents and children to live more fully God's intentions for them. Still, when a family takes out a loan to buy a home that is "better and bigger" than they need, simply to satisfy a materialistic urge, they have become dominated.

Finally, in looking at Jesus' teachings on wealth and its usage, we noted how Jesus upsets economic norms. Specifically, in several of Jesus' parables, short-term economic concerns are flagrantly disregarded in pursuit of something of value, whether that be a pearl of astounding beauty, or a feast with close friends. What might this theme in Jesus' teaching on wealth and its usage imply for our economic lives? Simply put, it implies that we should place the things of highest value in our lives before economic concerns, to the point that we would sacrifice our very subsistence for them if need be. The parables also imply that such actions result from great faith, and commend to us such profligate faith. What things are of greatest value in our lives? Are you willing to defy the norms of economics to pursue them? Is our faith in God's provision strong enough to allow us to pursue kingdom values rather than financial security?

On the Socio-Economic Context of Luke-Acts and the Theme of Wealth and its Usage in Luke-Acts

You may have noticed that many of the scriptures listed in this chapter come from the Gospel of Luke. The reason for this is simple: the author of the Third Gospel had a particular interest in the subject of poverty and riches, and waxed eloquently on the subject. He, more than any other New Testament writer, wrestled with the implications of the Gospel for how Jesus' followers used wealth, and included in his gospel more of Jesus' teachings on the subject than did the other evangelists. The author of Luke, who also wrote the book of Acts, spelled out the Gospel as, above all, "good news for the poor" (Lk 4:16-30). And in Acts, he chose to tell the story of Jesus' earliest followers in a way that emphasized the revolutionary economic life of that community, in which those with possessions sold their goods to provide for the needs of everyone in the community. Why did Luke work this emphasis into his writings?

Philip Esler, a biblical scholar who has written extensively about Luke-Acts, suggests that the answer lies in the Christian community

Luke was a part of, and the struggles they faced as disciples of Jesus. Esler, in his book *Community and Gospel in Luke-Acts*,[55] argues that the community Luke was involved in, who were also likely the audience that Luke-Acts was written for, was comprised of both elites and very poor members (more on this below). Esler believes the relationships between these Christians and the inequalities among them provided the impetus for Luke's wrestling with the economic implications of Jesus' life and ministry, and for his telling of the Gospel in a way that addresses the issue of wealth and its usage among Christians. Luke stressed that the Gospel is good new for the poor, but he also emphasized the stark challenge Jesus poses to wealthy believers.

Because of this latter emphasis, the writings of Luke are of particular importance for middle—and upper-class Christians. We need to pay close attention to them. The message they bear speaks, in many ways, to those of us who constitute the global elite in our day. Just as the elites in Luke's congregation needed to rethink the issue of poverty and riches and to view it in light of their new life as Christians, so we desperately need to reexamine it. Luke did the elites in his congregation a favor by not brushing over Jesus' "difficult" words on the subject. Had he done so he would have told them only part of the story, and made it both innocuous and effectively irrelevant to their lives. But, he did not brush over Jesus' teachings on poverty and riches, or soften Jesus' words to the rich. Instead he told the story of Jesus' life and ministry in a way that was painfully relevant for elites.

Why this emphasis? What compelled Luke to include more of Jesus' teaching on wealth and poverty, and to intensify that element in his sources?

The Gospel of Luke is generally believed to have been written in an urban setting either in Rome, or in the eastern provinces of the Roman Empire. Luke probably interpreted and articulated the story of Jesus to Christians while living in the shadow of Greek or Roman temples, the shimmering palaces of Roman magistrates, the ever-present Roman military, and the overwhelming stench of urban poverty. He wrote in a city like Ephesus, or Rome, or Antioch. He was familiar with outrageous inequalities between rich and poor.[56] Luke seems to have come from the upper echelons of his society. Of all the New

Testament writers, his command of the Greek language and familiarly with various literary genres are the most advanced, suggesting that he enjoyed very high social status, or had at one time. Something, however, had turned his heart toward the poor. Various New Testament writers make references to Christian communities comprised of both very rich and poor members (i.e. the authors of Acts, Corinth, and James). Could it be that Luke's community knew this kind of diversity?

It doesn't take a great deal of imagination to assume that Luke's community included destitute members. Luke characterized the desperately poor as the primary beneficiaries of the good news, and particularly blessed in the kingdom of God. Would someone with this worldview have been a part of a Christian community that had few or no poor members? Probably not. It is more of a stretch to imagine that his community included elites. For one thing, elites were a very small percentage of the population. Nonetheless, there is evidence in Luke-Acts that Luke tailored parts of his gospel to speak directly to elites.[57] It is unlikely he would have chosen this emphasis if it was irrelevant to his own community and audience.

There is ample evidence, therefore, that Luke tailored his writings to speak both to the destitute and the rich, and that both groups were represented in Luke's Christian community. In his gospel, Luke went to great lengths to portray Jesus instructing the wealthy to share with the have-nots, and issuing stark warnings to those who hoarded riches. In the book of Acts, Luke proceeded to describe the successes and struggles of the early Jesus movement in living out Jesus' vision of the new family of God, meeting one another's needs. Even if, as some scholars suggest, Luke presents an idealized picture, it is clear that Luke shares this vision. It is likely that Luke's understanding of Jesus' vision for his followers, and Luke's desire that economic justice characterize the church was born out of his context. Perhaps he had seen great damage done within his own community as a result of inequality and greed.

Throughout this chapter we have discussed Jesus' teachings on wealth and its usage, including those teachings found in Luke. It is intriguing that Luke chose his words to address the problems of acute inequities among believers. In all times, economic inequality has been a reality with which Christians have had to grapple. It is no less so in our day. If Luke was writing, in part, for those on the privileged end of the economic spectrum, he was writing for people like you and me. My point here is: we should pay attention.

In this chapter, I have dealt primarily with Jesus' instructions to his followers on the use of wealth, and the ways in which his followers were called to view poverty and riches in an entirely new way. I have said little about Jesus' characterization of money, or Mammon, as an idol competing with God for our allegiance (Lk 16:13). This is because Jesus' personification of Mammon as a rival power is not elaborated on in the gospels. But "powers and principalities" do get attention elsewhere in the New Testament, especially in the Pauline writings, and Jesus' characterization of Mammon, or wealth, as a power is best interpreted in light of Pauline reflections on the subject. Consequently, it is to those reflections we now turn.

Chapter Six

Pauline Christology and the Powers

> The ultimate expression of [the] Christian attitude toward the power of money is what we will call *profanation*. . . . This profanation . . . means uprooting the sacred character, destroying the element of power. We must bring money back to its simple role as a material instrument. When money is no more than an object, when it has lost its seductiveness, its supreme value, its superhuman splendor, then we can use it like any other of our belongings, like any machine.
>
> . . . Now this profanation is first of all the result of a spiritual battle, but this must be translated into behavior. There is one act par excellence which profanes money by going directly against the law of money, an act for which money is not made. This act is *giving*.
>
> Jacques Ellul[1]

Introduction

It did not take long after Jesus' death and resurrection for his disciples to find themselves eyeball-to-eyeball with some daunting powers. Following the first recorded public acts of the disciples after Pentecost, the healing of a crippled man by Peter and John along with Peter's address to the astonished onlookers, the disciples encounter the powers

(Acts 4:1f.). They are arrested and taken before the "rulers of the people" (v.8b), who ask, "by what power" they have healed. It is the first of many recorded confrontations between Jesus' followers and the powers of state, religion, and economics (which, in their day, were all tied together).

Among the representatives of these powers who recognized the Jesus movement for the threat that it was, a threat to their claims of dominion, was an impassioned young Pharisee named Saul, who later became the Apostle Paul. Saul believed that the institution of Law was God's rightful representative on Earth, and he devoted himself wholeheartedly to upholding and protecting that institution against those who might usurp it. According to his best understanding, Jesus' followers were flouting the Law, and thus challenging God's rule. They were seducing people, leading them astray. He would do his best to stop them. It wasn't until he encountered Jesus in a piercing light on the road to Damascus that it dawned on him who the real usurper had been. If Jesus was alive and was God's true representative, then the authorities who killed Jesus must have been anything but. Paul's view of reality came unhinged.

It would take years for Paul to rethink his theology in light of this experience, and to develop a worldview consistent with his new faith in Jesus, but in time he did. And, of course, he eventually articulated these ideas in the form of letters. In Paul's writings, we see that Paul's understanding of the world, of God, and of Jesus included a well-developed understanding of power, of the structures that order earthly existence and the spiritual forces undergirding them, as well as the consequences of Jesus' death and resurrection for these. Few people would have been better suited to wrestle with and articulate these ideas than Paul, a person who had been so well-acquainted with the claims and agenda of the powers. He had been as devout a servant of the powers as any man.

In this chapter, I reflect on what the Pauline writings have to say about wealth and its usage. But rather than highlighting Paul's instructions on giving to the poor, or his collection for the needy Christians in Jerusalem (which we will discuss, to some extent, later), I focus on Pauline teaching regarding the powers and principalities. This teaching explains the role of the powers, including the power of Mammon as mentioned by Jesus, in our lives and our world, and enlightens us about the freedom we can have from their domination. It is impossible for Christians to fully grasp the New Testament perspective on wealth without understanding the role of the powers and principalities. What, or who, are these powers that are mentioned in the Pauline writings?

Principalities and Powers in the Pauline Writings

First, let us look at the various Pauline passages[2] in which powers and principalities are mentioned:[3]

"For I am convinced that neither death, nor life, nor angels, nor *principalities*, nor things present, nor things to come, nor *powers*, nor height, nor depth, nor anything else in all creation, will be able to separate us from the love of God in Christ Jesus our Lord." Romans 8:38-39

"None of the *principalities* of this age understood this; for it they had, they would not have crucified the Lord of glory." 1 Corinthians 2:8

"Then comes the end, when he hands over the kingdom to God the Father, after he has nullified every *principality* and every authority and *power*. For he must reign until he has put all his enemies under his feet. The last enemy to be nullified is death." 1 Corinthians 15:24-26[4]

"God put this power to work in Christ when he raised him from the dead and seated him at his right hand in the heavenly places, far above all *principality* and authority and *power* and dominion, and above every name that is named, not only in this age but also in the age to come. And he has put all things under his feet and has made him the head over all things for the church." Ephesians 1:20-22

"You were dead through the trespasses and sins in which you once lived, following the course of this world, following the *principality* of the *power* of the air, the spirit that is now at work among those who are disobedient." Ephesians 2:1-2

" . . . so that through the church the wisdom of God in its rich variety might now be made known to the *principalities* and authorities in the heavenly places." Ephesians 3:10

"For our struggle is not against enemies of blood and flesh, but against the *principalities*, against the authorities, against the cosmic *powers* of this present darkness, against the spiritual forces of evil in the heavenly places." Ephesians 6:12

" . . . for in him all things in heaven and on earth were created, things visible and invisible, whether thrones or dominions or *principalities* or *powers*—all things have been created through him and for him. He himself is before all things, and in him all things [are systematized] . . . and through him God was pleased to reconcile to himself all things, whether on earth or in heaven, by making peace through the blood of his cross." Colossians 1:16-17, 20

"He set this aside, nailing it to the cross. He disarmed the *principalities* and authorities, and made a public example of them, triumphing over them in it." Colossians 2:14b-15

These passages reveal some important things about the powers. In every passage but one, it is implied that the powers and principalities are inimical to God's purposes. Yet in Colossians 1:16, we learn that the powers (the general term I will use for both "principalities" and "powers") are among the "visible and invisible" things that God created through and for Christ. They, along with thrones and dominions were part of God's good creation. Simply put, these passages reveal that the powers are fallen. Though they were created by God to order and maintain human society, they have become enemies of God. What kind of enemies are the powers?

Often the powers have been misunderstood or dismissed as angels, or personalized spirits of a non-earthly realm. This is misguided. The powers as elucidated in the Pauline writings are far more multi-dimensional than this. In Romans 8:38-39, they are listed alongside "angels," which would suggest that they themselves are not angels. In fact, in this passage, principalities seem to be the opposite of angels in the way that death is the opposite of life, and present is the opposite of future. Does this mean that principalities are simply the evil counterpart of good angelic beings?

In one passage it is stated that the principalities crucified Jesus (1 Cor 2:8). And in another passage it is said that the principalities and powers were exposed and disarmed through the crucifixion (Col 2:14b-15). These passages implicate the powers in Jesus' death. Now, we know that Jesus was crucified by Roman authorities, with the encouragement of the Judean religious establishment. What does it mean, then, to equate the powers with those who killed Jesus? In another passage, the powers are aligned with the ways of this world. The Ephesians are told that they had once walked "according to the course of the world," which is equated with the "principality of the power of the air," a spirit prompting the disobedient actions of humankind (Eph 2:1-2). And in Col 2:8 and v.20, the "elemental spirits," or *stoicheia*, a term used in conjunction with "principalities" and "powers" in the Pauline writings, are equated with the "human traditions" to which Christ's followers have died. In the Colossians passages, *stoicheia* are aligned particularly with the purity laws of the Israelite religion (Col 2:21). In Galatians 4:1-11, the *stoicheia*, or elemental spirits, have the same meaning: the earthly institution of the law (Gal 4:3-5).

These passages are illuminating. They show that the powers are indeed "spiritual," but that they are manifested in human actions and institutions, and they are revealed through the corruption of human society. The composite picture of the powers one gets from these passages has many facets. The powers comprise "visible and invisible" elements; they are the spiritual underpinnings of earthly powers, such as kingdoms or dominions, *along with* those visible powers themselves, powers which act in this world and dominate human affairs. Other passages state that the powers are God's enemies who must be dethroned before the kingdom of God can be fully realized (1 Cor 15:24-25, Eph 1:20-21), yet they are also the ones to whom the church must witness (Eph 3:10), making known to those powers the "wisdom of God." How does the church witness to the powers? The answer would seem to be: by witnessing to the earthly power structures in which the powers reside, and through which they work. In the New Testament, we see the apostles carrying out such witness.

The powers and principalities are not merely spiritual forces, nor are they merely human. "Our struggle is not against enemies of blood and flesh," says Eph 6:12. But neither is our struggle with invisible, ghostly spirits separate from human social realities. We wrestle against God-defying, non-human powers that find expression in the human lives they seek to dominate *by way of* the structures and dominions that bear upon our lives. These dominions include such things as Religion, a power with which the Apostle Paul repeatedly wrestled, and Mammon, a power Jesus warned against in the bluntest terms, and the power of the State, the power that crucified Jesus. Paul could characterize the Law as an idol, and Jesus could characterize Mammon as a rival god. They saw the spiritual implications of these earthly institutions. Yet the legal system and the monetary system are, of course, not strictly spiritual, or non-human, entities. The fact is, both systems are administered by human beings and impinge upon such matters as what to eat and what to drink, as well as who gets to eat and drink. Can it get much more flesh-and-blood than that? But Paul and Jesus recognized that earthly institutions and structures are more than the sum of their human components and human intentions. At the core, they are spiritual, imbued with forces or powers which work to dominate the human spirit and seduce people away from God's intentions for humanity. This is the New Testament perspective on human systems.

Some may dismiss the New Testament teaching on the powers as merely a reflection of an antiquated worldview, one which sees earth, heaven, and hell as separate tiers in the universe, and which blames natural phenomena, such as illnesses, on the malevolence of mischievous, personal spirits from beyond, enjoying forays into the physical world. It is true that this ancient view of the universe cannot always be adopted by people in the twenty-first century who know there are scientific explanations for what was once explained as spirit possession. Nonetheless, the New Testament teaching on the powers can also provide support for an *integrated* worldview, the view that creation has both an interiority and an exteriority, both a spiritual and a physical manifestation which are not separate, but intertwined. Walter Wink,

in his outstanding book on the powers, does a good job of explaining
the differences between the ancient worldview and the "integral
worldview" we are talking about here. I quote him at length:

> There were, in the first century, both Jews and Christians
> who perceived in the Roman Empire a demonic spirituality
> that they called Sammael or Satan. But they encountered
> this spirit in the actual institutional forms of Roman life:
> legions, governors, crucifixions, payment of tribute, Roman
> sacred emblems and standards, and so forth. The spirit that
> they perceived existed right at the heart of the empire, but
> their worldview equipped them to discern that spirit only
> by intuiting it and then projecting it out, in visionary form,
> as a spiritual *being* residing in heaven representing Rome in
> the heavenly council.
>
> In the ancient worldview, where earthly and heavenly
> reality were inextricably united, this view of the Powers
> worked effectively. But modern Westerners are, on the whole,
> incapable of maintaining that worldview . . .
>
> What is necessary is to complete the projection process
> by *withdrawing* the projections and recognizing that the
> real spiritual force that we are experiencing is emanating
> from an actual institution. In the ancient worldview, a seer
> or prophet was able to sense the diseased spirituality of an
> institution or state, and then bring that spirituality to
> awareness by projecting it in visionary form onto the
> heavenly realm and depicting it (even *seeing* it) as a demon
> on high. Our task today, working with a unitary worldview,
> is to withdraw that projection from on high and locate it in
> the institution in which it actually resides.[5]

In no way does Wink's analysis downplay the realness of the spiritual.
In fact, it makes it impossible for us to downplay "spirits" by projecting
them into another realm apart from our own. Nor does his analysis see
our world and its people as possessed by ubiquitous demons; a paranoid
worldview that has gained ascendance among many fundamentalists.

Rather, Wink asserts that human systems and powers have an "interiority" that is spiritual. According to the Pauline writings, the spirituality of these earthly institutions is not neutral. Like all good creations of God, they are part of a fallen world and have arranged themselves in opposition to God. This analysis proves true as we observe the oppressiveness, intransigence, waste and destructiveness of systems and institutions in our world. Such systems are not corrupt because they are comprised of individuals who have been possessed by demons. Nor are they corrupt because they are controlled by evil people, though the leadership of such institutions may include people guided by vengeance, greed, and selfishness. Ultimately, they are corrupt because at the core of earthly institutions are spiritual forces, forces which have turned away from God.

All human institutions are shaped by human ingenuity and ideas. In the early stages of development, such institutions are under the control of human beings. However, as they advance, systems become greater than humanity's ability to control them. They take on a life of their own. Jacques Ellul, a French thinker who wrote extensively about the powers in the decades following World War II, explains it thus:

> . . . a social factor like religion, political power, technology, or propaganda will still be the work of man in it earliest forms, so that at its commencement it can still be modified by man. Man is its master and the arbiter of its destiny. But as this factor solidifies in its means and methods, as it extends its sphere of application, as it invests itself with spiritual meaning, man progressively loses his possibilities of intervention and modification. A reversal takes place. Man no longer organizes the object. The object has its own life and develops like a true organism according to its own necessity. The more it obeys this law of its own development the more it forces itself on man and becomes a necessity for him. . . . It should be noted, however, that this could happen only because there was not merely an inner mechanism but because man consented to go along with it. Man is not stripped of his mastery apart from or contrary to himself.[6]

The "inner mechanism" Ellul mentions denotes the spirituality of an institution. It is the spiritual force that finds expression in human life *in and through* that institution and the claims the institution makes upon people's lives. But, as Ellul states, earthly institutions come to have this kind of power because humanity, at some point, allows it. We allow these created institutions to take the form of gods, and to determine our existence. It is essentially the story of the Fall enacted over and over again, with created powers usurping the place of the Creator. Like Adam, the quintessential human, we allow ourselves to be seduced. And once the reversal takes place, the created powers forever rival God for our allegiance. As William Stringfellow explains, in the post-Fall world, the powers have gained oppressive control over the human beings they were intended by God to serve:

> Pretending autonomy from God, these creatures [the principalities and powers] are autonomous from human control. In reality they dominate human beings. Relying upon the biblical description, I have come to think of the relationship of the principalities and persons as if the Fall means that there has been not only a loss of dominion by human beings over the rest of Creation but, more precisely than that, an inversion or a reversal of dominion. So, now, those very realities of Creation—traditions, institutions, nations—over which humans are said in the Genesis Creation story to receive dominion and the very creatures which are called thus into the service and enhancement of human life in society exercise, in the era of the Fall, dominion over human beings (Gen 1:26).[7]

It is apparent at times that human systems, whether they be governmental regimes or economic systems or religious institutions, take on lives of their own, completely apart from the human beings making decisions within them. Things are done a certain way *because that is just the way the system works*, and every actor within the system is constrained to act according to the system's preordained patterns, regardless of whether they agree with them. The system comes first, and human actions follow along its course. People working within the system might want things to be done differently, might want to make decisions that radically diverge from the norm, but they find it is impossible to do so. Elected politicians find it is impossible to act according to their consciences and still get reelected. Aspiring politicians find it impossible to follow their consciences and get elected in the first place. Religious leaders find it impossible to speak the truth people most need to hear without being replaced by someone who instead says what people want to hear. Business people find it impossible to make ethical business choices and remain viable.

Imagine the following: a woman decides she wants to design and make clothing in a way that does not oppress the workers sewing that clothing, does not pollute the environment, and does not promote materialism with all its waste and domination. It does not take her long to figure out that she cannot pay her workers fair wages and still locate her business close to her North American customers, because her competitors pay rock-bottom wages in factories overseas. She cannot compete with them. They are able to sell their clothing for the cost of her overhead. Now, she could decide to use factories in the global south, but she is committed to paying an international living wage. If she sets up shop overseas and pays her overseas factory workers a living wage, she cannot pay her North American staff the high salaries that the industry has taught executives to expect. She would have a very difficult time keeping these employees. Besides all this, she is aware of the massive pollution that would result from transporting her product thousands of miles between the point of production and the points of sale. Finally, there is the dilemma of how to let people know about her product without taking advantage of the manipulations of advertising, and thus promoting materialism. All in all, the system has her stymied. If she wants to participate in it, she will have to lay aside her concerns about social justice and environmental stewardship, and act in the spirit of greed in order to survive.

The system, you see, is comprised of all kinds of good individuals. But each of them has about as much freedom of action as does the woman in this example, which is to say, very little. They have inherited an economic system that, if they choose to participate in it, predetermines their actions. As Wink writes, the people who participate in such an economic system "need not be greedy for profit at all; *the system is greedy on their behalf.*"[8]

The powers have a way of making people feel stuck, of limiting the choices we can make, of coercing us. Is this the intention of the myriad human beings who in small ways shaped and are shaping the systems that we now have? Probably not. The systems we collectively mold and participate in seem to be quite out of our control. Never is this more evident than in geopolitics, where the war machine, once it gets moving, runs roughshod over everyone's best intentions and thoroughly out of human control. According to the biblical worldview, this in not merely because of human frailty and error, but because spiritual forces are at work in and through fallen human institutions, deceiving and dominating humanity.

We live in a notably materialistic age. For the most part, western societies see and seek material causes and solutions for every human problem. Those who consider themselves to be people of faith might believe in spiritual forces, yet many operate as materialists or, more precisely, as dualists, separating out the spiritual from all things earthly and physical, and keeping their everyday earthly lives compartmentalized, segregated from their "spiritual lives." Spiritual things impinge upon such invisible entities as the soul, or the heart, and upon little else. Therefore we see zealous drives for the conversion of individual souls alongside zealous support for violence, nationalism, and luxurious living. Some may see this as a perfectly modern approach to things, a way to be spiritual without holding to an antiquated worldview. Yet this otherworldly kind of religion, based as it is on abstraction and myth, is age-old. It is essentially non-incarnational, and bears more resemblance to pagan religions than to biblical Christianity.[9] This otherworldly interpretation of Christianity focuses on the salvation that will happen in another life, and in another realm. According to this worldview, Jesus came to set accounts right on some cosmic, spiritual plane, and faith in Jesus primarily affects the afterlife, and one's "spiritual life."

The Bible, on the other hand, tells the story of a God actively engaged in and concerned with the everyday existence of God's children. Salvation, in the biblical sense, is profoundly "earthy" *and* spiritual. Indeed, the two are inseparable. In the biblical story, salvation entails rescue from the God-denying, death-worshipping powers at work in earthly systems and institutions. Furthermore, Christians profess faith in a Savior who became a man and ministered to very human, earthly needs, who proclaimed the in-breaking of God's kingdom into our very world of family relationships and money and anger, who was crucified by the powers, and who, in the end, triumphed over them in the flesh-and-bloodness of the cross and resurrection. Biblical Christianity is profoundly *incarnational*, meaning that truth and redemption take on flesh-and-blood relevance, completely altering our existence both "in earth and in heaven." In the biblical sense, to say that Jesus set us free from sin is to say that Jesus set us free from all the ways that sin binds people, both in the course of our lives and eternally. It is to say that we *are* free, and will be free forever. Biblical ethics always have to do with how people live out of their faith in God, and in Christ, in everyday, earthly existence in the era of the Fall.[10]

Our materialistic worldview can also move people in a direction quite opposed to the dualism described above, yet equally destructive. It can lead us to deny the spiritual altogether. We can deny the presence of God and other spiritual forces in earthly affairs, and attribute all movements in human history solely to human actors. While this may keep us from "demonizing" the structures we do not like, it may also keep us from acknowledging the fallenness of our own agendas and ideologies. We devote ourselves completely to promoting causes or movements without recognizing the ways in which those seemingly good causes begin to dominate us, and to rob us of perspective, or to recognize the way those apparently benign movements, once victorious, adopt the strategies of the systems they once opposed.

Still, there are times when the fallen spiritual forces residing in and working through human institutions create such a din that even the staunchest materialists perceive them. Many people in and around Germany during the rise and reign of the Third Reich noticed that evil was "in the air," that a dehumanizing, manipulative power had taken hold, something mightier than any human being. Destructive spiritual forces were palpably present in the earthly systems at work in Germany under Hitler—palpable, perhaps, because of the extent to which they had gained ascendancy. Likewise, in the days following the incomprehensible destruction of the World Trade Center in New York City by terrorists, many people commented on the dark spirituality perceptible in the world, a force that felt like hatred, and moved with the destructive subtlety of fire.

Yet it is harder to see the fallen spirituality of institutions one holds dear. As I sit and write this in the Fall of 2002, many people around the world watch the Bush Administration concoct a war with Iraq, slowly and methodically shaping people's perceptions to win them over to a completely offensive and massive war plan, and we sense a destructive spiritual force moving in world affairs. Something deeper and more sinister than politics seems to be at work in our institutions of government, yet the majority of Americans have gotten on the war wagon. Our Congress and Senate have just handed the President permission to stage a "preemptive" war, lending legitimacy to a plan that could have catastrophic consequences in our time. Many of the leaders and people of my country seem to be swept along by a current of revenge, greed and myopia controlled by no one, claimed by no one, and seemingly irresistible. The powers and principalities keep moving us along, and we march to the beat of their drums.

A fallen spiritual force was perceptible when a friend of mine recently attended a court trial in support of a woman whose child had been taken away by the medical system. It was certainly not perceptible, however, to those who had proffered their loyalty to the institution. The mother had chosen not to put her son, in the late stages of cancer, through the chemotherapy treatments which doctors admitted would only delay her son's death by a few years, years which would be devoid of any quality of life. The medical system, so committed to its own "treatment" programs, reacted to her decision by giving custody of her child to the state. In the landmark court case, the dying child was returned to his mother. But the situation provided a vivid example of the way the powers work. Their own self-preservation becomes primary. Any threat to the established way of doing things meets with violent resistance. Does this mean that the doctors who had the boy taken from his mother, and who testified against her were acting with violent, evil intentions, or that they were possessed by evil spirits? No. The system, itself undergirded by a fallen spirituality the doctors could not see, was and is violent on their behalf. The doctors believed they were doing the best thing for the child. Threatening the parents who refuse to comply with recommended treatment programs is apparently just the way things are often done in hospitals today. Several parents of children who had cancer and had died from the effects of the radical chemical treatments told my friend that they had been threatened by hospitals. They had been told that if they did not put their children in chemo and radiation treatment, their children would be taken away.

The powers do not prioritize their own self-preservation merely to avoid extinction, but because they are wholly devoted to their own programs and agendas. They are able to delude people into believing that they are God's representatives, that they are the vehicles through which God is carrying out God's will in the world, and to convince people to submit to their control. People working within such human systems become convinced that this is true and devote themselves to guarding the system from extinction at almost any cost. But their intentions in doing so may be very good; they may truly believe that their particular church, or political program, or social movement, or economic theory, or healthcare system is what humanity most needs. They believe that they are furthering the common good by giving their unquestioning allegiance to the power. But pretty soon, without their realizing it, the power has become their god, and supporting the power has taken precedence over obeying the one, true God.

And yet, there is good news in all this talk of the powers. According to the Pauline teaching, the powers were both created by God and are fallen. But they are also among the "all things" reconciled to God through the cross. They have been redeemed, and will one day submit to the lordship of Christ. God created the powers to provide order to human society. The powers are not evil in themselves, but were created by a loving God to fulfill a function in the created world. It is not possible to function in human society without such things as an economic system, or a political system. Such systems may be fallen, but they also maintain much needed organization, as they were created to. As Christians, we cannot allow them to dominate us; we do not owe them any allegiance. Our Lord is Jesus. Yet the powers are needed to fulfill their created purpose, and we must continually remind them of and call them to this purpose, which is to serve the needs of humanity and to glorify Christ (Col 1:16). Hendrik Berkhof, in his watershed study of the New Testament teaching on the powers, written in post-World War II Europe, acknowledges that the powers have an important preserving role in the world, which does not recognize the leading of Christ. He describes the powers as "the dikes with which God encircles His good creation, to keep it in His fellowship and protect it from chaos." Berkhof goes on to say: "the believer's combat is never to strive *against* the Orders, but rather to battle for God's intention for them, and against their corruption."[11]

In the imagery of Revelation, the powers, after the defeat of God's enemies, appear in the "new heaven and earth" of God's kingdom. Here the powers are pictured as nations and kings, and it is stated that they will walk by the light of the glory of God. All the glory of kings and nations come to be centered in the temple, the symbol of God's reign (Rev 20-21). These are the nations who, earlier in Revelation, are pictured as having "drunk of the wine of the wrath of [Babylon's] fornication," and the kings who are said to have "committed fornication with her" (Rev 18:3). In Revelation, "Babylon" symbolizes the Roman Empire, the supreme earthly power during the author's lifetime. Despite the waywardness of the powers, they, along with all things in creation, submit to and are reconciled to God in the end, and glorify God in the "new heaven and earth." Though Revelation was not written by Paul, or connected with him, it reflects the same thinking on the powers as reflected in the Pauline writings. The powers are created, fallen, and finally, redeemed. As it is stated in Colossians, God chose "to reconcile to himself all things, whether on earth or in heaven" (Col 1:20). While in this era between the cross and the fullness of God's kingdom the powers continue to operate in defiance of God's purposes, we live in the hope and the knowledge that one day they will be redeemed.

The fact that the powers will be redeemed must not be interpreted to mean that particular systems, such as capitalism, or communism, or socialism, or particular nations, such as Denmark, or Korea, or the

United States, will be present and redeemed as part of God's kingdom. But it does mean that the institutions and systems which order and maintain society will be submitted to God and devoted to serving God by fulfilling the role God has designed for them. We cannot presume to know how this will look, since none of us have experienced it. Still we live in the New Testament hope that it will be so.

According to 1 Cor 15:24-26, the powers will, in the end, be "nullified." The Greek word that is used in this passage, *katargein*, can be translated either "to destroy," or "to nullify, make ineffective." The passage does not seem to mean "destroy," as in "to do away with altogether," since the powers exist in some way in the new heaven and new earth, and are under Christ's rule in the age to come (Eph 1:21). The powers as they are presently expressed, however, as dominating forces rivaling God for the allegiance of humanity, will be nullified. In the coming age, they will be made new, and will fulfill the role they were always intended to have. Essentially, they will be "dethroned," a word preferred by some scholars as the translation of *katargein*. Their dominion over human affairs will be brought to an end.[12]

The New Testament teaching on the powers can assist us in thinking about the global economy. The economic system we have inherited and which orders our economic relationships for better or worse is, like all economic systems in this age, a fallen power. We have called it neoliberal economics or the "global economy"; others call it global capitalism. This power has gained unfathomable influence in recent generations, and dominates the lives of almost every person on the planet. It is both dehumanizing, not least of all because it equates the worth of each individual with the wealth he or she holds, as well as profane, in that it elevates its agenda above that of God. According to global economics, the ultimate goal of human societies is to allow the unhindered quest for personal wealth and luxury. This goal so dominates the lives of those who grant their allegiance to this system that virtues such as selflessness, radical generosity, and justice become anathema. They are treated with the utmost disdain and suspicion by the powers. They represent a rival agenda that must be stopped. On the other hand, sins such as gluttony, greed, envy, pride and lust come to be praised and stroked. They are the vehicles through which societal goals, which are one and the same with economic goals, are reached. Nowhere is this more evident than in the distorted ads in places like fashion and automotive magazines. Obedience to the teachings of Jesus is viewed not only as a nuisance and a hindrance to the agenda of this power, it is often violently opposed.

In the language of Colossians, Jesus "disarmed" such powers, "making a public example of them" (2:15). The crucifixion of Jesus by the powers and his subsequent resurrection revealed the powers to be impostors. Through being exposed they were disarmed, deprived of their primary weapon, which is illusion. The illusion of their sovereignty and dominion is forever destroyed for those who understand the death and resurrection of Jesus. By destroying the control that the powers had over our perceptions of them, Jesus destroyed their ability to seduce and manipulate us. But this is only true to the extent that we participate in the death and resurrection of Jesus, to use Paul's language, and allow ourselves to die to the old order of things (see Rom 6). In this death is true freedom. [13]

The meaning of the key word used for the powers by Paul (*archee*) essentially means "forces which subjugate." The powers keep people dominated and blind-sided. They render people immobilized, unable to serve God with their full potential because they have become servants of the powers. This means that the greatest freedom we can experience comes from dying to the powers. In this sense, freedom is: freedom to see the world clearly, without distortion and illusion, freedom to serve God with our full potential, freedom to act conscientiously, and freedom to actively love.

In this time between the times, when the kingdom of God is a partial, emerging reality, the powers continue to exert their control in this world. Nonetheless, Jesus has triumphed over the powers. Their control is limited. Even now we can have freedom from the domination of the powers in our lives through faith in Christ and the effect of his death and resurrection. We need only trust and allow Christ to loosen the grip they have on us. Paul in his letters to various churches was repeatedly appealing to his readers to let that work be done in them, to let themselves experience the freedom and new life Christ offered. Paul's particular concern was with the power of Law, but his words rally all those constrained by the various powers. In Gal 4:9, Paul writes: "Now, however, that you have come to know God, or rather to be known by God, how can you turn back again to the weak and beggarly elemental spirits? How can you want to be enslaved to them again?" In the passage that precedes this, Paul characterizes the elemental spirits as guardians and trustees in this world. They provide order and control, yet they do so by enslaving those under them. According to this imagery, all those who are under the domination of the powers are enslaved and must be redeemed, as a slave or a minor must be given their freedom (see Gal 4:1-9). According to Paul's analogy, the gift of Jesus was God's extension of freedom to those who would accept the gift. It was God's plan for our emancipation.

The redemption of which Paul speaks frees us from all dominating powers, including the power of Mammon, or the economic structures in which resides the spiritual force Jesus called Mammon. As we participate in the death and resurrection of Jesus, we die to this power. What an exciting prospect! But the fact is, we continue to live in the world of the powers, and we participate in the fallen economic systems and institutions that order this world. How, then, are Jesus' followers, who have been set free from bondage to the powers, to relate to the powers in this world where participation in fallen structures and institutions is inevitable?

Fortunately, the Pauline writings do illuminate this issue, and provide some instruction to Christians on how to relate to the powers. First, Romans 13 affirms that Christians will continue to be under the authority of fallen earthly institutions and that, *insofar as these carry out their God-ordained purposes*, Christians are to obey them. But the instruction of the Pauline writings does not end there. They also recommend resistance to the powers, and witness to them.

The posture of Christians to the powers is, in part, defensive. In Ephesians 6:12-17, readers are told to put on the armor of God in order to withstand the "principalities and powers" (see vv.12-13). The armaments that are commended for combating the powers are, incidentally, *defensive* armaments. They are armaments designed to help Christ's followers resist the domination of the powers in order that they might remain free to serve God entirely. These include: the belt of truth, the breastplate of righteousness, shoes for one's feet (which make one free to proclaim the gospel of peace), the shield of faith, the helmet of salvation, and the sword of the Spirit (vv.14-17). Truthfulness, righteousness, courageousness in proclamation and peacemaking, faith, salvation, and God's spirit all protect us from the deception and domination of the powers, including fallen economic systems. These are the things that equip us to *resist*, but they are likewise the means through which our allegiance to God is nurtured and expressed.

Christ's followers are also to *bear witness* to God's intentions for creation before the powers (Eph 3:10). The powers need to be reminded of the purposes for which they were created: to meet the needs of humanity and to honor Christ (Col 1:16). This witnessing function requires us to engage and confront the powers, and to proclaim a bold witness to them. Our witness before the systems and institutions of this world will likely bring varying degrees of persecution. The powers do not want to be reminded that they are accountable to God, that their agendas must be left behind and subordinated to God's agenda. They especially cannot bear to be told that their efforts at self-preservation are idolatrous.

Essentially, the church is called, through the work of resistance and witness, to embody an alternative to the world's domination by the powers. As a people devoted to God and freed from the illusions and agendas of the powers, we are to embody God's love, and mercy, and order. We are to live according to God's reign. The Pauline writings challenge readers to let this be so in their lives and communities. One way Paul challenged his readers to embody an alternative to life under the powers was through the collection for the saints. During Paul's ministry, a famine afflicted large portions of Palestine. The Christians in Jerusalem were experiencing grinding hardship as a result, and needed their non-Palestinean Christian brothers and sisters to share with them, to be God's open hands in providing for their needs. That Paul saw such giving and receiving as a vital part of the Christian life is evident by his dedication to facilitating the collection. Paul risked his life to gather and deliver the collection to the saints in Jerusalem (Rom 15:27; 1 Cor 16:1-4; 2 Cor 9:1-5; Acts 20:22-24, Acts 21).

Paul knew that the collection for Jerusalem Christians was not only important because Christians in Jerusalem had empty bellies, but because the church was to embody an alternative to the economic systems of the world which promote self-aggrandizement and self-sufficiency. The non-Palestinean Christians were to be "of service to [the saints in Jerusalem] in material things" (Rom 15:27; see also 1 Cor 16:1-4, 2 Cor 9:1-5). This kind of action, inimical as it is to the agenda of the powers, constitutes resistance. It honors God's agenda, namely service and generosity toward others, above the agenda of fallen economic systems. From the perspective of the powers it is subversive and threatening. By honoring the values of God's kingdom rather than the values of fallen earthly institutions, the church embodies an alternative in this world, and the grip of the powers on humanity is weakened. Hendrik Berkhof, puts it this way:

> All resistance and every attack against the gods of this age will be unfruitful, unless the church herself *is* resistance and attack, unless she demonstrates in her life and fellowship how men can live freed from the Powers. We can only preach the manifold wisdom of God to Mammon if our lives display that we are joyfully freed from his clutches. To reject nationalism we must begin by no longer recognizing in our bosoms any difference between peoples. We shall only resist social injustice and the disintegration of community if justice and mercy prevail in our own common life and social differences have lost their power to divide. Clairvoyant and warning words and deeds aimed at state or nation are meaningful only in so far as they spring from a church whose inner life is itself her proclamation of God's manifold wisdom to the "Powers in the air."[14]

Jacques Ellul, in the quote that opened this chapter, describes *giving* as the ultimate expression of resistance to the power of Mammon. Through giving we use money for a purpose antithetical to the purposes the powers would choose. They desire it to be used for personal gain, for leverage against others, and for over-consumption. Yet giving takes money and uses it in an act of resistance against the powers. It subverts the agenda of the idol Mammon, which glories in our worship of self. In Ellul's parlance, giving *desacrilizes* money. It denies the sacredness of money, and demotes it to a mere instrument for meeting real needs.

Still, giving is not the only way in which we can resist and desacrilize the power of Mammon. There are myriad ways in which the system of global economics dominates and dehumanizes people all around the world. We should resist this domination and dehumanization in every way possible. This does not mean that we will strive to overthrow this economic system and replace it with another. But we *are* told to defend ourselves against its deception and manipulation, and to call this power to honor God's intentions for creation. We, the church, are called to embody an alternative way of relating to one another and to God's creation. As we resist and witness we not only find that the control which the powers once had over our lives languishes, but we awaken those around us to new possibilities. We help them to see the kingdom of God at work in the world, mending that which is broken and bringing glory to our Creator. We become like a city on a hill by which travelers can navigate through the oppressive night, and find there way to true freedom.

How does Christian resistance and witness to the powers look in the real world of global economics? To answer that question, let us turn to the next and last chapter of this book.

Chapter Seven

Decisions that Matter:
Living Humanly in the Global Economy

What needs to be seen is rather that the primary social structure through which the gospel works to change other structures is that of the Christian community. Here, within this community, men are rendered humble and changed in the way they behave not simply by a proclamation directed to their sense of guilt but also by genuine social relationships with other people who ask them about their obedience.

John Howard Yoder[1]

If our best chance for a global household of justice is the democratization of economy, this would require radical changes in the way we form, accumulate, and distribute capital; in our understanding of property, work, and consumption; and in our tax, insurance, welfare, and security systems. These changes can only be made politically. But where are the communities that could envision and bear such a politics? The church is not itself meant to be such a political community, but it is meant to be a community that makes such communities possible.

M. Douglas Meeks[2]

Introduction

On a recent sun-spilled autumn morning my husband walked into the kitchen and stated, in a winded but upbeat voice, "Doing the right thing is hard work!" He was taking a short break after hours of chopping wood for the woodstove we installed this year, to heat our house by burning wood rather than natural gas. It was late on a Saturday morning and I had already spent hours in the kitchen, doing things like wrapping green garden tomatoes in newspaper to preserve them for winter ripening and putting away an order of bulk food from the food co-op we use. I heartily concurred with his statement. But we agreed, standing in the slanted light of the kitchen window, that the hard work was well worth it.

In fact, we enjoyed a good morning. While my husband split the wood of a damaged tree that had to be cut down, my daughter played in the brisk light of a breezy fall morning, with dead leaves and "helicopters seeds" streaming down from the canopy of trees surrounding our house. She was working up some kind of one-girl theatrical production, as she usually does. Our two chickens hopped around the woodpile looking for insect treasures. One found a large bucket full of soil and nestled down to lay an egg. Wood smoke drifted through the air and the faded flowers of summer yielded the spotlight to flaming perennial mums and the deepening magenta of old hydrangea blooms.

In the kitchen I finished up my chores by mixing up a large batch of granola, made from my friend Karah's recipe which has become rather famous among our circle of friends. In our house, this hearty, healthy granola has almost completely replaced store-bought cereals, with all of their waste and advertising hype. As the kitchen filled with the warming scent of toasted nuts and grains, sweetened with honey from my next-door-neighbor's bees, I called my family in for a lunch of grilled-cheese sandwiches and cantaloupe from the local organic farm where we are community gardeners. It was not a bad way to spend a Saturday morning.

Several people I know are rethinking how they do consumption. Granted, we all must consume. We eat, we drink and bathe; we go places. We need shelter and warmth, and clothing. But for far too long we have been encouraged to consume in excess, to take whatever we can get and never be satisfied. We are seduced into believing we must have the latest fashions and the most advanced technology in order to be acceptable. We are encouraged to not think about the origins of what we consume, or about how they may someday run out. We are more and more distanced from the production of what we consume and have been encouraged, for some time, to go about our consumption blissfully ignorant of the processes and politics that go into our food, clothing, gasoline, and just about everything else.

Yet for many of us, the jig is up. We see the destructiveness and deception of the lifestyle commended to us by our consumer culture, and we know we are being used. We are waking up to the costs of irresponsible consumption, not only in dollars, but in peace and security, in healthy relationships, in soil and air quality, and in plain old contentment. We do not want to support the oppression of the weak in the way we spend our money, to use more than our fair share of the world's resources, or to ravage God's creation. We want to be informed. We want to know, for example, from whence came the food we eat, what was added to it, how the workers involved in its production were treated, and so on. The desire of many consumers to be knowledgeable and conscientious is reflected in the growing outcry against sweatshops and the demand for "full disclosure" by corporations, by the increasing demand for organic foods, by the surge in support for local farmers' markets, by the demand for sustainable energy and transportation alternatives, by the growth of the "fair trade" movement, and the like. It is heartening to see how many people truly care, and to see the effort many people are willing to put forth to learn about the origins and nature of what they consume. This is all the more significant because corporations are resisting transparency and accountability with a vengeance.

In this chapter, readers will be introduced to several people who are seeking to live their lives and to use their wealth in ways that are both honoring to God and loving to their global neighbors. All of the people highlighted in the following case studies are Christians whose actions have been motivated by their Christian faith. None of their economic choices are unique to Christians. Still, these particular people are all, in some way, responding with their lives to the Christian story and to the Christian communities where they have experienced that story and been drawn into it. Their lives exemplify God's emancipation, as they gradually experience the freedom from the powers that is bespoken in the New Testament. They demonstrate to me what it means to be free people.

William Stringfellow, in one of the most important books ever written about the powers,[3] bluntly states that the only human way to live in the era of the Fall is in resistance to the powers. Since the primary purpose of the powers is to subject people to themselves, to dehumanize us and render us less than the beings God created us to be by immobilizing our minds and misleading us, the most humanizing act is to refuse to submit. And, as Stringfellow says, whenever we say "no" to the powers we simultaneously say "yes" to God, acknowledging God's sovereignty over all created powers and reminding the powers that they are subject to God. Resistance to the powers is thus an act of worship, and an act of witness. It is how we make real our devotion to God and our submission to God's order. Our resistance is, then, redolent with hope and with joy! It is not just a matter of nay-saying the ways of the world and struggling against the tide of our culture, it is a way of holding up, like a brilliant pearl, something vastly more glorious and attractive. Our "no" to the powers is not merely a choice *against* something, but is much more a choice *for* something, for the justice, love, reconciliation, and fecundity of God's kingdom.

The friends featured in this chapter—they are people I know personally—have lives that emanate joy and beauty and creativity. They are not ascetics or Puritans. They are lovers; lovers of God and creation and humankind. Their lifestyle choices are not heroic, but simple acts. Yet such simple acts fill us with hope that we too can set our feet on a different path, one step at a time. As these words from historian Howard Zinn remind us, such acts are also what bring healing and transforming love into our world:

> To be hopeful in bad times is not just foolishly romantic. It
> is based on the fact that human history is a history not only
> of cruelty, but also of compassion, sacrifice, courage, kindness.

What we choose to emphasize in this complex history will determine our lives. If we see only the worst, it destroys our capacity to do something. If we remember those times and places—and there are so many—where people have behaved magnificently, this gives us the energy to act, and at least the possibility of sending this spinning top of a world in a different direction.

We don't have to engage in grand, heroic actions to participate in the process of change. Small acts, when multiplied by millions of people, can transform the world.[4]

Case Studies: Decisions that Matter

Brenda and Bill Jolliff: On Using a Food Cooperative. Bill and Brenda Jolliff both grew up on farms in the Midwest. Brenda's home sat on a relatively modest plot of land that marked one end of a well-traveled route between the farm and the conservative Mennonite church her family visited at least twice a week. The big farm of Bill's childhood dwarfed the uneasy farmhouse it surrounded, and produced crops like an outdoor factory. While Brenda attributes her passion for raising food to her upbringing on a farm, she carried into adulthood concerns that were not raised during her childhood. She doubts the word "organic" ever passed the lips of her parents in those years. Bill's misgivings about the state of contemporary farming run deep as Lake Erie. They stem in part from his awareness, stretching back into childhood, that the appealing country life of his grandparents had rapidly devolved into a way of life beset with unrelenting pressures and problems, and partially responsible for the demise of arable land in our country.

Early in their marriage, Brenda and Bill, who now have three children, sought to provide food for their family in ways that were more responsible than running down to the local grocery store for whatever they needed. They have been using food cooperatives ever since. Some of their earlier motivations for using food co-ops, such as cheaper prices on bulk food items, have lessened in the face of deeper inspirations. Today they are primarily concerned to live in a way that is more just and sustainable. The food co-op they presently use and have been using for eight years, Azure Standard, which is based in the Northwest, specializes in organic foods, smaller, independent food producers, and food of greater nutritional value than the typical, mass-marketed fare. Azure Standard sells a wide variety of food items, including several grains grown at Azure Farms, an organic farm located about 100 miles from the Jolliff's Oregon home.

Bill and Brenda share the conviction that the shift to industrialized, homogenized farming, where a few mammoth farms devoted to growing one or two crops in mass quantities replace dozens of smaller, diversified family farms, hurts farmers, communities, and the land. In communities where this shift takes place, people become less dependent on one another and more dependent on government subsidies, creditors, chemical companies, and transnational corporations. Soil depletion and soil loss occur at mind-blowing rates as a result of mass-production farming methods which resemble exploitation more than husbandry. Farmers are strapped with an often unmanageable amount of stress and financial pressure, and often die young, or foreclose. And the poor suffer. Not only does contemporary farming hurt poor families in the US, who have fewer and fewer opportunities than in previous generations to raise food and to live, to some degree, off of the land, but it hurts the world's poor. Farmers in the global south are increasingly pitted against US agribusiness. As in Haiti and Mexico mentioned earlier in this book, when markets in developing countries open up to US agriculture, small farmers cannot stay afloat due to the tidal wave of cheap imports. Not only are farmers forced out of business by the "dumping" into their countries of surplus, subsidized grains for less than the cost of production, but also by the ability of US farmers to raise and sell grain more cheaply than farmers using small-scale, sustainable farming practices.

The misgivings about contemporary farming shared by Brenda and Bill are interwoven with their faith and their commitment to Christian peacemaking. Obviously, they desire to help rather than hurt the poor. They are concerned about overconsuming when many people go hungry. Brenda states that her interest in providing food for her family in thoughtful, responsible ways is primarily motivated by her desire to live as she thinks Jesus would live in our day. "I always see

[Jesus] as intimately involved with the needs of the poor," she says, "and so I see it as my duty to be aware of and responsive to those needs as well." But Brenda and Bill are also unnerved by the connections between US agriculture, geopolitics, and oil. They know the amount of fossil fuel that goes into the typical American diet. Both the production and transportation of mass-marketed food burn an unfathomable amount of gasoline and diesel. (The average food item sitting on the American dinner table traveled 1,300 miles to get there!) When one tunes in to the connection between oil and lethal conflicts simmering around the globe, it is difficult to reconcile one's oil-reliant diet with one's commitment to Christian peacemaking.

Food cooperatives like Azure Standard give people the opportunity to buy more local foods which have not been trucked thousands of miles between the point of production and their kitchens. This dramatically lessens the amount of oil burned to put food on their plates. Brenda and Bill have become increasingly conscientious about the distance their food has traveled and are striving to buy more products originating in their home state or the states adjoining it. Checking labels to determine the origin of foods has become a part of shopping for the Jolliffs. Of course, they do this not only to lessen fossil fuel usage. They also want to support food producers from their own area, and thus to nurture their local community and economy.

Other advantages provided by food co-ops include the opportunity to buy foods in bulk, and to support organic farmers. Co-ops tend to offer many options for buying bulk foods such as dry goods, honey and spices, which both cuts down on packaging and makes frequent trips to the grocery store unnecessary. Since Brenda is convinced of the health advantages of grinding grains at home, she buys corn in 25 lb. quantities and mills it in a grinder. Azure Standard, like many food cooperatives, specializes in organic foods as well. This appeals to Bill and Brenda, who are trying to shift to a more organic diet. Like a growing contingent of Americans, the Jolliffs question the wisdom of heaping poisonous pesticides and herbicides on the food supply. What are the health consequences of such farming methods? How do these methods affect farmers who become reliant on transnational chemical companies? How is the richness of our farmland affected? How is the practice sustainable when pests and weeds are continually developing the capacity to resist the poisons, leading to the use of greater quantities of stronger pesticides and herbicides? How do the chemicals affect our water supply and wildlife? There are myriad questions being raised about our nation's chemically-dependent crops.

The Jolliff children, all in various stages of adolescence, do not always revel in their parents' healthful, ethical food choices. However, neither do they frequently complain. They were raised with less of the sugary, over-processed, over-packaged food abundant in the diet of American children, and without the constant barrage of television telling them they couldn't live without it. (Of course, they love junk food whenever they *do* get it.) Brenda gardens with a passion and cultivates as much food as she can on the small plot of land surrounding the Jolliff's home, which sits on a cul-de-sac in a non-pretentious, small-town neighborhood. Everything from corn and onions to tomatoes and plums is beckoned from the soil. The kids, who have always been homeschooled, give periodically to the local food bank where Brenda has, in the past, volunteered.

The Jolliffs will not tell you that buying organic food or food locally produced will necessarily save you money. In fact, eating "justly" can, at times, cost more in terms of dollar amount. Nonetheless, Brenda and Bill—who work as parttime nurse and literature professor, respectively—try to assess the cost of what they eat in less immediate terms, and to see conscientious food choices as far less costly in the long run. The long term cost-savings of taking care of our bodies and the natural world around us, as well as sharing with the poor and contributing to our local economies rather than to transnational corporations, far outweighs the price increases we may encounter by eating responsibly. This assessment runs contrary to capitalist sensibilities, but it coincides well with the value system of God's kingdom, which lifts up wholeness, justice, and peace. For the Jolliffs, it comes down to this. Though they are quick to emphasize that they have much further to go in bringing their food-purchasing and eating habits into line with their convictions about justice and simplicity, they are working at it, and keeping God's kingdom in view.

To learn more about food cooperatives, see the website of the National Cooperative Business Association (www.ncba.org/food.cfm), or call them at (202) 638-6222. There are three basic types of food co-ops: 1) co-op food buying clubs, 2) retail, store-front food co-ops, and 3) cooperative food warehouses.[5] The NCBA website is a good place to begin learning about the different types and how to use them. One can also find an online directory of retail food co-ops at: www.cooperativegrocer.com/coopdir.html. It is now possible to buy some organic, locally-produced foods at certain transnational grocery store chains, especially those which have "nutrition centers." For some, this may be the only way to get such foods. But food cooperatives and locally-owned markets have the advantage of cutting monolithic multinational grocery chains out of the picture, and thus lessening their control over the food supply. More importantly, they help our local economies become more vibrant and sustainable.

Jessica Phillips: On No-Sweat Clothing. Sweatshops were far from Jessica Phillip's mind as a girl, as she watched her Mexican-American mother tailor clothing in a small Houston, Texas shop. She remembers how her mother always provided for her needs, despite a limited income, not only adequately, but beautifully. It wasn't until college, when Jessica became more aware of international business practices, that a seed of concern about sweatshops took root in her mind and began to grow. She learned about the workers in the global south who toil without rights, for pennies an hour, to sew clothing for people like herself. Around that time, Walmart announced plans to construct a superstore in the town of her small college, and Jessica hit the streets with likeminded friends to oppose it. It was the beginning of a journey in resisting the powers that would take Jessica to places she hadn't dreamt of as a little girl playing among the ribbons and remnants of her mother's shop.

Jessica, a former elementary school teacher in Chicago and a full-time member of Christian Peacemaker Teams presently working in Grassy Narrows, Ontario, equates the work done in sweatshops to slave labor. When people work under deplorable sanitary and safety conditions, earn barely enough to survive, are forced to work 11 to 16 hours a day whether sick or well, and are threatened into silence about these conditions, it is akin to slavery. In cases where debt bondage is involved, it *is* slavery. The first and third chapters of this book provide vivid descriptions of sweatshops, so I need not repeat them here. As the image of the global sweatshop began to form in Jessica's mind, her habits began to change.

Deep concerns about materialism have been with Jessica since high school, when she awoke to the effects of overconsumption, including her own. At that time she made a concerted effort to buy less, and to opt out of the struggle to wear the "right" labels or conform to society's impossible standards of female beauty. Still she was not yet thinking about *what* she bought, or how she participated in oppression through her purchases. As the issue of sweatshops entered her consciousness, she knew she had to consider these questions. In college, she began buying the majority of her clothing from second-hand stores, and shared clothing with roommates in a sort of informal "clothing co-op." Now in her early thirties, Jessica continues to buy recycled clothing, and sews a portion of what she wears. When she cannot find something she needs secondhand, it poses a dilemma. Her low income does not allow her to buy a pair of shoes made in Europe, for example, where she knows workers were treated fairly. And though she can purchase some items from fair trade sources (more will be said on fair trade near the end of this chapter), many things, such as shoes, are not available via fair trade. In such cases, Jessica labors over her decisions and admits she struggles to make choices with which she is comfortable. To avoid such dilemmas, Jessica takes good care of what she has and repairs things that warrant repairing. In her opinion, there is no excuse for the rate at which things are thrown away in our country.

The reasons Jessica desires to "do justly" in her economic choices are not distinctly Christian. She wants to live in a way which does not harm others. She is moved by compassion, by a genuine concern for those who are vulnerable, and by a sense of connection with all who suffer. She shares these motivations with people of many faiths. Yet when Jessica traces her development as a person of compassion and conscience, she recognizes the vital role her Christian community played in this development. In significant ways, Jessica was shaped by the Christian community she was a part of during her years at Bethel College, a small college in Kansas. She still looks to this community for support and inspiration. Jessica's desires for justice were nurtured and developed in this environment where she saw Christians living out compassion and peacemaking. It was at Bethel that her Christian faith was born, and where she began to make connections between faith and a compassionate way of living and interacting in the world. "In college," Jessica explains, "I became aware of simple Christian lifestyles. This expanded what I was already feeling into the spiritual realm. It was no longer about not fitting in [to a destructive, materialistic culture], but about how Christians lived in a world where many suffer and a few of us live high on the hog."

Jessica harbors no illusions that she will single-handedly change the global economic system or eliminate sweatshops by refusing to buy sweatshop-made clothing. But she sees her actions as part of a much larger process which she has stepped into, and which stretches out toward the horizon far beyond her, a process of resistance. Whether or not her actions will help change the shape of global economics remains to be seen, but her actions are definitely changing her, and it is liberating.

Typically when people are presented with stories like the two preceding case studies, at least a few people respond with something like the following: "Wouldn't even greater poverty result if western consumers stopped buying products made in sweatshops?" "What would the people who are desperate enough to work in sweatshops do to survive without them?" Or, "wouldn't farmers in the global south be worse off if Americans started purchasing only organic produce from local farmers?" "What would happen to farmers overseas who depend on income from exports to the US?" And so on.

In a way these question trails are moving in the right direction. They get us thinking about the impact of our decisions on people around the world, whose lives are interlaced with ours in this age of global economics. Do our economic choices reverberate in the remote villages of Central America? Absolutely! Do our movements stir up the winds of change in our wake? Well, yes they do! Therefore, it is important that we be intentional about the *kinds* of changes we are promoting. Yet the questions above are also misleading. They imply that the only way we can truly help the poor is by supporting the status quo (i.e. the neoliberal model of development), and that radical changes in our lifestyles will necessarily have grave consequences in the global south. It is no wonder people have these fears, since on the level of governments and international financial institutions, liberalized trade is promoted as the sole route to development for "developing nations." Most Americans are fed a steady media diet telling them that the best way to help the poor is to buy lots of their stuff. The most powerful institutions of our time devote volcanic efforts to convincing us that the neoliberal economic model is the only hope for stability and prosperity the world over.

I have good news for you. *There are ways we can promote development in the global south that do not involve purchasing items made in sweatshops or buying food produced thousands of miles from our homes.* Indeed, it has already been argued that sweatshops and corporate agribusiness overseas do not, in the long—or short-run, prosper many in the global south who are not directly involved with transnational corporations or the political elite in their countries. And that is a meager percentage.

Those of us who desire to assist our global neighbors who lack the essentials for living are hesitant, however, to completely withdraw from global economic relationships. We don't want to simply keep our dollars in our local communities when they are desperately needed elsewhere. Fortunately, there are many ways in which funds given by the wealthy citizens of the world are being put to use to bring sustainable development and betterment to our neighbors in the global south. These efforts are known as "micro-development." I encourage people who make the shift from supporting transnational corporations to supporting their local economies, to simultaneously begin supporting micro-development work in the global south (see the Resources List at the back of this book for ideas). Our surplus is desperately needed to spark the processes of sustainable community and economic development in the global south. But these processes are best carried out by citizens of the global south.

Right Sharing of World Resources: On Promoting Development. This case study diverges from the two preceding ones, but with good reason. It features a group or organization rather than a family or individual, since, as Christians, we do not merely make decisions as individuals, or even families. We are part of the corporate life of the church, and often act corporately. I feature Right Sharing of World Resources (RSWR) in part because it is an example of what Christians have done to further economic justice *as a group*. It also exemplifies the alternatives available to Christians who desire to promote lasting development in poor countries. Together, we can do a lot to assist our neighbors around the world who have needs, and doing so does not require going to the mall. The work of RSWR empowers the poorest of the poor to develop their own communities and village economies, promotes better health among the poor with whom they work, and starts communities on the path of providing for each other's needs into the future. RSWR is one small group, yet they are representative of an approach to development being advanced by many people and organizations around the world to great effect. "Micro-development," as this approach is called, is helping communities, one-by-one, to transform themselves, putting their best skills and resources to use for the betterment of entire communities.

The work of Right Sharing of World Resources has two emphases, one being US-based education about global poverty and the need for simplicity, and the other being grant-making. In this study, I highlight the latter. RSWR is a project of the Religious Society of Friends (Quakers) in the United States, and is currently functioning as an independent organization. One paid staff person, General Secretary Roland Kreager, two consultants, and a small Board of Trustees administer the work of RSWR, which is funded by private donations. A friend of mine, Colin Saxton, is on the Board. Colin speaks of the integrity of this group of people, who share deep-rooted convictions about living simply and sustainably, and of how they inspire change in his life. Despite their size, they accomplish impressive goals.

Currently, RSWR makes grants[6] to small organizations (NGOs) in India, Nepal, Pakistan, Rwanda, Kenya, Republic of the Congo, and Sierra Leone. During 2002, they funded thirty-nine projects in these seven countries, distributing $160,000 in grants. They call these grants "seed money." Each one seeds a project that will, with proper nurturing, grow and provide fruit to seed additional projects. In this way the impact of RSWR's work extends far beyond the original groups receiving the grants. It is immeasurable. In poor villages all around the world, groups of individuals come together to spawn ideas for income-generation within their communities, and to share resources. Micro-development rests on the assumption that small organizations like this, which have a connection to and a vested interest in their communities, are the points at which sustainable development begins. Yet these groups, which may have abundant creativity, knowledge of the local context and access to local resources, often lack even the minute amounts of capital needed to turn their ideas into viable income-generating projects. This is where micro-development organizations come in.

By awarding grants to groups like this in the seven countries listed above, RSWR helps them to convert their ideas into reality. Their grants can be up to $US 5,000 per year, for a maximum of five years. By giving *small* grants, RSWR is able to "prime the pumps" of many different groups, and to encourage the groups' own initiative. RSWR supports small NGOs focused on income-generation and development of sustainable agricultural practices. Each year the Board reviews grant applications submitted by such NGOs, and funds as many as their limited budget allows, favoring those which: 1) are directed by women (the most vulnerable population in the places they work); 2) promote community-building; and 3) involve good stewardship of the environment.[7] Some of the NGOs with which RSWR works have developed small savings and credit operations to which grants are repaid, with interest, while others begin such operations as part of the project being funded by RSWR. The repaid money is then redistributed by the NGOs to other local groups similar to theirs. The seed money multiplies. RSWR, with the help of project partners in the sites where they work, provide support throughout the process. Accountability happens within the groups themselves, as the members are all responsible to one another, and dependent on one another. The groups with whom RSWR has worked have almost invariably repaid their loans and passed on their blessings; however, when a group has been incapable of repaying a loan, their "debt" has been graciously forgiven.

Below are two examples of RSWR's work in India:[8]

In Ariyalur District, Tamil Nadu (India), fifty women from self-help groups were enabled to participate in a one-year project with a $3,675 grant from RSWR. The women of the region struggle due to a lack of continuous and/or permanent employment. In this area cashew cultivation is predominant but, normally, collection of cashew fruit and separation of the nuts gives employment only in April, May and June of each year (off-peak agriculture time). Furthermore, cashew nuts are typically removed manually, and the shells and fruit are discarded in a way which pollutes the area. The aim of the RSWR-funded project is to develop regular employment in the cashew process in an eco-friendly manner.

There are three components of the project: 1) the self-help groups will get nut removal work in two ways: by contracting work with big farmers and business people, and by purchasing just-harvested cashew nuts. 2) The project will perform an experiment in cashew fruit jam production, and sell the product. (This type of jam is not a commercial product so far.) And 3) cashew shell oil will be extracted and sold for use in the paint industry in India. With these three efforts, all administered by the women themselves, they will get regular employment and waste material from cashew processing will be properly used. It is anticipated that in eight months a total of $815 can be generated (after the $.80/day wages for each of the women, at 6-8 hours of work/day). This profit can then be used to assist other self-help groups in starting up similar projects. For the desperately poor women of rural India with whom RSWR works, who earn wages around $.50/day during the agricultural season and nothing during the rest of the year, this program inspires great hope.

In the village of Ammapettai, Tiruchirapalli District, Tamil Nadu (India), forty women, 20 from each of two self-help groups, were enabled to participate in a one-year project with a $4,075 grant from RSWR. The two self-help groups own 25 acres at the edge of the village. In the first month, the land was reclaimed by plowing and building bunds [dividers in a field]. Flowers and herbal inter-cropping plants were then planted. After this, the women received training in compost production. When the flowers begin blooming, bees will be introduced and the women trained in bee-keeping. Once the herbs have grown sufficiently, the women will be trained in the production of herbal medicines.

The initial investment is $80 for each of the 40 women. This investment pays for the land preparation, water, purchase of bee hives, and the herb seedlings and saplings. This total investment, $3200, is the revolving fund amount. Beginning in the 4th month, the women began repaying their loan. Once production is at capacity, the total income per acre per year will be $1,500 ($1,325 from the sale of flowers, $10 from honey, $165 from the sale of herbs) for each woman. Expenses will be $945 for labor (5 workers for 9 months) and purchase of water. Net income will be $550 per month, $6,600 per year. This is about $28.50 per month for each woman.

In order for the project to be viable, a sidha doctor [practitioner of traditional medicine] will be needed to treat people. The doctor will assist the women in preparing medicines from the harvested herbs.

Projects such as these genuinely advance the wellbeing of the world's poorest citizens. The women participating in these projects not only receive needed income as a result, but they learn how to implement businesses and acquire a wide variety of practical skills. They are in charge of the projects. Over time, their businesses become more established and less vulnerable, their skills are honed, and their profits increase. Compare the effects of such micro-enterprises to the effects of sweatshop labor where women are treated like cattle, where they do repetitive labor from which they acquire few skills of practical value, where they work for factories which pollute their communities, where they can be fired for becoming pregnant or sick, where they produce something (products, such as clothing, for export) that is of no value to their local economies and communities, where they are forced to work an average of 14 hours a day,[9] where their bosses are from other countries and do not respect or understand their culture, and where their employers can pull out of their communities at a moment's notice, leaving them stranded. Clearly the micro-enterprise model is superior. Yet we have been told that the free movement of trade and capital across borders is the surest means to development for poor countries, and that the proliferation of factories producing for export (sweatshops) is the best that developing countries can hope for.

Roland Kreager of RSWR hopes for better. His rejoinder to the neoliberal model of development is this: to the degree that organizations promoting global economics ignore the social, political, cultural, and environmental costs of global economics, their model of development is bad for the developing world. "There is, however, a different vision of development," states Kreager optimistically. His is a vision of sharing, where we who have plenty support those who do not have enough, equipping them to begin to meet their own needs locally. It is a vision, Kreager describes, "in which communities are locally self-reliant and in which trade is based on local surpluses. Communities are interdependent, neither autonomous nor dependent."

Contact information for RSWR is listed in the Resource List at the back of this book. Other organizations doing micro-development work around the world include Heifer Project International and World Vision. They too can be found in the Resource List.

Jared and Jody Jones: On Being Community Gardeners. The jungled hills of northern Guatemala became home to Jared and Jody a year and a half after their marriage. Together they drank up the enveloping blue of the Central American sky, the woven rainbows of traditional Mayan dress, and the welcoming laughter emanating from mouths of silver-capped teeth. They worked their roots into new soil and began to learn how to do the jobs they'd been sent there to do. An international Christian community development organization called Food for the Hungry, which focuses on equipping families with sustainable and appropriate skills to meet their basic needs, employed Jared and Jody to educate the Ixil

Mayan people about household health techniques, gardening, nutrition, and grain storage. Motivating the organization's work is the desire to enable people to fulfill God's intentions for them as children of God. The experience proved enlightening for Jared and Jody, in part because they cultivated a rich understanding of the often-frustrating issues related to poverty in Central America. But also because they came to see the impact of US agribusiness in the global south from the other side of the cavernous gap separating the haves from the have-nots in the global economy. It was not an easy sight.

Jody and Jared lived three years in Guatemala. Now home in the States they carry the impact of those years with them every day, like a pouch of coins with which they have been entrusted, to spend with care and intention: the coin of awareness, the coin of compassion, the coin of responsibility. Sometimes it feels like a lot to hold. They told me a story about the farmers in the area where they worked. It is a memory that sits dormant at the back of their minds until they are standing in the grocery store considering the purchase of some imported produce. Then it creeps to the foreground like a tenacious vine.

The farmers in the highlands of Guatemala are subsistence farmers. They grow the corn, beans, squash, and seasonal vegetables, and raise the animals, that feed their families. Yet most years these provisions do not last. As a result, farmers are compelled to migrate for portions of each year to the coastal plantations devoted to growing huge quantities of sugar and coffee for export. On these plantations, migrant farmers can earn some extra cash, though pay is meager and living conditions are poor. The social costs of the migrations, however, devastate communities. Farmers often return to fragmented families, and bring with them alcoholism and disease. In light of this, one of the Jones' tasks in Guatemala was to help farmers get maximum production from their land, and to find local sources of needed cash in order to make migrations unnecessary.

One year during Jody and Jared's stay in Guatemala, a large broccoli company came to their area and gave the farmers a sweet-sounding offer. They convinced the farmers to plant broccoli for export and said they would buy the broccoli from them at the end of the season for a healthy profit, enough to feed their families throughout the year. The catch? To raise enough broccoli on their small plots of land, the farmers would have to plant far fewer of their usual subsistence crops. Still, to the farmers it sounded like a great idea, despite the risks. Though they would have to purchase more of their families' food, they would have enough money to avoid the yearly migration. So, they planted broccoli. The farmers, unfortunately, were gambling their families' livelihoods on a very unstable international market and, as it turned out, it was not a good year for broccoli. Demand was low. The company, which may have had good intentions for the farmers, ended up refusing to purchase most of the farmers' broccoli, stating it was not of superior quality. In the end, the farmers were left without cash, without enough corn, beans, and vegetables to feed their families throughout the year, and without the safety nets available to farmers in western nations (i.e. contracts and government subsidies). What they had in abundance were fields of rotting broccoli.

When Jody and Jared see imported produce in the market, they see the suffering of poor, small farmers like their friends in Guatemala. It's enough to make them lose their appetites. Though some small farmers in the global south may benefit by exporting produce, they wonder how many are taken advantage of. And this is not the only thing that comes to Jody and Jared's minds as they are gazing at the mounds of cheap peppers, beans, and bananas in the grocery store. They also think about the miles the food has traveled, the environmental costs of that transportation and refrigeration, and how climate change induced by carbon emissions is devastating farmers in places like Africa. They think about the impact of chemical pollution on fishermen who have lost their livelihoods as waters have become tainted with chemical run-off from industrial farms. They think about the fertile soil being lost due to the large-scale tilling done on those farms, soil spilling into rivers and streams, never to be recovered. It is becoming increasingly difficult for Jody and Jared to buy imported produce with a clear conscience.

Instead of supporting the model just described, the Jones' support a local organic farm where they have been community gardeners since their return from Guatemala in 1999. Community gardening, which is available to many people throughout the US, allows people to work on small family farms in exchange for produce. At Mustard Seed Farms, where Jared and Jody are community gardeners, adults pay $5 at the beginning of the summer season (May through October), and put in 12 hours of work throughout those months. In the winter season (November through April), they pay $2 each and work 3 hours. In exchange for these relatively small contributions, community gardeners have access to all the produce and berries they can use of the farm's bounty. Mustard Seed Farms grows a wide variety of vegetables during the summer, and keeps members supplied with winter veggies, as well as a variety of greenhouse offerings, during the winter. In the Fall, people from all over the community come to Mustard Seed Farms to buy their pumpkins and winter squashes, which include several heirloom varieties like a deep red Cinderella Pumpkin which looks as though it could morph into a stagecoach at any moment.

Fortunately, Mustard Seed Farms is just one of numerous family farms around the country which provide food for community gardeners in exchange for labor. Community gardening is a terrific way to get local, usually organic, produce inexpensively. However, as the Jones' have discovered, it is much more than that. It is an opportunity to feel connected with the land that gives them sustenance, through every seedling carefully planted in the ground, every row hoed, and every weed pulled. The farm is a thing of beauty, settled beneath sun-slanted hills and bursting with colorful possibilities. It is a pleasant place to go, and to take their young son.

For those who do not have the time to do labor on local farms, there are other ways to support local small farmers and to get one's hands on fresh local produce. One opportunity is through CSA farms (Community Supported Agriculture). CSA programs both assist small, family farms and connect non-farmers with food produced in their regions. CSA memberships work something like this: CSA members pay a lump sum to a particular farmer at the beginning of a season and, in exchange, receive so many "units" of produce from that farm.[10] These units are either delivered to or picked up by members throughout the season. CSA farms keep popping up all over the country, and now exist within geographical reach of most Americans. For those who can handle the outlay of money required of CSA members at the start of a season, and who do not desire to contribute labor to a farm, CSA membership is a great opportunity.

Last year was the first in which Jared and Jody, both teachers, made a concerted effort, even during winter, to eat only fresh produce they had gotten from the farm, or other in-season fresh fruit and vegetables produced within a reasonable distance of their home. They allowed exceptions for special occasions like holidays. Though the Jones' found this challenging at times, it was also enriching. They could finally understand the enthusiasm children had experienced long-ago when they received one whole orange for Christmas, and little else. How sweet that rare winter fruit must have tasted! In the dead of winter they do begin to miss the summer bounty they enjoyed months earlier. But they know it will return. Most of the time they fail to see the wait as a huge sacrifice. While their fellow Americans are slicing up anemic-looking imported tomatoes with the texture of mashed potatoes, grown for transportability and ripened with a blowtorch, the Jones' look forward to eating richly-colored, juicy, vine-ripened beauties from the farm which explode with flavor in one's mouth. The same can be said for the strawberries the farm provides, which taste so superior to the banal, mammoth berries sold in the stores that one wonders how anyone gets away with selling the store-bought berries. According to the Jones', fresh, in-season, picked-when-ripe produce is worth the wait.

Aside from all the benefits Jody and Jared reap as community gardeners, they feel that supporting local, small farmers is a wise investment in the future. They worry about the decline of small-scale farming in the US, and about what it will cost in the long run. "Small farmers had to know their land well to make it produce," explains Jody. "They had to know the micro-climates on their acreage leading to much more diversity in the variety [of produce] . . . They had to know how to keep the soil fertile with the by-products of their production (organic material). We fear that as the small farmer leaves his land, that specific knowledge is lost. The loss is a problem because somehow or other the day is going to come when it will no longer be feasible to ship food all over the planet, and when it does, who will be the ones who know how to get local land to produce enough to feed the community? . . . By being a part of a community farm, we feel we are doing something to preserve knowledge of how to feed our area, and keeping a small family in the farming business."

If you, like the Jones', are interested in supporting small farms in your area, or if you would like to learn more about CSA, see the website of the Alternative Farming Systems Information Center at: www.nal.usda.gov/afsic/csa. Click on "database" for a directory of CSA farms in your area.

Jerry and Molly Mechtenberg-Berrigan: On Living Sustainably in Community. Jerry and Molly know about community. When Jerry came into the world, he was born to a community as much as to a family. The people of Jonah House, the community his parents helped found in Baltimore, Maryland, played an immense role in his upbringing until the time he ventured off to college. A year after completing college, Jerry, along with Molly, began living and working at a Catholic Worker house, and continued with the Catholic Worker community until their arrival at Anathoth Farm in northwestern Wisconsin in January 2002. For all the challenges and sacrifices of sharing life with a community, it is something they plan to continue. Spending much time with them, one gets the impression they are on to something. It is something the rest of us could stand to learn, something about the vision Jesus had for his followers, something about being God's family.

When I arrived as a visitor to Anathoth Farm in November 2002, it was a brisk, starry night. The two houses visible from the gravel driveway looked solid and simple, built tall with natural wood siding and metal roofs and many south-facing windows which reflected the moon's light. They perched on grassy hills. Smoke lifted from the chimney of the Common House, where I was to stay, and clothing nodded on the lines out front. I could see the ghostly outlines of two large greenhouses standing in the nearly two-acre garden just south of the buildings. Huge stacks of wood were visible on either side of the Common House, which stood against a grove of hardwood trees clutching the last of their fall leaves. Even in the dark I could tell this place was unique.

Anathoth Farm is a community of ten people who share the farm and its work, while maintaining outside, part-time jobs. Together they hold a commitment to nonviolence and a commitment to living sustainably, in a manner that requires fewer of the world's resources and does less damage to the environment. Sustainable technologies abound in the four permanent homes on the farm, all of which were constructed or reconstructed by the owners for less than $15,000, using many recycled materials. The warmth and beauty of the small, simple homes are striking. There are little cubbyholes and nooks around every corner, as well as various openings between rooms to circulate heat. Lofts are used to maximize space and circulation, giving a tree-house feel to the interiors. Books and musical instruments are in ample supply. Artwork adorns the walls. Containers of bulk foods are everywhere— colorful pastas and beans, and grains of every persuasion: oats, rice, quinoa.

The first house built on the farm was constructed largely of donated logs from a 1892-era log home, and is filled with curiosities, such as a cryptic-looking door in the kitchen floor which leads to the basement and attached greenhouse. In the greenhouse one finds a solar-heated and solar-pumped shower, as well as a greywater system that recycles water from the kitchen sink for use in the garden. In this house, water is also circulated through copper coils atop the woodstove to provide hot water during colder months. Natural wood predominates in the construction of the homes, which are all flooded with natural light through the many windows. Thick, window-blanket blinds keep out the cold on cloudy days and nights. Four of the five homes on the farm have composting toilets, and only two have running water. All the buildings on the farm are wood-heated. The Common House has the one non-solar water heater on the farm. It is heated with wood.

The goal of maximizing renewable resources and lessening reliance on nonrenewable ones motivates the community's use of sustainable technologies. One of the homes on the property is completely off-grid. It uses solar electricity, along with a battery system to store power for cloudy days. This particular house also features a half-inside/half-outside refrigerator which, during the depths of winter, is cooled solely by the frigid Wisconsin temperatures. Throughout the rest of the year, it is the one appliance in the house that runs on propane. The homes are all built tightly enough to make heating with a single woodstove adequate, especially since the buildings are skirted with hay bales in the fall for additional winter insulation.

Fifteen acres of the community's 57-acre property produce hay. Not only do the bales provide warmth, but a thick layer of hay is spread over the huge garden each year for mulch and fertilization. It creates an ideal environment for the microorganisms essential to organic gardening. A third of the Anathoth property is wooded. During the winters, community members harvest maple sap for syrup from the trees in their woods, and sell the syrup to help pay property taxes. They stoke a huge fire under a fairytale-sized black kettle and boil down the gallons of collected sap until it turns to rich, marvelous syrup for canning. The remaining two acres of the farm are devoted to the garden. Those acres, upon which sit the two large greenhouses, provide most of the produce consumed on the farm. Innovative usage of the greenhouses allows them to harvest greens throughout the winter, and tomatoes well into the colder months. Community members nurture those two acres with great care, and the land rewards them lavishly.

The way of life at Anathoth immediately appealed to Jerry when he completed an internship on the farm in 1995. It drew him and Molly as a couple to leave the urban-centered lives they had led since childhood in order to join the community in January 2002. The members of Anathoth all strive to live light on the land. For Molly and Jerry, this desire directly connects with their faith in Christ, and their desire to walk in the way Jesus led, which in their estimation, has a lot to do with sharing and caring for the needs of one's neighbors. Though they are ministering to the needy less directly on the farm than in their Catholic Worker days, when they fed and offered hospitality to the homeless in the inner-city, they see the value of the radical simplicity practiced on the farm. Not only does it allow them to "share" the world's resources rather than hoarding them, but it allows community members to live below taxable income, and in so doing, to avoid paying for the weapons of war. Molly and Jerry harbor hopes that in the future they will find ways to connect with the poor more directly while living on the farm.

Resistance to violence and to the patterns of behavior that precipitate violence, are the main focuses of the Anathoth community. Molly works for the non-profit organization based at Anathoth Farm, Nukewatch, a watchdog group for the nuclear industry. She carries out research related to nuclear weapons manufacturing and proliferation, and writes articles. Jerry's concerns about these issues are deeply ingrained in his life and character. As the son of activist Philip Berrigan, who had spent about eleven years in prison for acts of civil disobedience against the US military before his death in late 2002, Jerry is familiar with our country's love affair with violence. The folks at Anathoth are part of a a deep stream of nonviolent resistance flowing consistently through the history of our country.

One way Jerry and Molly, as well as their fellow community members, resist violence is by striving to live according to alternative economics. The word "economics" which, in its original sense, implies caring for the needs of a household, describes well the manner of living at Anathoth. As a community, they want to live in a way that would allow *all* members of the human household to thrive. It is a matter of striving to not use more than their fair share. It is about acknowledging that the world and its bounty do not belong to us, but are temporarily entrusted to our care. It is living in a spirit of sharing and stewardship. They view this lifestyle as inextricable from their work of nonviolence, not only because it allows them to avoid paying war taxes, but because the inequitable distribution of resources in our world is a key precipitator of violence and unrest. The fact that Americans comprise only 6% of the world's population and use 30% of the world's resources, and are behooved to fight on many fronts to protect this position of privilege, leads to war. All around the world, people are fighting over resources, whether they be oil, water, or land. Molly states gravely her opinion that greed is one of the biggest problems plaguing our world. "Yet there's plenty for everybody," she continues. "It's just a matter of people opening their hearts and sharing a little bit." She and Jerry view the acquisitiveness bred into us by a consumer culture as starkly opposed to Jesus' teachings. For them, living at Anathoth helps them to better live the way Jesus desires for his followers. "Living here," continues Molly, "and being careful with our resources and realizing that they're not ours, and the earth isn't ours to exploit, is so important." Still, she is constantly humbled by the fact of her privilege, and the amount of progress she has to make. She fears becoming complacent, and desires most of all that she continue to be challenged to give more, to serve more.

When asked what motivates his lifestyle choices, Jerry speaks both of responsibility and of the example of Christ. Integral to his worldview is the idea that we are all responsible for others, that "God has given us responsibility for each other and for ourselves." In light of this, he finds it impossible to view the needs of people across the world with indifference. "Someone sleeping on the street over there *is* my problem," he explains. This sensitivity compels him to question his own habits and actions and to try to live in a way that helps rather than harms others. Community living lies at the center of his and Molly's vision of how this is done. "It is interesting that one of the first things Jesus did was to gather a community," Jerry says. Community living makes it possible for Jesus' followers to embody his ideas about wealth, and about caring for each others' needs as the family of God. "When you share and give, you will *always* have what you need," Molly remarks, summarizing the essence of real community.

Jerry describes this dynamic as the "economics of grace." As evidence of grace economics, he cites the home in which they live. Members of the Anathoth Community all build their own houses. When Jerry and Molly arrived at Anathoth, they had, obviously, not yet built a home on the farm. So they dove into fixing up a small trailer on the property, with help from other community members, in order to have a place to call their own. As the work progressed, however, it became apparent that the dank little trailer had leaks in every corner and joint, and was not suitable for long-term habitation. They wondered where they would live. But just in time, the brother of one of the community members donated a good, two-bedroom mobile home to the farm. It was given to Jerry and Molly. In this way, their needs have been met, and they extend to others the same generosity that has been extended to them. At times the demands of hospitality on the farm are arduous. Student groups come on "alternative Spring Breaks" a couple times a year, and other groups, both small and large, visit frequently. Community members at times feel overwhelmed, providing talks and meals to guests in addition to the demands of their jobs, and their many chores. Yet they always accommodate. As Jerry explains: "We have been so blessed. We feel it is our duty to share what we have, even if we feel stretched at times."

Though the families at Anathoth Farm all live in separate houses and own their own cars, they share several things in common, such as a tractor, work truck, tools, and a washing machine. And the houses on the farm are part of a land trust; they are not privately owned. Sharing land and possessions, as well as the work of the farm, makes possible the simplicity, sustainability, and generosity one witnesses at Anathoth. Could this be how Jesus envisioned his followers living, when he told them to forgo self-sufficiency for radical generosity? Molly and Jerry would answer with a resounding "Yes." Jesus' vision of a new community, one that would support one another and see that one another's needs were met, makes sense of Jesus' teachings about such things as wealth. Yet Western Christians, who tend toward stubborn individualism, frequently ignore the first step—community—and thus dismiss Jesus' teachings as impractical.

Molly and Jerry do not diminish the difficulties of communal living, which Molly describes as the "best and worst of human relationships." According to Jerry, every community he knows closely has suffered major rifts in relationships at some point. Nevertheless, he and Molly see something profoundly right about the helpfulness and cooperation that happens in community. Especially when community events take place, or at times of harvest and syrup preparation, people come together in a way that is not only productive, but life-giving for those involved. The intimacy of relationships experienced in community is a familial sort of intimacy, which can be a blessing and a curse. But in a society where many feel lonely and disconnected, it is powerful. Jerry, who works in log-home restoration with two other members of Anathoth, speaks of the high points in community, times when "we all pull each other toward the good . . . It kind of keeps you honest," he says, "and keeps you doing the work that needs to be done, that you couldn't do alone." This kind of connectedness and common vision sustains the Anathoth community through hard times. "It's really nice to know there are people right down the way," Molly adds. "I can just go in their house. You never even knock on the doors here, you just walk in." For her, the greatest thing about life at Anathoth is this "feeling of community, and having good times with the people, either individually or collectively . . . We've had some really memorable times." A highlight for Jerry has been bonfires where everyone shows up and pulls out their instruments to play.

Jerry and Molly do not know at present whether they will build a house on the farm and spend a large portion of their lives there. At times, Molly feels drawn back to the city, and to the model of the Catholic Worker to which she feels a strong affinity. Other times, the amount of work required to live as they do weighs heavily on their shoulders. It requires them to do things the rest of us never have to consider, such as building a fire under the water heater an hour before one can take a warm shower, or heating a large pot of water on the stove before one can wash the dishes, or having to haul water to one's house. But whether or not they make the changes necessary to become long-term members of the Anathoth community, the community is changing them. Among other things, they are learning new ways of envisioning economics, and are thinking about the resources they use. They will carry these ideas wherever they go.

In the meantime, the things they sacrifice to live at Anathoth are given in exchange for the incredible blessings of rich, deep relationships, stewardship of and connectedness to the natural world, and living justly. "Looking at our lives," Jerry says, "I don't see deprivation at all. I see abundance."

There are many *more* things one could do to "live humanly" in the global economy than the actions highlighted above. Indeed, the people featured in this chapter are doing many more exciting things in this regard than what I've mentioned. My intention in this chapter was not to provide a comprehensive list of possible decisions one can make or actions one can take in order to bring one's economic choices into line with the values held up in scripture. Instead, I have chosen to introduce readers to people who are striving to bring those things into alignment in their lives. As relational beings, we humans tend to be inspired and shaped by people more than by abstract concepts. You've just met some of the people who have inspired and shaped me.

Fair Trade

Before concluding, I want to say a bit about fair trade, or "alternative trade," since it only received passing mention above. Fair trade is a promising, growing movement that is improving the lives of workers and farmers in the global south and the US, while making their products available for purchase at fair prices. Companies and organizations which sell fair trade products support living wages and safe, healthy conditions for workers in the developing world. According to the Fair Trade Federation, the following criteria are used in determining whether a small business qualifies for the label "fair trade." They must be:[11]

- paying a fair wage in the local context[12]
- offering employees opportunities for advancement
- providing equal employment opportunities for all people, particularly the most disadvantaged
- engaging in environmentally sustainable practices
- being open to public accountability
- building long-term trade relationships
- providing healthy and safe working conditions within the local context
- providing financial and technical assistance to producers whenever possible.

Fair trade companies and organizations, all of which conform to these criteria, are listed in the Resource List at the back of this book. Among those listed are nonprofit organizations that primarily sell craft items produced in the global south, items which are especially useful for gift-giving occasions. But one will also find a few for-profit companies that sell fairly-traded clothing, some of which is produced in developing countries, and some in the United States. Available via many avenues is fair trade coffee. Buying fair trade coffee is tremendously important, especially in light of the devastation looming over the world's coffee producers after the drop in global coffee prices (See Chapter Three). Our purchasing fairly-traded coffee instead of the usual brands could mean the difference between starvation and survival for hundreds of thousands of coffee farmers. In the case of products like coffee and tea, fair trade products are distinguishable by the black and white "Fair Trade Certified" label. Many other fair trade products are not so clearly labeled. However, purchasing items from fair trade stores and organizations which are members of the Fair Trade Federation, or the International Federation for Alternative Trade, guarantees that one is supporting truly fair and sustainable trade.

Conclusion

As I conclude this book, I am struck by how much has happened since it was begun. Today the US government is hurling our country into a "war on terror," with apparent aspirations to outdo the Cold War. A thorough restructuring of the federal government has just been approved under the name of "Homeland Security." Terror attacks against Westerners increase in frequency every day, all over the world. The US economy limps along in recession, as the length of unemployment lines grows. Protest against the neoliberal economic agenda builds up volcanic pressure in such places as Argentina and Venezuela. And people in sub-Saharan Africa face disease and famine like another broken record. We find ourselves in very uncertain times. Part of us senses we are on the cusp of some major shifts in the course of history, yet we cannot make out the outline of what those shifts will be. The signs of the times point to patterns and eventualities we cannot bear to face. Yet the signs of God's kingdom dawning around us, visible in the healing, restoring, resisting, self-sacrificing work of our modern-day saints, at times raise our hope to the point of boiling over. So it has been for millennia. So it is to live in the era of the Fall with eyes open to God's presence in and sovereignty over all of creation. In the cross and resurrection of Jesus, the powers were exposed, and we were set free from bondage to them, set free from the illusion of their sovereignty, set free from their domination over us. Let us receive our freedom.

More boldly than ever, the powers of Mammon and militarism are asserting their false claims on us. We are told our security depends on our devotion to these gods, that all hell will break loose if we do not build ever-higher walls around our wealth and resources, and if we do not gird ourselves with ever-more destructive weapons and security systems. In such a climate, our "no" must be resoundingly firm and clear. But our "no" is like golden, sweet honey on our lips. It fills the air like the stirring rise of a symphony. When our "no" is born out of our deep convictions about God's sovereignty, and redemptive purposes, and love for all humanity, it is a booming "yes" to the kingdom of God. Our "no" is worship, as true as the "no" of the biblical Daniel and his intransigent young friends.

So let us say "no" to the idolatry of the market that says we need beautiful things more than we need justice in our world. Let us say "no" to a soul-consuming desire for *more* to eat, *more* to wear, *more* with which to amuse ourselves, *more* resources to consume. So many of the things proffered to us on a daily basis have been swiped from under the feet of the world's poor, who are violently pushed aside and left with little for themselves. Let us say "no" to these things, and "yes" to a God who shares their burdens. *The earth is the Lord's and all the things in it.* "Yes!," we'll say. Yes.

Notes

Chapter One

Bought and Sold: The Global Economy Introduced

1 Williams, Dar "Bought and Sold", *End of the Summer*, Razor and Tie Entertainment, 1997.

2 What I call the "global justice movement" is often wrongly titled the "anti-globalization movement". Most of the people represented in the movement do not oppose globalization as a whole. They do not, for example, oppose globalizing access to communication or information technology, nor do they oppose the interchange of world cultures, or even international trade. It is the global economy as it now stands that they oppose, because they find it empowers corporations while disempowering the poor and hurting the environment. For this reason, I will refer to the movement as the "global justice movement" rather than the "anti-globalization movement".

3 Greider (1997) 334.

4 Jacobs, Michael (2001).

5 Gray, John (1998) 55.

6 Nayyar (1997) 15f. As Nayyar explains, "World exports increased from $61 billion in 1950 to $315 billion in 1970 and $3447 billion in 1990" (p.15).

7 See Nayyar (1997) 27-28, and Black (1999) 100.

8 Phrase coined by John Gray (1998) 57.

9   Gray (1998) 62.

10   Roddick (2001) 199.

11   Witness for Peace (2001a) 7.

12   Witness for Peace (2001a) 7.

13   WTO representatives are appointed by government officials.

14   "Under the proposed rules [of the WTO], the recommendations of the review panel are automatically adopted by the WTO sixty days after presentation unless there is a *unanimous* vote of WTO members to reject them. This means that over 100 countries, including the country that won the decision, must vote against a panel decision to overturn it—rendering the appeals process virtually meaningless" (Korton [1995] 176).

15   For example, US environmental laws have come under attack by the WTO. A US law protecting dolphins was overturned by the WTO (called GATT at the time) in the early 90's, and another law protecting sea turtles was overturned by the WTO in 1998. Similarly, the US Clean Air Act was challenged by Venezuela before the WTO and had to be softened. For more information, see various articles on the Public Citizen website at: http://www.citizen.org.

16   Public Citizen (2001).

17   Gray, John (1998) 62-63.

18   Because of the unpopularity of the IMF's Structural Adjustment Programs, the IMF chose to change the name of their "Structural Adjustment Facility" to the "Poverty Reduction Strategy Program." Their policies, however, remain the same.

19   Barber (1995) 81.

20   Korten, David (1995) 38.

21   See England (1997) for a critique of GNP as a measure of progress, and for a proposed alternative way of measuring income and wellbeing.

22   Mansfield (1994) 240-241.

23   For more information on the globalization of the arms trade, see the Campaign Against Arms Trade website (www.caat.org.uk).

24   Hostetler, Lynen, and Raphaelidis (2001) 6.

25   Witness for Peace (2001) 2.

26   Parker (2002) 24.

27 Statistics from economist Jeff Gates, cited in Roddick (2001) 186.

28 Statistics from economist Jeff Gates, cited in Roddick (2001) 186.

29 Witness for Peace (2001) 2.

30 Statistics from economist Jeff Gates, cited in Roddick (2001) 210.

31 Okay, Monopoly experts, try to overlook the fact that this would not leave any money in the bank.

32 Economist staff (2000).

33 Rosenberg, Tina (2002) 30.

34 For further reading see: Sanders (1993), Worster (1993), Hawken (1994), Rowell (1996), Gorringe (1999), Shiva (1999), Hawken, Lovins, and Lovins (2000), Freyfogle (2001), Mander (2001), Hessel and Rasmussen (2001), Lofdahl (2002), Tabb (2002), Kingsolver (2002), Jensen (2002), Brown (2001, 2003), and the many essays of Wendell Berry. See Bibliography for bibliographical information.

35 The "tax-holidays" granted to TNCs are usually limited in time from 5-10 years. But most corporations either flee at the end of the tax-holiday, close and open up shop under a new name, or get an extension of their tax exemption status (Klein [1999] 209).

36 In the Philippines, companies must apply for a waiver from the minimum wage requirement. In many countries, this step is not even necessary (Klein [1999] 211). In 1999, there were 52 EPZs in the Philippines; 124 in China. The International Labor Organization estimated at that time that there were 850 EPZs operating in the world, an estimate that was likely conservative (p.205).

37 Klein (1999) 205.

38 During the year 1999, at least 140 trade unionists from 113 countries were assassinated, "disappeared," or committed suicide after receiving death threats, and nearly 3,000 were arrested, according to a study by the International Confederation of Free Trade Unions. Another 700 trade unionists received death threats (ICFTU [2000]).

39 Information for this section was gleaned from a report by the National Labor Committee (2001a) and from a New York Times article dating February 6, 2001. Both reports were based on US Department of Labor records.

40 Though the factory took Social Security deductions from the workers' pay, they never actually paid into Social Security for the workers.

41 In March of 2001, the Korean owner of the Daewoosa factory, Lee Kil-soo, was arrested by FBI agents for violations of slavery statutes. Also, with the help of the Vietnamese-American community, 170 of the Vietnamese workers from Daewoosa were flown to the US to testify in the investigation against Daewoosa (San Jose Mercury News, April 3, 2001). In February, 2003, he was found guilty of "human traffickking" and faces 20 years imprisonment for each of the 11 counts for which he was convicted.

42 Gray, John (1998) 84.

43 For more on the effects of structural adjustments, see Chapter 3. Also, see Gorringe (1999) 61-76.

44 See http://poverty.worldbank.org/library/subtopic.php?topic=4351&sub=8602.

45 United Nations Development Program, *Human Development Report* (1998, 2000). Data shows a significant decrease in per capita income for South Asia, South-East Asia and Pacific Region, Latin America/ Caribbean, and Sub-Saharan Africa over the past twenty years.

46 Parker (2002) 24.

47 Korten (1995) 49.

48 Information on Haiti's rice industry was gleaned from Aristide (2000) 11-12. For a summary of the devastating consequences of structural adjustments in other areas of the Caribbean under the Caribbean Basin Initiative, see Black (1999) 108-109.

49 US rice growers came from the US government (Aristide [2000] 12).

50 Bello (1999) 45-50, 61-63.

51 In the following summary of the debt crisis I am indebted to the excellent summary by Hostetler, Lynen, and Raphaelidis (2001) 5-6.

52 Hostetler, Lynen, and Raphaelidis (2001) 7.

53 For information, see their website at www.jubilee2000uk.org.

54 In early 2002, a bipartisan bill entitled the "Debt Relief Enhancement Act of 2002" was introduced in the Congress and Senate. If the act passed, it would direct the US Treasury to pressure the World Bank, IMF, and regional development banks to carry

out substantial debt relief to poor countries. The legislation also authorizes a US contribution of $43 million per year to assist regional development banks which cancel debts. Commendably, the Senate version of the bill opposes some of the structural adjustment conditions placed on previous debt relief plans (www.thirdway.com/wv/article.asp?a_ID=85). Overall, passage of the Debt Relief Enhancement Act would be a significant step forward.

55 See, for example, Black (1999) 100.

56 Kaufman and Gonzalez (2001).

57 Kaufman and Gonzalez (2001).

58 Though this is viewed as a hardship by Gap, and runs counter to capitalist sensibilities, it should be noted that the Gap CEO earned a $660 million salary in 1995 alone. By pointing out the difficulty of one company trying to effect change I am not implying that the difficulty and sacrifices are too much to ask. From an ethical standpoint, they are imperative. And, as one can see, companies like Gap could afford the costs of people-centered business practices if priorities were different.

59 Kaufman and Gonzalez (2001).

60 See http://www.us.ilo.org for information on the International Labor Organization, a specialized, independent agency of the United Nations.

61 NAFTA contains a "labor side agreement" that allows workers under the agreement to file complaints when their government is not enforcing its own labor laws. However, the agreement is virtually useless. First of all, there are no serious mechanisms in place to provide remedies for worker's concerns. Furthermore, the agreement does not provide a way for workers to file complaints against corporations or factories who are abusing human rights, or to address the acute problem of weak national labor laws (Maquila Solidarity Network, April 2001).

62 Simply setting standards, such as labor and environmental standards, without reconfiguring the system at its foundations, is counterproductive. As one campaigner against neoliberal economics, Asbjørn Wahl, explains: "To liberalise and deregulate

the markets and then think that you can protect the workers by introducing formal labour standards, is like opening the floodgates of the regulated waterfall and then forbidding the water to fall."

63 Understanding the powers to include earthly rulers and dominions (as Col 1:15-16 states) does not mean one denies *spiritual* powers. Rather, such an understanding recognizes the integral unity between God-denying earthly structures and the demonic powers underpinning them. See Chapter Six.

64 Greider (1997) 388.

Chapter Two

Portraits of Global Economics from the Global North

1 Marx, Karl and Friedrich Engels (1967) *The Communist Manifesto*, trans. A. J. P. Taylor (Middlesex, England: Penguin Books) 83-84.

2 Quoted in *The Nation* (Bangkok), Sept 7, 1993.

3 Nader 1993: 5.

4 Witness for Peace (2001:) 7. Statistics for period from 1994 to 2000.

5 "Fast-track" was developed in 1974, during the Nixon administration, and has been used only five times since. Congress granted President Clinton fast-track authority during the NAFTA negotiations, authority which expired in 1994. In Summer 2002, President Bush, Jr was granted fast-track authority by Congress for negotiating the FTAA, the Free Trade Agreement of the Americas, which would expand the NAFTA free trade zone to encompass almost all of Central and South America and the Caribbean Basin.

6 NAFTA, and the proposed FTAA agreement, are so focused on investor protections and provisions some have suggested they be called "investor agreements" not trade agreements. For more information on NAFTA's Chapter 11 investor protections, see Public Citizen (2001).

7   Currently, in a case against the State of California, the Canadian corporation Methanex is asking for compensation of nearly $1 billion for California's decision to phase out of use a gasoline additive called MTBE, which has contaminated ground and surface water in California. At the time of this publication, a determination has not been made in the case. (Public Citizen 2001, 2004a).

8   Public Citizen 2004b.

9   Public Citizen 2004b.

10 Gribskov 2001.

11 For more on the conflict in Chiapas, see Chapter Three.

12 Gribskov 2001: 14.

13 Not all anarchist groups espouse violence. The ones who do, unfortunately, steal the show.

14 To their credit, the Clinton Administration did, in Seattle, begin to push for greater openness by the WTO. They proposed that the WTO make more documents public, and that they allow interest groups to fill briefs in dispute. Non-US delegates to Seattle, and especially delegates from the EU, opposed such proposals (Paulson, *Seattle Post-Intelligencer*, Dec 3, 1999). Unfortunately, the push for greater WTO openness has been stymied.

15 Sunde, *Seattle Post-Intelligencer*, Dec 1, 1999. According to the National Lawyers Guild, which had 150 legal observers present at the protests, the Seattle police used excessive force. Besides using rubber bullets on occasion, the police were observed, among other things, beating a television cameraman and chasing down a woman to douse her with pepper spray (Sunde, Dec 1, 1999).

16 Sunde, *Seattle Post-Intelligencer*, Dec 1, 1999.

17 Sunde, *Seattle Post-Intelligencer*, Dec 2, 1999.

18 Sunde, *Seattle Post-Intelligencer*, Dec 2, 1999.

19 *Seattle Post-Intelligencer* (staff writers), Dec 3, 1999.

20 *Seattle Post-Intelligencer* (staff writers), Dec 4, 1999.

21 *Seattle Post-Intelligencer* (staff writers), Dec 3, 1999.

22 *Business World* (Philippines), Dec 26, 2000.

23 The following information was garnered from Vidal and Connolly, *The Guardian* (London), Sept 27, 2000.

24 Vidal and Connolly, *The Guardian* (London), Sept 27, 2000.

25 Huggler, *The Independent* (London), Oct 1, 2000.

26 Lloyd, *Financial Times* (London), Feb 24, 2001.

27 de Guy, *Financial Times* (London), Jan 24, 2001.

28 de Guy, *Financial Times* (London), Jan 24, 2001.

29 *The Toronto Star* (staff writers), Feb 10, 2001.

30 Pandora News Service, in *The Independent* (London), Jan 31, 2001.

31 Reuters, Apr 19, 2001.

32 Cohen, Tom, *The Oregonian*, Apr 22, 2001.

33 Krahn (2001).

34 Ahronheim (2001).

35 "G8" indicates the seven wealthiest nations of the world, the United States, Japan, Germany, France, Britain, Canada, and Italy, plus Russia.

36 Kennedy, *The Independent* (London), July 19, 2001.

37 D'Emilio, *The Independent* (London), July 20, 2001.

38 Boggan, *The Independent* (London), July 27, 2001.

39 Kennedy and Harris, *The Independent* (London), July 30, 2001.

40 Staff writers *The Independent* (London), July 22, 2001.

41 The following information on the final statement on the G8 summit in Genoa from Castle, *The Independent* (London), July 24, 2001.

42 Quoted in Castle, *The Independent* (London), July 24, 2001.

43 Quoted in Castle, *The Independent* (London), July 24, 2001.

44 The proposed US foreign aid budget for the fiscal year 2003 is $16.1 billion, out of a total budget of $2,128 billion. In other words, foreign aid is less than 1% of the total budget, and the $16.1 billion *includes military aid* to foreign countries. In comparison to the foreign aid budget, the US defense budget towers at $396 billion for current military expenditures. Benefits for veterans and interest on the portion of the national debt created by military spending are far over and above this figure.

45 Staff, *The Independent* (London), July 23, 2001.

46 Buncombe, *The Independent* (London), Aug 31, 2001.

47 Thornton, *Financial Times* (London), Nov 10, 2001.

48 Denny, *The Guardian* (UK), Nov 12, 2001.

49 Williams, Frances, *Financial Times* (London), Nov 13, 2001.

50 Staff writer, *The Guardian* (UK), Nov 14, 2001.
51 Kuttner (1997), Gray (1998), Barber (1995), Korten (1995), Sine (1999), and Klein (1999), Kelly and Greider (2003).
52 See Thom Hartmann (2004), Marjorie Kelly and William Greider (2003), Barbara Ehrenreich (2001), Schlosser (2001), Anthony Giddens (2000), Russell Mokhiber and Robert Weissmann (1999), Naomi Klein (1999), Walden Bello (1999: 86-115), William Greider (1997), Robert Kuttner (1997), Benjamin Barber (1995), Browne and Sims (1993), and Neil Postman (1985).

Chapter Three

The Global Economy at Work in the Global South

1   Sen (2002).
2   Ortiz (2001) 102.
3   Ortiz (2001) 102.
4   UPI, Feb 13, 1995. Chase Manhattan distanced itself from this statement after the statement had brought on copious public scorn. However, their disavowal does not explain why the statement by this advisor was printed in a Chase Manhattan newsletter and distributed to business partners as an official document. In the same document, the advisor also subtly recommends the use of electoral fraud in Mexico (UPI, Feb 13, 1995).
5   Table 1 supports indigenous autonomy and grants indigenous people land rights and rights over their land's natural resources.
6   At the end of 2001, hundreds of these refugees returned to their homes after more than four years of displacement.
7   Hernández (2000) 209-212.
8   In the year 2000, the US military opted to change the name of the School of the Americas to the Western Hemisphere Institute for Security Cooperation. Opponents of the US training ground for Latin American military leaders continue to know it by the nickname "School of the Assassins".
9   Kaufman (2001) 232.
10 Kaufman (2001) 233.

11 Las Abejas support the indigenous struggle, and the goals of the Zapatistas, but as Christian pacifists, do not support the taking up of arms. They believe the Zapatista cause can only be successful using nonviolent resistance. It should be pointed out that the Zapatistas' use of violence has been extremely limited since the ceasefire of January of 1994, but they are an army, and do carry weapons.

12 Kaufman (2001) 230-231.

13 SIPAZ (1998) 217-220.

14 Kaufman (2001) 228.

15 I have no doubt that many young men serving in Mexico's military give out handouts with good intentions. In a country where minimum wage is not enough to live on, one cannot help but feel compassion for young men who choose the military as their best financial option. I suspect many young men join the Mexican Army for this reason, without fully understanding the nature of the conflict they are entering into.

16 In 2001 there were 1,111 autonomous communities or "communities of resistance" (Ortiz [2001] 107).

17 Plan Puebla Panama (PPP) is a neoliberal economic plan Fox announced shortly after taking office as President of Mexico in 2000. It is a plan to open up for foreign investment the area from Puebla State in SE Mexico to the Panama Canal. The plan primarily involves 1) opening ports on both sides of Central America, as well as building railroads and highways to facilitate export, 2) opening *maquila* sectors (sweatshops) throughout the region, and 3) opening access to the region's natural resources for extraction. The plan would facilitate oversea transportation of goods produced in southern Mexico and Central America. To corporations in the US and Canada, the plan's appeal is in the way it would allow products to be shipped back and forth from the east coast of the US or Canada to and from Mexico, or to be shipped from Mexico on to markets in East Asia. The plan would also make the region, rich as it is in natural resources and biodiversity, available for exploitation by transnational corporations. PPP would be a $10 billion dollar program financed by loans from international financial

institutions to benefit corporations. Yet the loans would be repaid by the citizens of Mexico, including those dispossessed of their lands and livelihoods by the plan, in the form of taxes and loss of government jobs and programs. Much needed infrastructure, such as clean water systems and rural roads, would be neglected while the government developed a transport system suitable for semi-trucks and cargo ships. For more information on PPP, see Witness for Peace (2002) 3-4.

18 Keady (2000).

19 Interfaith Center on Corporate Responsibility (1998) 8.

20 These figures are taken from Keady (2000). In 2001, the minimum wage in Indonesia, as well as Nike's basic wage, went up to 426,000Rp. However, inflation also caused the prices of food, medicine, electricity, etc. to rise proportionately. Furthermore, the crash of the value of the rupia over the past few years has meant that the pay increase has cost Nike very, very little in terms of US dollars.

21 http://nikebiz.com/labor/faq.shtml.

22 Keady (2000).

23 Educating for Justice (2000b).

24 Sider (1997) 144.

25 Information of Tiger Woods and Phil Knight from Educating for Justice (2001).

26 Many corporations have "codes of conduct" which spell out the standards they aim to meet as a company. These codes can include labor standards for the factories outsourcing for them. Though codes of conduct are a promising idea, they have been rendered meaningless by the way corporations openly disregard their own codes.

27 Educating for Justice (2000b).

28 Figures from Educating for Justice (2000a).

29 Educating for Justice (2000b).

30 See Educating for Justice (2000b), and Press for Change (1999).

31 In 1998, President Suharto stepped down.

32 Greider (1997) 391-393.

33 Buchori and Bahagijo (2001).

34   Pettifor (2001).

35   Pettifor (2001).

36   Oxfam (2001).

37   Ferrer, *Asia Times Online*, Dec 12, 2001.

38   Jeffrey, *Pacific News Service*, Sept 4, 2001.

39   *BBC News Online: Business*, Jan 17, 2001.

40   Social Justice Committee (2001a).

41   Ferrer, *Asia Times Online*, Dec 12, 2001.

42   Ferrer, *Asia Times Online*, Dec 12, 2001.

43   Statistics from Hostetler, Lynen, and Raphaelidis (2001) 9.

44   Statistics from Hostetler, Lynen, and Raphaelidis (2001) 9.

45   United Nations Development Program, *Human Development Report* (1998, 2000). Data shows a significant decrease in per capita income for South Asia, South-East Asia and Pacific Region, Latin America/ Caribbean, and Sub-Saharan Africa over the past twenty years.

46   Hostetler, Lynen, and Raphaelidis (2001) 7.

47   Social Justice Committee (2001b). See the IMF "Article IV" consultation staff report, Oct 2, http://www.imf.org/external/pubs/cat/longres.cfm?sk=15389.0.

48   Rossi (2002).

49   http://www.nestle.com/investor_relations/mr2000/pdf/productsgb.pdf

50   Crawshaw (2001).

51   Jeffrey, *Pacific News Service*, Sept 4, 2001.

52   Statistics from the National Labor Committee Report (2001b) 56.

53   National Labor Committee (2001b) iii.

54   At the time of this writing: Arizona State Univ., Central Michigan Univ., Columbia Univ., Cornell Univ., De Paul Univ., Illinois State Univ., Miami Univ. of Ohio, Northern Illinois Univ., Northwest Univ., Purdue Univ., Tulane Univ., Univ. of Arizona, Univ. of California at Santa Barbara, Univ. of Connecticut, Univ. of Michigan, Univ. of Minnesota, Univ. of New Hampshire, Univ. of North Carolina at Chapel Hill, Univ. of Washington, and Univ. of Wisconsin at Madison, and Stevens Point.

55   National Labor Committee (2001b) 4.

56   National Labor Committee (2001b) 4-7.

57   National Labor Committee (2001b) 27.

58   National Labor Committee (2001b) 50.

59   On the issue of child labor, I highly recommend the book *Free the Children*, by Craig Kielburger (1998). The book was written when Kielburger himself was still a child, after his travels in South Asia, and his founding of the organization *Free the Children*, which is working to bring an end to child labor.

60   Rothstein (1994).

61   For eyewitness stories of children bonded laborers, see Kielburger (1998).

Chapter Four

Biblical Economics, Part I: Ancient and Modern, A Contemporary Conversation

1   Thoreau (1893) 91.

2   Thoreau (1893) 91-92.

3   "Wealth" is used here to denote "material possessions," which means that anyone who owns anything has *some* wealth. A very destitute man might only own the clothing on his back. In the sense that we are meaning, that clothing would constitute his wealth.

4   For the Greeks, "economy" meant "housekeeping," or dividing up goods to provide for the needs of those in the "house." They believed all resources were limited, and "economy" denoted the system by which those limited resources were allocated justly.

5   Hanson (1997) 2.

6   Information on preindustrial, "agrarian" economies can be found in Polanyi, Arensberg, and Pearson (1957), Sjoberg (1960), Rohrbaugh (1978) 29-52, Lenski (1984), and Finley (1985).

7   It is impossible to know the specific dates of Abraham's life. He is usually placed sometime in the period between 2000 and 1700 BCE.

8   The work of Richard Rohrbaugh (1978:29-41) was especially helpful in this summary of the features of agrarian societies.

9   Rohrbaugh (1978) 30-31.

10 On the importance of the kin-group for the Hebrews, especially during in the pre-monarchical period, see Wright (1990) 44-103.

11 Ostensibly, some of the laws within the Pentateuch reflect periods of time significantly later than the Exodus, specifically, the periods in which the Pentateuch was edited and finalized. Nonetheless, the Mosaic laws on wealth tell us something of what the generations of Israelites believed to be a right use of wealth, and one finds no reason to doubt that the core of the tradition lies with Moses. The fact that the laws about wealth were preserved so well points to the integral nature of these laws to the Hebrew understanding of God.

12 "In-group" and "out-group" are anthropological terms that are useful in talking about kin-group-based societies. One's in-group includes one's family and those who are like family and, in certain contexts, one's fellow villagers and ethnic group. In-group members command one's loyalty. Out-group members are presumed to be in competition for life's limited resources, and are thus treated with suspicion.

13 Albright (1963).

Chapter Five

Biblical Economics, Part II: Jesus' Teaching on Wealth and its Usage

1 Esler (1987) 170.

2 Honor in Mediterranean terms is defined as: "the value of a person in his own eyes, but also in the eyes of his society. It is his estimation of his own worth, his *claim* to pride, but it is also the acknowledgement of that claim, his excellence recognized by society, *his right* to pride" (Pitt-Rivers [1977] 1).

3 Hanson and Oakman (1998) 123-125.

4 After 6 CE, the regions of Judea, Samaria and Idumea were no longer under Herodian rule, but under the administration of Roman prefects and procurators. However, many of the taxes imposed throughout Palestine under Herodian rule continued to be collected in these areas, and simply redirected to Rome and her Judean clients.

5   Josephus, *The Antiquities of the Judeans* 20.213.

6   Lenski (1984) 228.

7   For analyses of that evidence, see Finley (1985), Oakman (1986), Garnsey and Saller (1987), Freyne (1995), and Hanson and Oakman (1998).

8   Hoehner (1972) 70.

9   Hanson and Oakman (1998) 114-115.

10 Oakman (1986) 167.

11 Hanson and Oakman (1998) 114-115.

12 Hoehner (1972) 77-78.

13 Josephus, *The Antiquities of the Judeans* 17.307-308.

14 Oakman (1986) 69.

15 Hoehner (1972) 70-71.

16 At the time, the Roman province of Judea included the regions of Samaria and Idumea.

17 See Hoehner (1972) 74-77.

18 These included a soil tax used to support the priests (at least one-tenth of the harvest [Deut 14:22], based on a man's income *before* governmental taxes had been deducted), a head tax (2 denarii, or a half-shekel), sacrifices (animals and agricultural products), and vows (dedicated materials goods) (Hanson and Oakman [1998] 114-115).

19 Herzog (1994) 182.

20 Oakman (1986) 47, 75.

21 Carney (1975) 181-182.

22 Certain elites also acquired land because it was given to them by the Herods (Goodman [1980] 58-59), or by Rome.

23 Oakman (1986) 72f.

24 Goodman (1987) 57.

25 Through careful consideration of the evidence, Oakman (1986) estimates that after the kinds of extractions listed above as well as the setting aside of seed for future harvests, a peasant family was left with only one-fifth to one-thirteenth of the produce they harvested.

26 See Horsley on peasant revolts (1987).

27 Malina (1993) 97.

28 Hoehner (1975) 70-71.
29 Josephus, *The Antiquities of the Judeans* 18.245.
30 See Freyne (1995).
31 Hanson and Oakman (1998) 107.
32 Josephus, *Jewish War* 3.4, Loeb translation.
33 Hanson and Oakman (1998) 104. See Lenski (1984) 199-200.
34 Hoehner (1975) 74-76.
35 Freyne (1995) 33-34.
36 Hanson and Oakman (1998) 87.
37 Josephus, *Jewish Antiquities* 18.118.
38 Hanson and Oakman (1998) 88.
39 For studies devoted entirely to Jesus and economics, see Mealand (1980), Oakman (1986), and Schmidt (1987).
40 According to the Q theory, the material in common between Matthew and Luke came from this common source. The theory has much to commend it, especially since the material shared by Matthew and Luke is often almost verbatim, and the theory is widely accepted among scholars as the best explanation for this shared material.
41 The proper meaning of the word usually translated "poor" in this verse. The Greek word *ptochos* implies absolute destitution.
42 Jerome Neyrey's essay "Loss of Wealth, Loss of Family and Loss of Honour" (1995) first got me thinking about the relationship between the Beatitudes and the costs of discipleship.
43 Luke's simpler version, which refers to economic poverty and physical hunger, is more congruent with Q's special attention to possessions and poverty (Mt 6:19-21=Lk 12:13-34, Mt 6:24=Lk 16:13, Mt 6:25-34=Lk 12:22-32, Mt 6:9-13=Lk 11:1-4, Mt 6:24=Lk 16:1-15).
44 There is evidence in Acts that the early church lived out this vision of Jesus to a large extent. In the communities that did so, some of the severe social and economic costs of discipleship mentioned in this section would have been lessened. However, Jesus' earliest followers in rural Palestine did not yet have the kinds of social networks among believers that are reflected in Acts, and thus experienced hardships as a result of following Jesus which many later Christians did not have to bear.

45   This breakdown came to mind as I was reading Oakman (1986), though he does not make it explicit.

46   For more on this, see Malina (1995) 63-89.

47   Finley (1973) 108-109.

48   Oakman (1986) 166.

49   Duling and Perrin (1994: 4).

50   Oakman (1986) 166f.

51   By Oakman's estimate, a denarius would provide two-week's sustenance for one person ([1986] 167).

52   Oakman (1986) 186.

53   For further reading on the kingdom of God, see Yoder (1972), Hauerwas (1983) chapters five and six, and Wink (1992) chapter six.

54   For further reading on the meaning of the cross, see Yoder (1972), Hauerwas (1983) chapter five, and Wink (1992) chapter seven.

55   Esler (1987), chapter Seven, "The Poor and the Rich," 164-200.

56   For descriptions of urban poverty and the opulent urban dwellings of the elite class in the Roman era, see Esler (1987) 171-179.

57   See Lk 7:1-10, 8:3, 23:27; Acts 8:26-39, 10:1f. 13:1 and 7, 17:12, 19:31.

Chapter Six

Pauline Christology and the Powers

1   Ellul (1984) 109-110.

2   In this section I am including books considered by many scholars to be "deutero-Pauline," namely Colossians and Ephesians, under the heading of "Pauline writings." These books have many characteristics that set them apart from "primero" works of Paul, such as very unique vocabulary, distinct writing styles, and some dissimilar theology. Such features lead many scholars to question whether Paul wrote these letters. The deutero-Pauline writings do, however, share many things in common with Paul's letters, so that even those who question Paul's authorship of them concede that they were written by people very close to Paul, perhaps by co-workers or students, who were writing in Paul's name and style,

and adapting his ideas for a new situation. It was extremely common in antiquity for students of a great teacher to write pieces using the name of their teacher, adopting their teacher's style and ideas.

It is not necessary in this study to have a position on whether or not Paul wrote Colossians or Ephesians. They were clearly written, at the very least, by someone close to Paul, who had been significantly impacted by Paul's theology and worldview. For this reason, we call these writings "Pauline," and leave it at that.

3   The translation below is based on the NRSV, though I have substituted the translation "principalities" for "rulers," which is used by the NRSV for the word *archee*. Italics have been added.

4   In this passage we have chosen the translation "nullify" for the Greek word *katargein* over the NRSV choice of "destroy." The reason for this is explained later in this chapter.

5   Wink (1992) 7-8.

6   Ellul (1976) 40-41.

7   Stringfellow (1973) 82.

8   Wink (1992) 78.

9   Stringfellow (1973) 43f.

10   Stringfellow (1973) 77.

11   Berkhof (1977) 29.

12   What about death, however, which according to 1 Cor 15:26 will be *katargeitai*? Won't death be *destroyed*? Perhaps it will. But it is also true to say that the power of death will be broken, or canceled, or nullified. The translation of *katargein* as "nullified" still remains preferable.

13   As G. B. Caird explains: "The Cross . . . was a personal victory for Christ which carried him beyond the dominion of the powers; . . . But the Cross was also a corporate victory. By identifying himself with men in their sinfulness and humiliation Christ had made it possible for men to be identified in his righteousness and triumph. He had become the Last Adam, the head of a new humanity, and in him all mankind had passed vicariously through death and resurrection into a new life over which the principalities and powers had no control . . . The rulers of this age would not have crucified the Lord of Glory if they had

known that in so doing they were not gaining control over Christ but losing control over all men [1 Cor 2:6-8]" (1956: 92).

14 Berkhof (1977) 51.

Chapter Seven

Decisions that Matter: Living Humanly in the Global Economy

1 Yoder (1972) 157.

2 Meeks (1995) 121-122.

3 Stringfellow (1973).

4 Zinn, Howard (2002) "Born Yesterday", *Tikkun*, May/June 2002: 30-32.

5 Azure Standard falls somewhere between a co-op food buying club and a food warehouse. In the case of Azure Standard, individuals order food from an online or printed catalog, and the food is delivered to one or more location (usually houses) in each town or area in the delivery zone. Individuals pick up their orders at their drop-off location. Deliveries range from once to twice a month. As already mentioned, many of the dry goods Azure Standard offers originate very near the warehouse, on the organic Azure Farms.

6 Though the grants are repaid, I call them grants rather than loans because a group will repay the money to a small savings and credit operation they form, and then distribute the repaid grant money to another NGO working in their community, who in turn passes on the blessing. The money is not repaid to RSWR, but shared with others in need of grants.

7 Other questions asked in the selection process include:

  1) Has the project been visited by a RSWR representative, and has it been recommended?

  2) How many people will benefit from the money invested?

  3) Does the project demonstrate a clear and thorough business plan for the micro-enterprise activities,

including the ability of the project to be self-sustaining once outside funding ends?

4)   Is the capital invested in the project ("seed money") to be used as a revolving loan?

5)   Is the project innovative?

6)   Is the project from a RSWR constituency group identified by the Board of Trustees?

8   Both project descriptions are adapted from the RSWR Second Quarter, 2002 newsletter.

9   This is the average work hours per day in factories producing for export (sweatshops) in neighboring Bangladesh. In contrast to this, women in the projects RSWR supports generally work 6 to 8 hours a day.

10   For example, at Mustard Seed Farms in 2002, a full CSA membership, or "share", cost $200 for the Summer Season, and $80 for the Winter Season. In exchange, full members received 100 units of produce in the summer, and 40 units in the winter. An example of a unit would be three pounds of carrots, or two heads of lettuce. The costs of CSA shares vary from farm to farm. At most CSAs, shares range from $450 per family per year on up.

11   http://www.fairtradefederation.com/memcrit.html.

12   In response to the question, "what is a fair wage?," the Fair Trade Federation offers the following answer: "Producers receive a fair wage when they are paid fairly for their products. This means that workers are paid at least the country's minimum wage. Since the minimum wage is often not enough for basic survival, whenever feasible, workers are paid a living wage, which enables them to cover basic needs, including food, shelter, education and health care for their families. Paying fair wages does not necessarily mean that products cost the consumer more. Since fair trade organizations bypass exploitative middlepeople and work directly with producers, they are able to cut costs and return a greater percentage of the retail price to the producers" (http://www.fairtradefederation.com/faq.html).

Resource List

(Updated 2004)

Fair Trade/"No Sweat" Clothing and Other Items

Maggie's Organics—www.maggiesorganics.com
Ten Thousand Villages—www.tenthousandvillages.org
American Apparel—www.americanapparel.net
SweatX—www.sweatx.net
The Union Mall—www.NoSweatShop.com
Sweetgrass Fibers—www.sweetgrassfibers.com
Serrv International—www.serrv.org
People Tree (UK)—www.ptree.co.uk
Fair Trade Federation—www.fairtradefederation.com

Fair Trade Certified Coffee and Tea

Equal Exchange—www.equalexchange.org
Green Mountain Coffee Roasters—www.greenmountaincoffee.com

Microdevelopment Organizations

Right Sharing of World Resources—www.rswr.org
Heifer Project, International—www.heifer.org
World Vision International—www.worldvision.org

Global Labor Issues/Global Labor Advocacy Groups

Behind the Label—www.behindthelabel.org
National Labor Committee—www.nlcnet.org
Educating for Justice—www.nikewages.org
Sweatshop Watch—www.sweatshopwatch.org
Interfaith Center for Corporate Responsibility—
www.iccr.org
U.S./Labor Education in the Americas Project—
www.usleap.org
Clean Clothes—www.cleanclothes.org
Resource Center of the Americas.org—www.americas.org
International Confederation of Free Trade Unions—
www.icftu.org
Maquila Solidarity Network—www.maquilasolidarity.org
Worker Rights Consortium—www.workersrights.org

Education about Neoliberal Economics

Witness for Peace—www.witnessforpeace.org
Jubilee Plus—www.jubileeplus.org
Global Exchange—www.globalexchange.org
Resource Center of the Americas.org—www.americas.org

Arms Trade

Campaign Against the Arms Trade—www.caat.org.uk

Bibliography

Ahronheim, Sara (2001) "What I Saw in Quebec: Eyewitness to Oppression", *The Oregon PeaceWorker*, June 2001: 1,5.

Albright, William F. (1963) *The Biblical Period from Abraham to Ezra* (New York, NY: Harper).

Aristide, Jean-Bertrand (2000) *Eyes of the Heart: Seeking a Path for the Poor in the Age of Globalization*, ed. Laura Flynn (Monroe, ME: Common Courage Press).

Arnold, Eberhard (1998) *Salt and Light: Living the Sermon on the Mount* (Farmington, PA: Plough Publishing House).

Atwood, Margaret, *et al.* (1993) *The Case Against Free Trade: GATT, NAFTA, and the Globalization of Corporate Power* (San Francisco/ Berkeley, CA: Earth Island Press/North Atlantic Books).

Barber, Benjamin R. (1995) *Jihad vs. McWorld* (New York, NY: Times Books).

BBC News Online Staff (2001) "Economic Struggle for Central America", *BBC News Online: Business*, January 17, 2001, http:// www.news.bbc.co.uk/low/english/business/newsid_1120000/ 1120117.stm.

Bello, Walden (1999) *Dark Victory: The United States and Global Poverty*, written with Shea Cunningham and Bill Rau (London: Pluto Press).

Berkhof, Hendrik (1977) *Christ and the Powers*, trans. John H. Yoder (Scottdale, PA: Herald Press).

Black, Jan Knippers (1999) *Inequity in the Global Village: Recycled Rhetoric and Disposable People* (West Hartford, CT: Kumarian Press).

Blomberg, Craig (1999) *Neither Poverty Nor Riches: A Biblical Theology of Material Possessions* (Grand Rapids, MI: William B. Eerdmans).

Boggan, Steve (2001) "Fury Over 'Brutal' Genoa Police", *The Independent* (London), July 27, 2001.

Bright, John (1981) *A History of Israel*, 3rd ed. (Philadelphia, PA: Westminster Press).

Brown, Lester B. (2001) *Eco-Economy: Building an Economy for the Earth* (New York, NY: W.W. Norton & Company).

—(2003) *Plan B: Rescuing a Planet Under Stress and a Civilization in Trouble* (New York, NY: W.W. Norton & Company).

Browne, Harry and Beth Sims (1993) *Runaway America: U.S. Jobs and Factories on the Move* (Albuquerque, NM: The Resource Center Press).

Buchori, Binny and Sugeng Bahagijo (2001) "Indonesia's Domestic Debt Must Be Paid by the IMF, says British Debt Expert", *INFID*, June 21, 2001, http://www.jubileeplus.org/media/jubileepluspress_release_archive/INFID_press_release.htm.

Buncombe, Andrew (2001) "Protesters Go Into Training for Summit in Washington", *The Independent* (London), August 31, 2001.

Business World (Philippines) Staff (2000) "The Year of Global Protest Against Globalization", *Business World (Philippines)*, December 26, 2000.

Caird, G. B. (1956) *Principalities and Powers: A Study in Pauline Theology* (Oxford: Oxford University Press).

Carney, Thomas (1975) *The Shape of the Past: Models and Antiquity* (Lawrence, KS: Coronado Press).

Castle, Stephen (2001) "G8 Leaders Promise a Great Deal While Delivering Next to Nothing", *The Independent* (London), July 24, 2001.

Christian, Jayakumar (1999) *God of the Empty-Handed: Poverty, Power and the Kingdom of God* (Monrovia, CA: World Vision).

Cleaver, Tony (1997) *Understanding the World Economy: Global Issues Shaping the Future* (New York, NY: Routledge).

Cohen, Tom (2001) "Police, Free-Trade Activists Clash as Thousands Protest Peacefully", *The Sunday Oregonian*, April 22, 2001.

Crawshaw, Steve (2001) "Coffee Prices are Slumping (not that you would know it in Starbucks)", *Organic Consumers Association*, May 2001, http://www.purefood.org/starbucks/slump.cfm.

Dawn, Marva J. (1999) "The Biblical Concept of 'the Principalities and Powers': John Yoder Points to Jacques Ellul", in *The Wisdom of the Cross: Essays in Honor of John Howard Yoder*, ed. Stanley Hauerwas, Chris K. Huebner, Harry J. Huebner, and Mark Thiessen Nation (Grand Rapids, MI: William B. Eerdmans).

D'Emilio, Frances (2001) "Protester 'Killed' in G8 Clash", *The Independent* (London), July 20, 2001.

Denny, Charlotte (2001) "Developed World Accused of Bully-Boy Tactics at WTO", *The Guardian* (UK), November 12, 2001.

Duling, Dennis and Norman Perrin (1994) *The New Testament: Proclamation and Parenesis, Myth and History*, 3rd ed. (Fort Worth, TX: Harcourt Brace College Publishers).

Economist staff (2000) "A Different, New World Order", *The Economist* (print edition), Nov. 9, 2000.

Educating for Justice (2000a) "Costs of Basic Needs", http://www.nikewages.org/cost_main.html.

—(2000b) "Group Interview", http://www.nikewages.org/interviews.html.

—(2001) "What Does Nike Pay Its People?", http://nikewages.org/index2.html.

Ehrenreich, Barbara (2001) *Nickel and Dimed: On (Not) Getting By in America* (New York, NY: Metropolitan Books).

Ellul, Jacques (1976) *The Ethics of Freedom*, trans. and ed. Geoffrey W. Bromiley (Grand Rapids, MI: William B. Eerdmans).

—(1984) *Money and Power*, trans. LaVonne Neff (Downers Grove, IL: Inter-Varsity Press).

England, Richard W. (1997) "Alternatives to Gross National Product: A Critical Survey", in *Human Well-Being and Economic Goals*, ed. by Frank Ackerman, et al (Washington, DC: Island Press) 373-402.

Esler, Philip (1987) *Community and Gospel in Luke-Acts* (Cambridge: Cambridge University Press).

Fatemi, Khosrow, ed. (1997) *International Trade in the 21st Century* (Tarrytown, NY: Pergamon).

Ferrer, Yadira (2001) "Slumping Coffee Prices Leave a Bitter Taste", *Asia Times Online*, December 12, 2001, http://www.atimes.com/se-asia/CL12Ae03.html.

Finley, Moses I. (1985) *The Ancient Economy* (London: The Hogarth Press).

Foster, George M. (1965) "Peasant Society and the Image of Limited Good", *American Anthropologist* 67: 293-315.

Freyfogle, Eric T. (2001) *The New Agrarianism: Land Culture, and the Community of Life* (Washington, DC: Island Press).

Freyne, Sean (1995) "Herodian Economics in Galilee: Searching for a Suitable Model", in *Modelling Early Christianity*, ed. Philip Esler (New York, NY: Routledge) 23-46.

Garnsey, Peter and Richard Saller (1987) *The Roman Empire: Economy, Society and Culture* (Berkeley, CA: University of California Press).

Giddens, Anthony (2000) *Runaway World: How Globalization is Reshaping our Lives* (New York, NY: Routledge).

Goodman, Martin (1987) *The Ruling Class of Judaea: The Origins of the Jewish Revolt against Rome A.D. 66-70* (Cambridge: Cambridge University Press).

Gorringe, Timothy (1999) *Fair Shares: Ethics and the Global Economy* (New York, NY: Thames and Hudson).

Gray, John (1998) *False Dawn: The Delusions of Global Capitalism* (New York, NY: The New Press).

Greider, William (1997) *One World, Ready or Not: The Manic Logic of Global Capitalism* (New York, NY: Simon and Schuster).

Gribskov, Margaret (2001) "Recent Trade Agreements Will Bankrupt Democracy", *The Oregon PeaceWorker*, November 2001: 14.

Guardian Staff (2001) "Done Deal in Doha", *The Guardian* (UK), November 14, 2001.

Gupta, Satya Dev, ed. (1997) *The Political Economy of Globalization* (Boston, MA: Kluwer Academic Pub.).

Guy, Jonquieres de (2001) "Power Elites at Davos Set to Vie with Protesters for Attention: World Economic Forum is Facing Stringent Security", *The Financial Times* (London), January 24, 2001.

Hamel, Gildas (1990) *Poverty and Charity in Roman Palestine, First Three Centuries C.E.* (Berkeley, CA: University of California Press).

Hands, A. R. (1968) *Charities and Social Aid in Greece and Rome* (Ithaca, NY: Cornell University Press).

Hanson, K. C. (1997) "The Galilean Fishing Economy and the Jesus Tradition", *Biblical Theology Bulletin* 27:99-111.

Hanson, K. C. and Douglas Oakman (1998) *Palestine in the Time of Jesus* (Minneapolis, MN: Fortress Press).

Hartmann, Thom (2004) *Unequal Partners* (Emmaus, PA: Rodale Press).

Hauerwas, Stanley (1983) *The Peaceable Kingdom: A Primer in Christian Ethics* (Notre Dame, IN: University of Notre Dame Press).

Hawken, Paul (1994) *The Ecology of Commerce: A Declaration of Sustainability* (San Francisco, CA: HarperBusiness).

Hawken, Paul, Amory Lovins, and L. Hunter Lovins (2000) *Natural Capitalism: Creating the Next Industrial Revolution* (Newport Beach, CA: Back Bay Books).

Hernández, Oscar (2000) "A New Cycle of Life for the Mayan People", in *Never Again a World Without Us*, by Teresa Ortiz (Washington, DC: EPICA) 207-216.

Herzog, William R., II (1994) *Parables as Subversive Speech: Jesus as Pedagogue of the Oppressed* (Louisville, KY: Westminster/John Knox Press).

Hessel, Dieter and Larry Rasmussen, eds. (2001) *Earth Habitat: Eco-Injustice and the Church's Response* (Minneapolis, MN: Fortress Press).

Hoehner, Harold W. (1972) *Herod Antipas: A Contemporary of Jesus Christ* (Grand Rapids, MI: Zondervan Pub.).

Horsley, Richard (1987) *Jesus and the Spiral of Violence: Popular Jewish Resistance in Roman Palestine* (San Franscisco, CA: Harper & Row).

Hostetler, Sharon, JoAnn Lynen, and Leia Raphaelidis (2001) *A High Price to Pay: Structural Adjustment and Women in Nicaragua* (Washington, DC: Witness for Peace).

Huggler, Justin (2000) "Britons Accuse Czech Police", *The Independent* (London), October 1, 2000.

Independent Staff (2001) "Genoa Must Be the Last of These Overblown Summits", *The Independent* (London), July 22, 2001.

—"Genoa Summit, What the Leaders Have Achieved: Extracts from the Final Statements of the G8 Summit in Genoa", *The Independent* (London), July 23, 2001.

Interfaith Center on Corporate Responsibility (1998) "Fact-finding Report on Footwear Manufacturing: Nike and Reebok Plants in Indonesia, Vietnam, China. March 1-12, 1998", *The Corporate Examiner*, July 31, 1998: 8.

International Confederation of Free Trade Unions (ICFTU) (2000) "Thousands of People Targeted for Trade Union Activities World-Wide", *Clean Clothes.org*, September 13, 2000, http://www.cleanclothes.org/news/00-09-13.htm.

Jacobs, Michael (2001) "Bridging the Global Divide", *The Guardian (UK)*, November 11, 2001.

Jeffrey, Paul (2001) "Central America's Silent Killer—The Man-Made Causes of Drought and Famine", *Pacific News Service*, September 4, 2001.

Jensen, Derrick (2002) *Listening to the Land: Conversations about Nature, Culture, and Eros* (San Francisco: Sierra Club Books).

Kaufman, Leslie and David Gonzalez (2001) "Labor Standards Clash with Global Reality", *New York Times*, April 24, 2001.

Kaufman, Mara (2001) "Whose Side are We On?: A Look at the US Role in Chiapas", in *Never Again a World Without Us*, by Teresa Ortiz (Washington, DC: EPICA) 227-234.

Keady, James (2000) "Jim's Journal", *Educating for Justice*, http://www.nikewages.org/journal_jim_1.html#Anchor-47857.

Kelly, Marjorie and William Greider (2003) *The Divine Right of Capital: Dethroning the Corporate Aristocracy* (San Francisco, CA: Berrett-Koehler Pub.).

Kennedy, Frances (2001) "Genoa Ringed by Steel as G8 Tension Mounts", *The Independent* (London), July 19, 2001.

Kennedy, Frances and Jonathon Harris (2001) "Italy Investigates Allegations of Police Brutality Against Protesters in Genoa", *The Independent* (London), July 30, 2001.

Kielburger, Craig (1998) *Free the Children: A Young Man Fights Against Child Labor and Proves That Children can Change the World*, written with help of Kevin Major (New York, NY: HarperPerennial).

Kingsolver, Barbara (2002) *Small Wonder* (New York, NY: Harper Collins).

Klein, Naomi (1999) *No Logo: Taking Aim at the Brand Bullies* (New York, NY:Picador).

Korten, David C. (1995) *When Corporations Rule the World* (West Hartford, CT/San Francisco, CA: Kumarian/Berrett-Koehler).

Krahn, Natasha (2001) "This is What Democracy Looks Like", *CPT Net* (www.prairienet.org/cpt/), April 24, 2001.

Küng, Hans (1998) *A Global Ethic for Global Politics and Economics* (New York, NY: Oxford University Press).

Kuttner, Robert (1997) *Everything for Sale: The Virtues and Limits of Markets* (New York, NY: Alfred A. Knopf).

Lasn, Kalle (1999) *Culture Jam: The Uncooling of America* (New York, NY: Eagle Brook).

Lenski, Gerhard E. (1984) *Power and Privilege: A Theory of social stratification* (Chapel Hill and London: The University of North Carolina Press).

Lofdahl, Corey L. (2002) *Environmental Impacts of Globalization and Trade* (Cambridge, MA: MIT Press).

Lloyd, John (2001) "Attack on Planet Davos", *The Financial Times* (London), February 24, 2001.

Longacre, Doris Janzen (1980) *Living More With Less* (Scottdale, PA: Herald Press).

Luttwak, Edward (1999) *Turbo-Capitalism:Winners and Losers in the Global Economy* (New York, NY: HarperCollins).

Malina, Bruce (1993) *The New Testament World: Insights from cultural anthropology*, rev. ed. (Louisville, KY: Westminster/John Knox Press).

Mander, Jerry (2001) "Globalization and the Environment: The Intrinsic Danger", *Tikkun* 16:33-40.

Mansfield, Edward D. (1994) *Power, Trade, and War* (Princeton, NJ: Princeton University Press).

Maquila Solidarity Network (2001) "Lessons from Mexico's Maquilas: Dispelling the Myths of Free Trade," http://www.maquilasolidarity.org/resources/maquilas/dispellingmyths.htm, April 2001.

Mealand, David (1980) *Poverty and Expectation in the Gospels* (London: SPCK).

Meeks, M. Douglas (1995) "God's *Oikonomía* and the New World Economy", in *Christian Social Ethics in a Global Era*, Max L. Stackhouse, ed. (Nashville, TN: Abingdon Press) 111-126.

Meshorer, Yaakov (1982) *Ancient Jewish Coinage*, 2 vols. (Dix Hills, NY: Amphora Books).

Mokhiber, Russell and Robert Weissman (1999) *Corporate Predators: The Hunt for MegaProfits and the Attack on Democracy* (Monroe, ME: Common Courage Press).

Myers, Bryant L. (1999) *Walking with the Poor: Principles and Practices of Transformational Development* (Maryknoll, NY: Orbis Books).

National Labor Committee (2001a) "'Made in the U.S.A.'? Nightmare at the Daewoosa Factory in American Samoa", *National Labor Committee Report*, March 2001.

—(2001b) "Bangladesh: Ending the Race to the Bottom", *National Labor Committee Report*, December 2001.

Nayyar, Deepak (1997) "Globalization: The Game, the Players, and the Rules", in *The Political Economy of Globalization*, ed. Satya Dev Gupta (Boston, MA: Kluwer Academic Pub.) 13-40.

Neyrey, Jerome H. (1995) "Loss of Wealth, Loss of Family and Loss of Honour: The Cultural Context of the Original Makarisms in Q", in *Modelling Early Christianity*, ed. Philip Esler (New York, NY: Routledge) 139-158.

Nhu, T. T. (2001) "U. S. Allows Vietnamese to Enter, Testify about Alleged Sweatshop", *San Jose Mercury News*, April 3, 2001.

Oakman, Doughlas (1986) *Jesus and the Economic Questions of his Day* (Lewiston, NY: Edwin Mellen Press).

Ortiz, Teresa (2001) *Never Again A World Without Us: Voices of Mayan Women in Chiapas, Mexico* (Washington, DC: Epica).

Oxfam (2001) "Bitter Coffee: How the Poor are Paying for the Slump in World Coffee Prices", *Oxfam GB News Release*, May 2001, http://www.oxfam.org.uk/whatnew/press/coffee.htm.

Parker, Richard (2002) "From Conquistadors to Corporations", *Sojourners*, May-June 2002: 20-25.

Paulson, Michael (1999) "Delegates Angered by U.S. Agenda on Labor", *Seattle Post-Intelligencer*, December 3, 1999.

Pettifor, Ann (2001) "Jubilee Plus Open Letter to the British Chancellor on Indonesia's Debt", *Jubilee Plus*, July 1, 2001, http://www.jubileeplus.org/jmi/jmi-campaigns/Gordon_Brown_letter_indo_010601.htm.

Polanyi, Karl, Conrad M. Arensberg, and Harry W. Pearson (1957) *Trade and Market in the Early Empires: Economies in History and Theory* (Glencoe, IL: Free Press).

Postman, Neil (1985) *Amusing Ourselves to Death: Public Discourse in the Age of Show Business* (New York, NY: Viking).

Press for Change (1999) "Cruel Treatment Working for Nike in Indonesia", *Urban Community Mission Survey Report*, December 1999, http://www.summersault.com/~agj/clr/crueltreatmentworkingfor NikeinIndonesia.html.

Public Citizen (2001) "On Trade Matters Related to the Free Trade Area of the Americas", http://www.citizen.org/trade/ftaa/articles.cfm?ID=4500.

—(2004a) "Statement of Lori Wallach, Director of Public Citizen's Global Trade Watch, on the Preliminary Decision in the NAFTA Chapter 11 Methanex Case Against California's Ban on MTBE", http://www.publiccitizen.org/pressroom/release.cfm?ID=1180.

—(2004b) "NAFTA Chapter 11 Investor-to-State Cases: Bankrupting Democracy", http://www.publiccitizen.org/publications/print_release.cfm?ID=7076.

Reuters Staff (2001) "Ring of Steel Greets Leaders at Summit of Americas", *Reuters News Service*, April 19, 2001.

Roddick, Anita (2001) *Take It Personally: How to Make Conscious Choices to Change the World* (Berkeley, CA: Conari Press).

Rohrbaugh, Richard (1978) *The Biblical Interpreter: An Agrarian Bible in an Industrial Age* (Philadelphia, PA: Fortress Press).

Rosenberg, Tina (2002) "The Free-Trade Fix", *The New York Times Magazine*, August 18, 2002: 28-33, 50, 74.

Rossi, Holly Lebowitz (2002) "Cuppa Joe, With a Twist", *Sojourners*, May-June 2002: 26-29.

Rothstein, Richard (1994) "The Global Hiring Hall: Why We Need Worldwide Labor Standards", *American Prospect*, March 21, 1994.

Rowell, Andrew (1996) *Green Backlash: Global Subversion of the Environmental Movement* (New York, NY: Routledge).

Sander, Scott Russell (1993) *Staying Put: Making a Home in a Restless World* (Boston, MA: Beacon Press).

Schlosser, Eric (2001) *Fast Food Nation: The Dark Side of the all-American Meal* (Boston, MA: Houghton Mifflin).

Schmidt, Thomas E. (1987) *Hostility to Wealth in the Synoptic Gospels* (Sheffield: Sheffield Academic Press).

Seattle Post-Intelligencer Staff (1999) "Police, Protesters Clash on Second Night of Curfew: Police Beef Up Presence; Hundreds Arrested", *Seattle Post-Intelligencer*, December 1, 1999.

Seattle Post-Intelligencer Staff (1999) "Anti-WTO Protests Escalate", *Seattle Post-Intelligencer*, December 3, 1999.

Sen, Amartya (2002) "How to Judge Globalism", *American Prospect*, January 1-14, 2002.

Shiva, Vandana (1999) *Stolen Harvest: The Hijacking of the Global Food Supply* (Cambridge, MA: South End Press).

Sider, Ron (1997) *Rich Christians in an Age of Hunger* (Dallas, TX: Word).

Sine, Tom (1999) *Mustard Seed vs. McWorld: Reinventing Life and Faith for the Future* (Grand Rapids, MI: Baker Books).

SIPAZ (1998) "Women and Low-Intensity Warfare", in *Never Again a World Without Us*, by Teresa Ortiz (2001) (Washington, DC: Epica) 217-224.

Sjoberg, Gideon (1960) *The Pre-Industrial City* (New York, NY: The Free Press).

The Social Justice Committee (2001a) "Drop in Coffee Prices Brings Misery for Some Nicaraguans", *Social Justice Committee Net*, December 2001, http://www.s-j-c.net/CoffeePrices.htm.

—(2001b) "IMF Tells Starving Nicaraguans to Tighten Their Belts, Cuts off Debt Relief", *Social Justice Committee Net*, October 2001, http://www.s-j-c.net/NicaraguaOct2001.htm.

Stringfellow, William (1973) *An Ethic for Christians and Other Aliens in a Strange Land* (Waco, TX: Word Books).

Suderman, Robert J. (1998) *Calloused Hands, Courageous Souls*. Trans. by W. Derek Suderman (Monrovia, CA: World Vision).

Sunde, Scott (1999) "Schell Orders a Curfew: National Guard Called In", *Seattle Post-Intelligencer*, December 1, 1999.

Sunde, Scott (1999) "Second Straight Night of Confrontations Rocks Capitol Hill: Hundreds of Protesters Held as Schell Vows 'Swift' Response", *Seattle Post-Intelligencer*, December 2, 1999.

Tabb, William K. (2002) *Unequal Partners: a Primer on Globalization* (New York, NY: New Press).

Thoreau, Henry David (1893) *A Week on the Concord and Merrimack Rivers*, in *The Writings of Henry David Thoreau*, v.1 (Boston, MA and New York, NY: Houghton Mifflin).

—(1906) "Slavery in Massachusetts," in *The Writings of Henry David Thoreau*, v.4 (Boston, MA and New York, NY: Houghton Mifflin).

Toronto Star Staff (2001) "Reaching Across the Battle Lines", *The Toronto Star*, February 10, 2001.

United Press International (1995) "U.S. Bank Disavows Newsletter on Mexico", *UPI News Service*, February 13, 1995.

Vidal, John and Kate Connolly (2000) "Barricades Burn in Battles of Prague: Polic e Lash out as World Bank Protest Ends In Major Riots", *The Guardian* (London), September 27, 2000.

Williams, Frances (2001) "Global Trade Deal Near After All-Night Talks in Doha", *Financial Times* (London), November 14, 2001.

Williams, William Appleman (1980) *Empire as a Way of Life: An Essay on the Causes and Character of America's Present Predicament Along with a Few Thoughts About an Alternative* (New York, NY: Oxford University Press).

Wink, Walter (1992) *Engaging the Powers: Discernment and Resistance in a World of Domination* (Minneapolis, MN: Fortress Press).

Witness for Peace (2001a) *A Hemisphere for Sale: The Epidemic of Unfair Trade in the Americas* (Washington, DC: Witness for Peace).

—(2002) "Plan Puebla Panama: Development for Corporations, Not for People", Witness for Peace Newsletter, Summer/Fall 2002: 3-4.

Worster, Donald (1993) *The Wealth of Nature: Environmental History and the Ecological Imagination* (Oxford: Oxford University Press).

Wright, Christopher J. H. (1990) *God's People in God's Land: Family, Land, and Property in the Old Testament* (Grand Rapids, MI: William B. Eerdmans).

Yoder, John Howard (1972) *The Politics of Jesus* (Grand Rapids, MI: William B. Eerdmans).